SRA Code of Conduct and Accounts Rules

LPC STUDENT EDITION

Other titles available from Law Society Publishing:

SRA Handbook (October 2015)
Solicitors Regulation Authority

Career Planning for Solicitors
Edited by Sue Lenkowski

Titles from Law Society Publishing can be ordered from all good bookshops or direct (telephone 0370 850 1422, email **lawsociety@prolog.uk.com** or visit our online shop at **www.lawsociety.org.uk/bookshop**).

SRA CODE OF CONDUCT AND ACCOUNTS RULES

Including the SRA Practice Framework Rules

LPC STUDENT EDITION

Solicitors Regulation Authority

The Law Society

© The Law Society 2016

ISBN 978-1-78446-059-4

Published in June 2016 by the Law Society
113 Chancery Lane, London WC2A 1PL

Typeset by Columns Design XML Ltd, Reading
Printed by TJ International Ltd, Padstow, Cornwall

FSC
www.fsc.org
MIX
Paper from
responsible sources
FSC® C013056

The paper used for the text pages of this book is FSC certified. FSC (the Forest Stewardship Council) is an international network to promote responsible management of the world's forests.

Contents

Important note

The materials here are extracted from the SRA Handbook.

Terms which are defined, and which are being used in their defined sense, appear in the text in italics and in a separate Glossary.

The extracts are taken from version 16 of the online SRA Handbook (which was published and came into effect on 1 April 2016). Please check the latest version for amendments to these or other provisions in the SRA Handbook in case they are modified from those shown here. The SRA Handbook is updated regularly and can be found at www.sra.org.uk.

June 2016

Important note

[A] Introduction

[A.1] Introduction to the SRA Handbook

Contents

1 Consumer interests and the general public interest are the key justifications for any regulatory scheme. Users of legal services are, therefore, the focus of the Solicitors Regulation Authority's (SRA's) regulatory framework.

2 This Handbook sets out the standards and requirements which we expect our regulated community to achieve and observe, for the benefit of the clients they serve and in the general public interest. Our approach to regulation (i.e. authorisation, supervision and enforcement) is outcomes-focused and risk-based so that clients receive services in a manner which best suits their own particular needs, and depending on how services are provided (e.g. whether in-house or through private practice).

3 Our Handbook brings together the key regulatory elements in the following sections:

(a) SRA **Principles** – these are the ten Principles which are mandatory and apply to all those we regulate and underpin all aspects of practice. They define the fundamental ethical and professional standards that we expect of all firms (including owners who may not be lawyers) and individuals when providing legal services. In some circumstances they apply outside practice.

(b) SRA **Code of Conduct** (**"the Code"**) – this section contains the "Outcomes" we require which, when achieved, benefit users of legal services and the public at large. These Outcomes are mandatory and, when achieved, will help ensure compliance with the Principles in the particular contexts covered by the various chapters in the Code. We recognise that these mandatory Outcomes may be achieved in a variety of ways depending on the particular circumstances, and we have supplemented the mandatory Outcomes with non-mandatory "Indicative Behaviours" to aid compliance. The Indicative Behaviours which we set out are not exhaustive: the Outcomes can be achieved in other ways. We encourage firms to consider how they can best achieve the Outcomes taking into account the nature of the firm, the particular circumstances and, crucially, the needs of their particular clients.

  (i) Introduction

  (ii) SRA Code of Conduct

(c) **Accounts** – this section contains the SRA Accounts Rules – requirements aimed at protecting client money.

  (i) Introduction

  (ii) SRA Accounts Rules

(d) **Authorisation and Practising Requirements** – this section includes key requirements for the training and admission for individuals intending to become solicitors; exercising higher rights of audience; acting as advocates in the criminal courts; for individuals and firms setting up in practice and for holding certain roles in a practice.

  (i)   Introduction

  (ii)   SRA Practice Framework Rules

  (iii) SRA Authorisation Rules for Legal Services Bodies and Licensable Bodies

  (iv)   SRA Practising Regulations

  (v)   Solicitors Keeping of the Roll Regulations

  (vi)   SRA Training Regulations:

    (A) 2014 – Qualification and Training Provider Regulations

    (B) 2011 Part 3 – CPD Regulations

  (vii) SRA Admission Regulations

  (viii) SRA Qualified Lawyers Transfer Scheme Regulations

  (ix)   SRA Higher Rights of Audience Regulations

  (x)   SRA Quality Assurance Scheme for Advocates (Crime) Regulations

  (xi)   SRA Suitability Test

(e) **Client Protection** – this section contains key elements for the financial protection of clients.

  (i)   Introduction

  (ii)   SRA Indemnity Insurance Rules

  (iii) SRA Indemnity (Enactment) Rules and SRA Indemnity Rules

  (iv)   SRA Compensation Fund Rules

  (v)   SRA Intervention Powers (Statutory Trust) Rules

(f) **Discipline and Costs Recovery** – this section contains provisions upon which our disciplinary and costs recovery powers are based.

  (i)   Introduction

  (ii)   SRA Disciplinary Procedure Rules

  (iii) SRA Cost of Investigations Regulations

(g) **Overseas Rules**

  (i)   Introduction

  (ii)   Overseas Rules

(h) **Specialist Services** – this section contains provisions which are only applicable when certain services are being provided to clients.

  (i)   Introduction

  (ii)   SRA Property Selling Rules

  (iii)   SRA Financial Services (Scope) Rules

  (iv)   SRA Financial Services (Conduct of Business) Rules

  (v)   SRA European Cross-border Practice Rules

  (vi)   SRA Insolvency Practice Rules

(i) **Glossary** – The Glossary is central to all the rules and regulations within the SRA Handbook. It comprises all terms used throughout the Handbook which are shown in italics, and sets out their definitions. The same terms in the SRA Handbook may appear as italicised text in some cases but not in others. Where they are not italicised, for reasons relating to the specific context, they are not being used in their defined sense and take their natural meaning in that context. The Glossary also contains interpretation and transitional provisions.

Additional information

1   Non-mandatory guidance and notes appear, as appropriate, throughout the Handbook as an aid to compliance.

2   Our approach to regulation has two elements: firm-based requirements and individual requirements. It focuses on the practices of regulated entities as well as the conduct and competence of regulated individuals. This approach allows us to take regulatory action against firms or individuals, or both, in appropriate cases. This could include action against anyone in the firm including non-lawyer owners, managers and employees. We exercise our regulatory powers in a proportionate manner, focusing on risk and outcomes for clients.

3   Firms will need to ensure that all employees (even if non-qualified and non-fee earners) receive appropriate training on the requirements in the Handbook, but only to the extent necessary for the role they undertake in the firm. For example, all staff will need to understand that they should keep clients' affairs confidential and behave with integrity; however it is likely that only those in fee-earning roles need be aware of the procedures required for checking for conflicts of interests and giving undertakings.

4   Although firms now have greater freedom in the way they offer services (e.g. outsourcing certain functions), they may not abrogate responsibility for compliance with regulatory requirements.

5   We are confident that the contents of this Handbook, coupled with our modern, outcomes-focused, risk-based approach to authorisation, supervision and effective enforcement will:

(a) benefit the public interest;

(b) support the rule of law;

(c) improve access to justice;

(d) benefit consumers' interests;

(e) promote competition;

(f) encourage an independent, strong, diverse and effective legal profession;

(g) increase understanding of legal rights and duties; and

(h) promote adherence to the professional principles set out in the Legal Services Act 2007.

6   The Handbook will, therefore, support not only consumers of legal services, but will also support the independence of the legal profession and its unique role in safeguarding the legal rights of those it serves.

7   These regulatory objectives can only be achieved if we and our regulated community work together in a spirit of mutual trust for the benefit of clients and the ultimate public interest.

[B] Principles

[B.1] SRA Principles 2011

PREAMBLE

The SRA Principles dated 17 June 2011 commencing 6 October 2011 made by the Solicitors Regulation Authority Board under sections 31, 79 and 80 of the Solicitors Act 1974, sections 9 and 9A of the Administration of Justice Act 1985 and section 83 of the Legal Services Act 2007, with the approval of the Legal Services Board under paragraph 19 of Schedule 4 to the Legal Services Act 2007, regulating the conduct of solicitors and their employees, registered European lawyers, recognised bodies and their managers and employees, and licensed bodies and their managers and employees.

PART 1: SRA PRINCIPLES

1: SRA Principles

These are mandatory *Principles* which apply to all.

You must:

1. uphold the rule of law and the proper administration of justice;

2. act with integrity;

3. not allow your independence to be compromised;

4. act in the best interests of each *client*;

5. provide a proper standard of service to your *clients*;

6. behave in a way that maintains the trust the public places in you and in the provision of legal services;

7. comply with your legal and regulatory obligations and deal with your regulators and ombudsmen in an open, timely and co-operative manner;

8. run your business or carry out your role in the business effectively and in accordance with proper governance and sound financial and risk management principles;

9. run your business or carry out your role in the business in a way that encourages equality of opportunity and respect for diversity; and

10. protect *client* money and *assets*.

2: SRA Principles – notes

2.1   The Principles embody the key ethical requirements on firms and individuals who are involved in the provision of legal services. You should always have regard to the Principles and use them as your starting point when faced with an ethical dilemma.

2.2   Where two or more Principles come into conflict, the Principle which takes precedence is the one which best serves the public interest in the particular circumstances, especially the public interest in the proper administration of justice.

2.3   These Principles:

(a)   apply to individuals and firms we regulate, whether traditional firms of solicitors or ABSs, in private practice or in-house. Where a firm or individual is *practising overseas*, the Overseas Principles apply;

(b)   will be breached by you if you permit another person to do anything on your behalf which if done by you would breach the Principles; and

(c)   apply to you to the fullest extent if a sole practitioner or manager in a firm, but still apply to you if you work within a firm or in-house and have no management responsibility (for example, even if you are not a manager you may have an opportunity to influence, adopt and implement measures to comply with Principles 8 and 9).

2.4   Compliance with the Principles is also subject to any overriding legal obligations.

Principle 1: You must uphold the rule of law and the proper administration of justice.

2.5   You have obligations not only to clients but also to the court and to third parties with whom you have dealings on your clients' behalf – see, e.g., Chapter 5 (Your client and the court) and Chapter 11 (Relations with third parties) of the Code.

Principle 2: You must act with integrity.

2.6   Personal integrity is central to your role as the client's trusted adviser and should characterise all your professional dealings with clients, the court, other lawyers and the public.

Principle 3: You must not allow your independence to be compromised.

2.7   "Independence" means your own and your firm's independence, and not merely your ability to give independent advice to a client. You should avoid situations which might put your independence at risk – e.g. giving control of your practice to a third party which is beyond the regulatory reach of the SRA or other approved regulator.

Principle 4: You must act in the best interests of each client.

2.8   You should always act in good faith and do your best for each of your clients. Most importantly, you should observe:

(a)   your duty of confidentiality to the client – see Chapter 4 (Confidentiality and disclosure) of the Code; and

(b)   your obligations with regard to conflicts of interests – see Chapter 3 (Conflicts of interests) of the Code.

Principle 5: You must provide a proper standard of service to your clients.

2.9   You should, e.g., provide a proper standard of client care and of work. This would include exercising competence, skill and diligence, and taking into account the individual needs and circumstances of each client.

2.10   For a *solicitor*, meeting the competencies set out in the Competence Statement forms an integral part of the requirement to provide a proper standard of service.

Principle 6: You must behave in a way that maintains the trust the public places in you and in the provision of legal services.

2.11   Members of the public should be able to place their trust in you. Any behaviour either within or outside your professional practice which undermines this trust damages not only you, but also the ability of the legal profession as a whole to serve society.

Principle 7: You must comply with your legal and regulatory obligations and deal with your regulators and ombudsmen in an open, timely and co-operative manner.

2.12   You should, e.g., ensure that you comply with all the reporting and notification requirements – see Chapter 10 (You and your regulator) of the Code – and respond promptly and substantively to communications.

Principle 8: You must run your business or carry out your role in the business effectively and in accordance with proper governance and sound financial and risk management principles.

2.13   Whether you are a manager or an employee, you have a part to play in helping to ensure that your business is well run for the benefit of your clients and, e.g. in meeting the outcomes in Chapter 7 (Management of your business) of the Code.

Principle 9: You must run your business or carry out your role in the business in a way that encourages equality of opportunity and respect for diversity.

2.14   Whether you are a manager or an employee, you have a role to play in achieving the outcomes in Chapter 2 (Equality and diversity) of the Code. Note that a finding of unlawful discrimination outside practice could also amount to a breach of Principles 1 and 6.

Principle 10: You must protect client money and assets.

2.15   This Principle goes to the heart of the duty to act in the best interests of your clients. You should play your part in e.g. protecting money, documents or other property belonging to your clients which has been entrusted to you or your firm.

Breach of the Principles

2.16   Our approach to enforcement is proportionate, outcomes-focused and risk-based. Therefore, how we deal with failure to comply with the Principles will depend on all the particular circumstances of each case. Our primary aim is to achieve the right outcomes for clients.

PART 2: SRA PRINCIPLES – APPLICATION PROVISIONS

The *Principles* apply to you in the following circumstances (and "you" must be construed accordingly).

3: Application of the SRA Principles in England and Wales

3.1   Subject to paragraphs 3.2 to 6.1 below and any other provisions in the *SRA Code of Conduct*, the *Principles* apply to you, in relation to your activities carried out from an office in England and Wales, if you are:

(a) a *solicitor*, *REL* or *RFL* who is *practising* as such, whether or not the entity through which you *practise* is subject to these *Principles*;

(b) a *solicitor*, *REL* or *RFL* who is:

  (i)   a *manager*, *employee* or *owner* of a body which should be a *recognised body*, but has not been recognised by the *SRA*;

  (ii) a *manager*, *employee* or *owner* of a body that is a *manager* or *owner* of a body that should be a *recognised body*, but has not been recognised by the *SRA*;

  (iii) an *employee* in a *sole practitioner's practice* which should be a *recognised sole practice*, but has not been recognised by the *SRA*;

  (iv) an *owner* of an *authorised body* or of a body which should be a *recognised body* but has not been recognised by the *SRA*, even if you undertake no work for the body's *clients*;

  (v)   a *manager* or *employee* of an *authorised non-SRA firm*, or a *manager* of a body which is a *manager* of an *authorised non-SRA firm*, when doing work of a sort authorised by the *SRA*, for that firm;

(c) an *authorised body*, or a body which should be a *recognised body* but has not been recognised by the *SRA*;

(d) any other person who is a *manager*, or *employee* of an *authorised body*, or of a body which should be a *recognised body* but has not been recognised by the *SRA*;

(e) any other person who is an *employee* in a *recognised sole practice*, or of a *sole practitioner* whose *practice* should be a *recognised sole practice*, but has not been recognised by the *SRA*;

and "you" includes "your" as appropriate.

3.2 The *Principles* apply to you if you are a *solicitor*, *REL* or *RFL*, and you are:

(a) *practising* as a *manager* or *employee* of an *authorised non-SRA firm* when doing work of a sort authorised by the *authorised non-SRA firm's approved regulator* or carrying on any other activity that is not precluded by the terms of your authorisation from the firm's *approved regulator*; or

(b) an *owner* of an *authorised non-SRA firm* even if you undertake no work for the body's *clients*.

3.3 The *Principles* apply to you if you are an *REL practising* as a *manager*, *employee*, *member* or *interest holder*, of an *Exempt European Practice*.

4: Application of the SRA Principles in relation to practice from an office outside England and Wales

4.1 The *Principles* apply to you if you are:

(a) a body practising from an office outside England and Wales only if you are required to be an *authorised body* as a result of the nature of your practice and you have been authorised by the *SRA* accordingly; or

(b) a *manager* of such a body.

Guidance note

(i) In most circumstances, overseas offices of authorised bodies based in England and Wales will not require authorisation with the SRA and will be governed by the SRA Overseas Rules. However, in some circumstances, because of the work that is being carried out from the overseas office, it will need to be authorised (see Rule 2.1(e) and have regard to Rule 2.1(g) of the SRA Overseas Rules). In those circumstances, the SRA Principles and Code of Conduct apply.

4.2 The *Principles* apply to you if you are an individual engaged in *temporary practice overseas*.

5: Application of the SRA Principles outside practice

5.1 In relation to activities which fall outside *practice*, whether undertaken as a *lawyer* or in some other business or private capacity, *Principles* 1, 2 and 6 apply to you if you are a *solicitor*, *REL* or *RFL*.

6: General provisions

6.1 You must comply with the *Principles* at all times, but the extent to which you are expected to implement the requirements of the *Principles* will depend on your role in the *firm*, or your way of *practising*. For example, those who are managing a business will be expected to have more influence on how the *firm* or business is run than those *practising* in-house but not managing a legal department, or those *practising* as *employees* of a *firm*.

PART 3: TRANSITIONAL PROVISIONS

7: Transitional provisions

7.1   For the avoidance of doubt, where a breach of any provision of the Solicitors' Code of Conduct 2007 comes to the attention of the *SRA* after 6 October 2011, this shall be subject to action by the *SRA* notwithstanding any repeal of the relevant provision.

7.2   [Deleted]

7.3   [Deleted]

7.4   [Deleted]

PART 4: INTERPRETATION

8: Interpretation

8.1   The SRA Handbook Glossary 2012 shall apply to these rules and, unless the context otherwise requires:

  (a)   all italicised terms within these rules shall be defined; and

  (b)   terms within these rules shall be interpreted,

in accordance with the *Glossary*.

[C]   Code of Conduct

SRA Code of Conduct 2011

INTRODUCTION TO THE SRA CODE OF CONDUCT

Overview

Outcomes-focused regulation concentrates on providing positive outcomes which when achieved will benefit and protect *clients* and the public. The SRA Code of Conduct (the Code) sets out our outcomes-focused conduct requirements so that you can consider how best to achieve the right outcomes for your *clients* taking into account the way that your *firm* works and its *client* base. The Code is underpinned by effective, risk-based supervision and enforcement.

Those involved in providing legal advice and representation have long held the role of trusted adviser. There are fiduciary duties arising from this role and obligations owed to others, especially the *court*. No code can foresee or address every issue or ethical dilemma which may arise. You must strive to uphold the intention of the Code as well as its letter.

The Principles

The Code forms part of the Handbook, in which the 10 mandatory *Principles* are all-pervasive. They apply to all those we regulate and underpin all aspects of *practice*. They define the fundamental ethical and professional standards that we expect of all *firms* and individuals (including owners who may not be *lawyers*) when providing legal services. You should always have regard to the *Principles* and use them as your starting point when faced with an ethical dilemma.

Where two or more *Principles* come into conflict the one which takes precedence is the one which best serves the public interest in the particular circumstances, especially the public interest in the proper administration of justice. Compliance with the *Principles* is also subject to any overriding legal obligations.

You must:

1. uphold the rule of law and the proper administration of justice;

2. act with integrity;

3. not allow your independence to be compromised;

4. act in the best interests of each *client*;

5. provide a proper standard of service to your *clients*;

6. behave in a way that maintains the trust the public places in you and in the provision of legal services;

7. comply with your legal and regulatory obligations and deal with your regulators and ombudsmen in an open, timely and co-operative manner;

8. run your business or carry out your role in the business effectively and in accordance with proper governance and sound financial and risk management principles;

9. run your business or carry out your role in the business in a way that encourages equality of opportunity and respect for diversity; and

10. protect *client* money and *assets*.

Structure of the Code

The Code is divided into 5 sections:

*   You and your client
*   You and your business
*   You and your regulator
*   You and others
*   Application, waivers and interpretation

Each section is divided into chapters dealing with particular regulatory issues, for example, client care, *conflicts of interests*, and *publicity*.

These chapters show how the *Principles* apply in certain contexts through mandatory and non-mandatory provisions.

Mandatory provisions

The following provisions are mandatory:

*   the outcomes;
*   the application and waivers provisions in Chapters 13 and 13A;
*   the interpretations; and
*   the transitional provisions in Chapter 15.

The outcomes describe what *firms* and individuals are expected to achieve in order to comply with the relevant *Principles* in the context of the relevant chapter. In the case of *in-house practice*, we have set out at the end of each chapter which outcomes apply and in some cases have specified different outcomes.

In respect of *in-house practice*, different outcomes may apply depending on whether you are acting for your employer or for a *client* other than your employer as permitted by rules 4.1 to 4.10 of the *SRA Practice Framework Rules*.

The outcomes contained in each chapter are not an exhaustive list of the application of all the *Principles*. We have tried to make them as helpful as possible.

Non-mandatory provisions

The following provisions are non-mandatory:

- indicative behaviours;
- notes.

The outcomes are supplemented by indicative behaviours. The indicative behaviours specify, but do not constitute an exhaustive list of, the kind of behaviour which may establish compliance with, or contravention of the *Principles*. These are not mandatory but they may help us to decide whether an outcome has been achieved in compliance with the *Principles*.

We recognise that there may be other ways of achieving the outcomes. Where you have chosen a different method from those we have described as indicative behaviours, we might require you to demonstrate how you have nevertheless achieved the outcome. We encourage *firms* to consider how they can best achieve the outcomes, taking into account the nature of the *firm*, the particular circumstances of the matter and, crucially, the needs of their particular *clients*.

Waivers

Due to the flexibility of approach this structure allows, we do not anticipate receiving many applications for waivers from the mandatory outcomes. The *SRA*, nonetheless, reserves power to waive a provision in exceptional circumstances.

Interpretation

Words shown in italics are defined in the *Glossary*.

Sources of help

You can access the Code and other elements of the Handbook and find information on particular issues on the *SRA* website. You can also seek guidance on professional conduct from our Professional Ethics Guidance Team.

List of contents of the Code

1st section: You and your client

Chapter 1 Client care
Chapter 2 Equality and diversity
Chapter 3 Conflicts of interests
Chapter 4 Confidentiality and disclosure
Chapter 5 Your client and the court
Chapter 6 Your client and introductions to third parties

2nd section: You and your business

Chapter 7 Management of your business
Chapter 8 Publicity
Chapter 9 Fee sharing and referrals

PREAMBLE

The SRA Code of Conduct dated 17 June 2011 commencing 6 October 2011 made by the Solicitors Regulation Authority Board under sections 31, 79 and 80 of the Solicitors Act 1974, sections 9 and 9A of the Administration of Justice Act 1985 and section 83 of the Legal Services Act 2007, with the approval of the Legal Services Board under paragraph 19 of Schedule 4 to the Legal Services Act 2007, regulating the conduct of solicitors and their employees, registered European lawyers and their employees, registered foreign lawyers, recognised bodies and their managers and employees and licensed bodies and their managers and employees.

1ST SECTION: YOU AND YOUR CLIENT

Chapter 1: Client care

This chapter is about providing a proper standard of service, which takes into account the individual needs and circumstances of each *client*. This includes providing *clients* with the information they need to make informed decisions about the services they need, how these will be delivered and how much they will cost. This will enable you and your *client* to understand each other's expectations and responsibilities. This chapter is also about ensuring that if *clients* are not happy with the service they have received they know how to make a *complaint* and that all *complaints* are dealt with promptly and fairly.

Your relationship with your *client* is a contractual one which carries with it legal, as well as conduct, obligations. This chapter focuses on your obligations in conduct.

You are generally free to decide whether or not to accept instructions in any matter, provided you do not discriminate unlawfully (see Chapter 2).

The outcomes in this chapter show how the *Principles* apply in the context of client care.

Outcomes

You must achieve these outcomes:

O(**1.1**) you treat your *clients* fairly;

O(**1.2**) you provide services to your *clients* in a manner which protects their interests in their matter, subject to the proper administration of justice;

O(**1.3**) when deciding whether to act, or terminate your instructions, you comply with the law and the Code;

O(**1.4**) you have the resources, skills and procedures to carry out your *clients'* instructions;

O(**1.5**) the service you provide to *clients* is competent, delivered in a timely manner and takes account of your *clients'* needs and circumstances;

O(**1.6**) you only enter into fee agreements with your *clients* that are legal, and which you consider are suitable for the *client's* needs and take account of the *client's* best interests;

O(**1.7**) you inform *clients* whether and how the services you provide are regulated and how this affects the protections available to the *client*;

O(**1.8**) *clients* have the benefit of your *compulsory professional indemnity insurance* and you do not exclude or attempt to exclude liability below the minimum level of cover required by the *SRA Indemnity Insurance Rules*;

O(**1.9**) *clients* are informed in writing at the outset of their matter of their right to complain and how *complaints* can be made;

O(**1.10**) *clients* are informed in writing, both at the time of engagement and at the conclusion of your *complaints* procedure, of their right to complain to the *Legal Ombudsman*, the time frame for doing so and full details of how to contact the *Legal Ombudsman*;

O(**1.11**) *clients' complaints* are dealt with promptly, fairly, openly and effectively;

O(**1.12**) *clients* are in a position to make informed decisions about the services they need, how their matter will be handled and the options available to them;

O(**1.13**) *clients* receive the best possible information, both at the time of engagement and when appropriate as their matter progresses, about the likely overall cost of their matter;

O(**1.14**) *clients* are informed of their right to challenge or complain about your bill and the circumstances in which they may be liable to pay interest on an unpaid bill;

O(1.15)   you properly account to *clients* for any *financial benefit* you receive as a result of your instructions;

O(1.16)   you inform current *clients* if you discover any act or omission which could give rise to a claim by them against you.

Indicative behaviours

Acting in the following way(s) may tend to show that you have achieved these outcomes and therefore complied with the *Principles*:

DEALING WITH THE CLIENT'S MATTER

IB(1.1)   agreeing an appropriate level of service with your *client*, for example the type and frequency of communications;

IB(1.2)   explaining your responsibilities and those of the *client*;

IB(1.3)   ensuring that the *client* is told, in writing, the name and status of the person(s) dealing with the matter and the name and status of the person responsible for its overall supervision;

IB(1.4)   explaining any arrangements, such as fee sharing or *referral arrangements*, which are relevant to the *client's* instructions;

IB(1.5)   explaining any limitations or conditions on what you can do for the *client*, for example, because of the way the *client's* matter is funded;

IB(1.6)   in taking instructions and during the course of the retainer, having proper regard to your *client's* mental capacity or other vulnerability, such as incapacity or duress;

IB(1.7)   considering whether you should decline to act or cease to act because you cannot act in the *client's* best interests;

IB(1.8)   if you seek to limit your liability to your *client* to a level above the minimum required by the *SRA Indemnity Insurance Rules*, ensuring that this limitation is in writing and is brought to the *client's* attention;

IB(1.9)   refusing to act where your *client* proposes to make a gift of significant value to you or a member of your family, or a member of your *firm* or their family, unless the *client* takes independent legal advice;

IB(1.10)   if you have to cease acting for a *client*, explaining to the *client* their possible options for pursuing their matter;

IB(1.11)   you inform *clients* if they are not entitled to the protections of the SRA Compensation Fund;

IB(1.12) considering whether a *conflict of interests* has arisen or whether the *client* should be advised to obtain independent advice where the *client* notifies you of their intention to make a claim or if you discover an act or omission which might give rise to a claim;

FEE ARRANGEMENTS WITH YOUR CLIENT

IB(1.13) discussing whether the potential outcomes of the *client's* matter are likely to justify the expense or risk involved, including any risk of having to pay someone else's legal fees;

IB(1.14) clearly explaining your fees and if and when they are likely to change;

IB(1.15) warning about any other payments for which the *client* may be responsible;

IB(1.16) discussing how the *client* will pay, including whether public funding may be available, whether the *client* has insurance that might cover the fees, and whether the fees may be paid by someone else such as a trade union;

IB(1.17) where you are acting for a *client* under a fee arrangement governed by statute, such as a conditional fee agreement, giving the *client* all relevant information relating to that arrangement;

IB(1.18) where you are acting for a publicly funded *client*, explaining how their publicly funded status affects the costs;

IB(1.19) providing the information in a clear and accessible form which is appropriate to the needs and circumstances of the *client*;

IB(1.20) where you receive a *financial benefit* as a result of acting for a *client*, either:

(a) paying it to the *client*;

(b) offsetting it against your fees; or

(c) keeping it only where you can justify keeping it, you have told the *client* the amount of the benefit (or an approximation if you do not know the exact amount) and the *client* has agreed that you can keep it;

IB(1.21) ensuring that *disbursements* included in your bill reflect the actual amount spent or to be spent on behalf of the *client*;

COMPLAINTS HANDLING

IB(1.22) having a written *complaints* procedure which:

(a) is brought to *clients'* attention at the outset of the matter;

(b) is easy for *clients* to use and understand, allowing for *complaints* to be made by any reasonable means;

(c) is responsive to the needs of individual *clients*, especially those who are vulnerable;

(d) enables *complaints* to be dealt with promptly and fairly, with decisions based on a sufficient investigation of the circumstances;

(e) provides for appropriate remedies; and

(f) does not involve any charges to *clients* for handling their *complaints*;

IB(1.23) providing the *client* with a copy of the *firm's complaints* procedure on request;

IB(1.24) in the event that a *client* makes a *complaint*, providing them with all necessary information concerning the handling of the *complaint*.

Acting in the following way(s) may tend to show that you have not achieved these outcomes and therefore not complied with the *Principles*:

ACCEPTING AND REFUSING INSTRUCTIONS

IB(1.25) acting for a *client* when instructions are given by someone else, or by only one *client* when you act jointly for others unless you are satisfied that the *person* providing the instructions has the authority to do so on behalf of all of the *clients*;

IB(1.26) ceasing to act for a *client* without good reason and without providing reasonable notice;

IB(1.27) entering into unlawful fee arrangements such as an unlawful contingency fee;

IB(1.28) acting for a *client* when there are reasonable grounds for believing that the instructions are affected by duress or undue influence without satisfying yourself that they represent the *client's* wishes.

In-house practice

Outcomes 1.1 to 1.5, 1.7, 1.15 and 1.16 apply to your *in-house practice*.

Outcomes 1.6 and 1.9 to 1.14 apply to your *in-house practice* where you act for someone other than your employer unless it is clear that the outcome is not relevant to your particular circumstances.

IHP(1.1) Instead of Outcome 1.8 you comply with the *SRA Practice Framework Rules* in relation to professional indemnity insurance.

Notes

(i) The information you give to *clients* will vary according to the needs and circumstances of the individual *client* and the type of work you are doing for them, for example an individual instructing you on a conveyancing matter is unlikely to need the same information as a sophisticated commercial *client* who instructs you on a regular basis.

(ii)   Information about the *Legal Ombudsman*, including the scheme rules, contact details and time limits, can be found at **www.legalombudsman.org.uk**.

Chapter 2: Equality and diversity

This chapter is about encouraging equality of opportunity and respect for diversity, and preventing unlawful discrimination, in your relationship with your *clients* and others. The requirements apply in relation to age, disability, gender reassignment, marriage and civil partnership, pregnancy and maternity, race, religion or belief, sex and sexual orientation.

Everyone needs to contribute to compliance with these requirements, for example by treating each other, and *clients*, fairly and with respect, by embedding such values in the workplace and by challenging inappropriate behaviour and processes. Your role in embedding these values will vary depending on your role.

As a matter of general law you must comply with requirements set out in legislation – including the Equality Act 2010 – as well as the conduct duties contained in this chapter.

The outcomes in this chapter show how the *Principles* apply in the context of equality and diversity.

Outcomes

You must achieve these outcomes:

O(2.1)   you do not discriminate unlawfully, or victimise or harass anyone, in the course of your professional dealings;

O(2.2)   you provide services to *clients* in a way that respects diversity;

O(2.3)   you make reasonable adjustments to ensure that disabled *clients*, *employees* or *managers* are not placed at a substantial disadvantage compared to those who are not disabled, and you do not pass on the costs of these adjustments to these disabled *clients*, *employees* or *managers*;

O(2.4)   your approach to recruitment and employment encourages equality of opportunity and respect for diversity;

O(2.5)   *complaints* of discrimination are dealt with promptly, fairly, openly, and effectively;

O(2.6)   you have appropriate arrangements in place to ensure that you monitor, report and, where appropriate, publish workforce diversity data.

Indicative behaviours

Acting in the following way(s) may tend to show that you have achieved these outcomes and therefore complied with the *Principles*:

IB(2.1)   having a written equality and diversity policy (which may be contained within one or more documents, including one or more policy documents, as appropriate) which is appropriate to the size and nature of the *firm* and includes the following features:

  (a)   a commitment to the principles of equality and diversity and legislative requirements;

  (b)   a requirement that all *employees* and *managers* comply with the outcomes;

  (c)   provisions to encompass your recruitment and interview processes;

  (d)   details of how the *firm* will implement, monitor, evaluate and update the policy;

  (e)   details of how the *firm* will ensure equality in relation to the treatment of *employees*, *managers*, *clients* and third parties instructed in connection with *client* matters;

  (f)   details of how *complaints* and disciplinary issues are to be dealt with;

  (g)   details of the *firm's* arrangements for workforce diversity monitoring; and

  (h)   details of how the *firm* will communicate the policy to *employees*, *managers* and *clients*;

IB(2.2)   providing *employees* and *managers* with training and information about complying with equality and diversity requirements;

IB(2.3)   monitoring and responding to issues identified by your policy and reviewing and updating your policy.

Acting in the following way(s) may tend to show that you have not achieved these outcomes and therefore not complied with the *Principles*:

IB(2.4)   being subject to any decision of a court or tribunal of the *UK*, that you have committed, or are to be treated as having committed, an unlawful act of discrimination;

IB(2.5)   discriminating unlawfully when accepting or refusing instructions to act for a *client*.

In-house practice

Outcomes 2.1 and 2.2 apply to all *in-house practice*.

Instead of outcomes 2.3 to 2.5 you must achieve the following outcome:

IHP(2.1)   if you have management responsibilities you take all reasonable steps to encourage equality of opportunity and respect for diversity in your workplace.

Notes

(i)   The obligations in this chapter closely mirror your legal obligations. You can obtain further information from the Equality and Human Rights Commission, **www.equalityhumanrights.com.**

(ii)   See also Chapter 1 (Client care) for the handling of *client complaints.*

(iii)   See also Chapter 7 (Management of your business) for your obligation to have in place appropriate systems and controls for complying with the outcomes in this chapter.

(iv)   For more information on collecting, reporting and publishing diversity data, including compliance with data protection legislation, please see guidance.

Chapter 3: Conflicts of interests

This chapter deals with the proper handling of *conflicts of interests*, which is a critical public protection. It is important to have in place systems that enable you to identify and deal with potential conflicts.

Conflicts of interests can arise between:

1.   you and current *clients* (*"own interest conflict"*); and

2.   two or more current *clients* (*"client conflict"*).

You can never act where there is a conflict, or a significant risk of conflict, between you and your *client*.

If there is a conflict, or a significant risk of a conflict, between two or more current *clients*, you must not act for all or both of them unless the matter falls within the scope of the limited exceptions set out at Outcomes 3.6 or 3.7. In deciding whether to act in these limited circumstances, the overriding consideration will be the best interests of each of the *clients* concerned and, in particular, whether the benefits to the *clients* of you acting for all or both of the *clients* outweigh the risks.

You should also bear in mind that *conflicts of interests* may affect your duties of confidentiality and disclosure which are dealt with in Chapter 4.

The outcomes in this chapter show how the *Principles* apply in the context of *conflicts of interests.*

Outcomes

You must achieve these outcomes:

SYSTEMS

O(3.1)   you have effective systems and controls in place to enable you to identify and assess potential *conflicts of interests*;

O(3.2) your systems and controls for identifying *own interest conflicts* are appropriate to the size and complexity of the *firm* and the nature of the work undertaken, and enable you to assess all the relevant circumstances, including whether your ability as an individual, or that of anyone within your *firm*, to act in the best interests of the *client(s)*, is impaired by:

    (a)   any financial interest;

    (b)   a personal relationship;

    (c)   the appointment of you, or a member of your *firm* or family, to public office;

    (d)   commercial relationships; or

    (e)   your employment;

O(3.3) your systems and controls for identifying *client conflicts* are appropriate to the size and complexity of the *firm* and the nature of the work undertaken, and enable you to assess all relevant circumstances, including whether:

    (a)   the *clients'* interests are different;

    (b)   your ability to give independent advice to the *clients* may be fettered;

    (c)   there is a need to negotiate between the *clients*;

    (d)   there is an imbalance in bargaining power between the *clients*; or

    (e)   any *client* is vulnerable;

PROHIBITION ON ACTING IN CONFLICT SITUATIONS

O(3.4) you do not act if there is an *own interest conflict* or a significant risk of an *own interest conflict*;

O(3.5) you do not act if there is a *client conflict*, or a significant risk of a *client conflict*, unless the circumstances set out in Outcomes 3.6 or 3.7 apply;

EXCEPTIONS WHERE YOU MAY ACT, WITH APPROPRIATE SAFEGUARDS, WHERE THERE IS A CLIENT CONFLICT

O(3.6) where there is a *client conflict* and the *clients* have a *substantially common interest* in relation to a matter or a particular aspect of it, you only act if:

    (a)   you have explained the relevant issues and risks to the *clients* and you have a reasonable belief that they understand those issues and risks;

    (b)   all the *clients* have given informed consent in writing to you acting;

    (c)   you are satisfied that it is reasonable for you to act for all the *clients* and that it is in their best interests; and

    (d)   you are satisfied that the benefits to the *clients* of you doing so outweigh the risks;

O(3.7)   where there is a *client conflict* and the *clients* are *competing for the same objective*, you only act if:

- (a)   you have explained the relevant issues and risks to the *clients* and you have a reasonable belief that they understand those issues and risks;

- (b)   the *clients* have confirmed in writing that they want you to act, in the knowledge that you act, or may act, for one or more other *clients* who are *competing for the same objective*;

- (c)   there is no other *client conflict* in relation to that matter;

- (d)   unless the *clients* specifically agree, no individual acts for, or is responsible for the supervision of work done for, more than one of the *clients* in that matter; and

- (e)   you are satisfied that it is reasonable for you to act for all the *clients* and that the benefits to the *clients* of you doing so outweigh the risks.

Indicative behaviours

Acting in the following way(s) may tend to show that you have achieved these outcomes and therefore complied with the *Principles*:

IB(3.1)   training *employees* and *managers* to identify and assess potential *conflicts of interests*;

IB(3.2)   declining to act for *clients* whose interests are in direct conflict, for example claimant and defendant in litigation;

IB(3.3)   declining to act for *clients* where you may need to negotiate on matters of substance on their behalf, for example negotiating on price between a buyer and seller of a property;

IB(3.4)   declining to act where there is unequal bargaining power between the *clients*, for example acting for a seller and buyer where a builder is selling to a non-commercial *client*;

IB(3.5)   declining to act for *clients* under Outcome 3.6 (*substantially common interest*) or Outcome 3.7 (*competing for the same objective*) where the *clients* cannot be represented even-handedly, or will be prejudiced by lack of separate representation;

IB(3.6)   acting for *clients* under Outcome 3.7 (*competing for the same objective*) only where the *clients* are sophisticated users of legal services;

IB(3.7)   acting for *clients* who are the lender and borrower on the grant of a mortgage of land only where:

- (a)   the mortgage is a standard mortgage (i.e. one provided in the normal course of the lender's activities, where a significant part of the lender's activities consists of lending and the mortgage is on standard terms) of property to be used as the borrower's private residence;

(b) you are satisfied that it is reasonable and in the *clients'* best interests for you to act; and

(c) the certificate of title required by the lender is in the form approved by the *Society* and the Council of Mortgage Lenders.

Acting in the following way(s) may tend to show that you have not achieved these outcomes and therefore not complied with the *Principles*:

IB(3.8)   in a personal capacity, selling to or buying from, lending to or borrowing from a *client*, unless the *client* has obtained independent legal advice;

IB(3.9)   advising a *client* to invest in a business, in which you have an interest which affects your ability to provide impartial advice;

IB(3.10)   where you hold a power of attorney for a *client*, using that power to gain a benefit for yourself which in your professional capacity you would not have been prepared to allow to a third party;

IB(3.11)   acting for two or more *clients* in a *conflict of interests* under Outcome 3.6 (*substantially common interest*) where the *clients'* interests in the end result are not the same, for example one partner buying out the interest of the other partner in their joint business or a seller transferring a property to a buyer;

IB(3.12)   acting for two or more *clients* in a *conflict of interests* under Outcome 3.6 (*substantially common interest*) where it is unreasonable to act because there is unequal bargaining power;

IB(3.13)   acting for two buyers where there is a *conflict of interests* under Outcome 3.7 (*competing for the same objective*), for example where two buyers are competing for a residential property;

IB(3.14)   acting for a buyer (including a lessee) and seller (including a lessor) in a transaction relating to the transfer of land for value, the grant or assignment of a lease or some other interest in land for value.

In-house practice

Outcomes 3.4 to 3.7 apply to your *in-house practice*.

Outcomes 3.1 to 3.3 apply if you have management responsibilities.

Chapter 4: Confidentiality and disclosure

This chapter is about the protection of *clients'* confidential information and the disclosure of material information to *clients*.

Protection of confidential information is a fundamental feature of your relationship with *clients*. It exists as a concept both as a matter of law and as a matter of conduct. This duty continues despite the end of the retainer and even after the death of the *client*.

It is important to distinguish the conduct duties from the concept of law known as legal professional privilege.

Bear in mind that all members of the *firm* or *in-house practice*, including support staff, consultants and locums, owe a duty of confidentiality to your *clients*.

The duty of confidentiality to all *clients* must be reconciled with the duty of disclosure to *clients*. This duty of disclosure is limited to information of which you are aware which is material to your *client's* matter. Where you cannot reconcile these two duties, then the protection of confidential information is paramount. You should not continue to act for a *client* for whom you cannot disclose material information, except in very limited circumstances, where safeguards are in place. Such situations often also give rise to a *conflict of interests* which is discussed in Chapter 3.

The outcomes in this chapter show how the *Principles* apply in the context of confidentiality and disclosure.

Outcomes

You must achieve these outcomes:

O(**4.1**) you keep the affairs of *clients* confidential unless disclosure is required or permitted by law or the *client* consents;

O(**4.2**) any individual who is advising a *client* makes that *client* aware of all information material to that retainer of which the individual has personal knowledge;

O(**4.3**) you ensure that where your duty of confidentiality to one *client* comes into conflict with your duty of disclosure to another *client*, your duty of confidentiality takes precedence;

O(**4.4**) you do not act for A in a matter where A has an interest adverse to B, and B is a *client* for whom you hold confidential information which is material to A in that matter, unless the confidential information can be protected by the use of safeguards, and:

    (a) you reasonably believe that A is aware of, and understands, the relevant issues and gives informed consent;

    (b) either:

        (i) B gives informed consent and you agree with B the safeguards to protect B's information; or

        (ii) where this is not possible, you put in place effective safeguards including information barriers which comply with the common law; and

    (c) it is reasonable in all the circumstances to act for A with such safeguards in place;

O(4.5) you have effective systems and controls in place to enable you to identify risks to *client* confidentiality and to mitigate those risks.

Indicative behaviours

Acting in the following way(s) may tend to show that you have achieved these outcomes and therefore complied with the *Principles*:

IB(4.1) your systems and controls for identifying risks to *client* confidentiality are appropriate to the size and complexity of the *firm* or *in-house practice* and the nature of the work undertaken, and enable you to assess all the relevant circumstances;

IB(4.2) you comply with the law in respect of your fiduciary duties in relation to confidentiality and disclosure;

IB(4.3) you only outsource services when you are satisfied that the provider has taken all appropriate steps to ensure that your *clients'* confidential information will be protected;

IB(4.4) where you are an individual who has responsibility for acting for a *client* or supervising a *client's* matter, you disclose to the *client* all information material to the *client's* matter of which you are personally aware, except when:

(a) the *client* gives specific informed consent to non-disclosure or a different standard of disclosure arises;

(b) there is evidence that serious physical or mental injury will be caused to a person(s) if the information is disclosed to the *client*;

(c) legal restrictions effectively prohibit you from passing the information to the *client*, such as the provisions in the money-laundering and anti-terrorism legislation;

(d) it is obvious that privileged documents have been mistakenly disclosed to you;

(e) you come into possession of information relating to state security or intelligence matters to which the Official Secrets Act 1989 applies;

IB(4.5) not acting for A where B is a *client* for whom you hold confidential information which is material to A unless the confidential information can be protected.

Acting in the following way(s) may tend to show that you have not achieved these outcomes and therefore not complied with the *Principles*:

IB(4.6) disclosing the content of a will on the death of a *client* unless consent has been provided by the personal representatives for the content to be released;

IB(4.7) disclosing details of bills sent to *clients* to third parties, such as debt factoring companies in relation to the collection of book debts, unless the *client* has consented.

In-house practice

The outcomes listed above apply to your *in-house practice*.

Notes

(i)   The protection of confidential information may be at particular risk where:

   (a) two or more *firms* merge;

   (b) when you leave one *firm* and join another, such as if you join a *firm* acting against one of your former *clients*.

(ii)   The following circumstances may make it difficult to implement effective safeguards and information barriers:

   (a) you are a small *firm*;

   (b) the physical structure or layout of the *firm* means that it will be difficult to preserve confidentiality; or

   (c) the *clients* are not sophisticated users of legal services.

Chapter 5: Your client and the court

This chapter is about your duties to your *client* and to the *court* if you are exercising a right to conduct litigation or acting as an advocate. The outcomes apply to both litigation and advocacy but there are some indicative behaviours which may be relevant only when you are acting as an advocate.

The outcomes in this chapter show how the *Principles* apply in the context of your *client* and the *court*.

Outcomes

You must achieve these outcomes:

O(5.1)   you do not attempt to deceive or knowingly or recklessly mislead the *court*;

O(5.2)   you are not complicit in another *person* deceiving or misleading the *court*;

O(5.3)   you comply with *court* orders which place obligations on you;

O(5.4)   you do not place yourself in contempt of *court*;

O(5.5)   where relevant, *clients* are informed of the circumstances in which your duties to the *court* outweigh your obligations to your *client*;

O(5.6)   you comply with your duties to the *court*;

O(5.7)   you ensure that evidence relating to sensitive issues is not misused;

O(5.8)   you do not make or offer to make payments to witnesses dependent upon their evidence or the outcome of the case.

Indicative behaviours

Acting in the following way(s) may tend to show that you have achieved these outcomes and therefore complied with the *Principles*:

IB(5.1)   advising your *clients* to comply with *court* orders made against them, and advising them of the consequences of failing to comply;

IB(5.2)   drawing the *court's* attention to relevant cases and statutory provisions, and any material procedural irregularity;

IB(5.3)   ensuring child witness evidence is kept securely and not released to *clients* or third parties;

IB(5.4)   immediately informing the *court*, with your *client's* consent, if during the course of proceedings you become aware that you have inadvertently misled the *court*, or ceasing to act if the *client* does not consent to you informing the *court*;

IB(5.5)   refusing to continue acting for a *client* if you become aware they have committed perjury or misled the *court*, or attempted to mislead the *court*, in any material matter unless the *client* agrees to disclose the truth to the *court*;

IB(5.6)   not appearing as an advocate, or acting in litigation, if it is clear that you, or anyone within your *firm*, will be called as a witness in the matter unless you are satisfied that this will not prejudice your independence as an advocate, or litigator, or the interests of your *clients* or the interests of justice.

Acting in the following way(s) may tend to show that you have not achieved these outcomes and therefore not complied with the *Principles*:

IB(5.7)   constructing facts supporting your *client's* case or drafting any documents relating to any proceedings containing:

     (a)   any contention which you do not consider to be properly arguable; or

     (b)   any allegation of fraud, unless you are instructed to do so and you have material which you reasonably believe shows, on the face of it, a case of fraud;

IB(5.8)   suggesting that any *person* is guilty of a crime, fraud or misconduct unless such allegations:

     (a)   go to a matter in issue which is material to your own *client's* case; and

     (b)   appear to you to be supported by reasonable grounds;

IB(5.9)   calling a witness whose evidence you know is untrue;

IB(5.10) attempting to influence a witness, when taking a statement from that witness, with regard to the contents of their statement;

IB(5.11) tampering with evidence or seeking to persuade a witness to change their evidence;

IB(5.12) when acting as an advocate, naming in open *court* any third party whose character would thereby be called into question, unless it is necessary for the proper conduct of the case;

IB(5.13) when acting as an advocate, calling into question the character of a witness you have cross-examined unless the witness has had the opportunity to answer the allegations during cross-examination.

In-house practice

The outcomes in this chapter apply to your *in-house practice*.

> *Notes*
>
> (i) If you are a litigator or an advocate there may be occasions when your obligation to act in the best interests of a *client* may conflict with your duty to the *court*. In such situations you may need to consider whether the public interest is best served by the proper administration of justice and should take precedence over the interests of your *client*.

Chapter 6: Your client and introductions to third parties

There may be circumstances in which you wish to refer your *clients* to third parties, perhaps to another *lawyer* or a financial services provider. This chapter describes the conduct duties which arise in respect of such introductions. It is important that you retain your independence when recommending third parties to your *client* and that you act in the *client's* best interests.

The outcomes in this chapter show how the *Principles* apply in the context of your *client* and introductions to third parties.

Outcomes

You must achieve these outcomes:

O(6.1) whenever you recommend that a *client* uses a particular *person* or business, your recommendation is in the best interests of the *client* and does not compromise your independence;

O(6.2) *clients* are fully informed of any financial or other interest which you have in referring the *client* to another *person* or business;

O(6.3) *clients* are in a position to make informed decisions about how to pursue their matter;

O(6.4)   you are not *paid* a *prohibited referral fee.*

Indicative behaviours

Acting in the following way(s) may tend to show that you have achieved these outcomes and therefore complied with the *Principles*:

IB(6.1)   any *arrangement* you enter into in respect of *regulated mortgage contracts, regulated credit agreements, general insurance contracts* (including after the event insurance) or *pure protection contracts,* provides that referrals will only be made where this is in the best interests of the particular *client* and the contract or agreement is suitable for the needs of that *client*;

IB(6.2)   any referral to a third party that can only offer products from one source is made only after the *client* has been informed of this limitation;

IB(6.3)   having effective systems in place for assessing whether any *arrangement* complies with the statutory and regulatory requirements;

IB(6.4)   retaining records and management information to enable you to demonstrate that any *payments* you receive are not *prohibited referral fees.*

Acting in the following way(s) may tend to show that you have not achieved these outcomes and therefore not complied with the *Principles*:

IB(6.5)   entering into any *arrangement* which restricts your freedom to recommend any particular business, except in respect of *regulated mortgage contracts, general insurance contracts* or *pure protection contracts*;

IB(6.6)   being an *appointed representative.*

In-house practice

The outcomes in this chapter apply to your *in-house practice.*

Notes

(i)   See Outcome 1.15, in relation to *financial benefits* that you may receive in respect of introductions to third parties.

(ii)   If the introduction is in connection with the provision of financial services, and your *firm* is not authorised by the Financial Conduct Authority, you will need to comply with the SRA Financial Services (Scope) Rules 2001 and the SRA Financial Services (Conduct of Business) Rules 2001. Where an introduction is not a *regulated activity* because you can rely on an exclusion in the *Regulated Activities Order,* you will need nevertheless to consider Outcome 1.15.

(iii)   This chapter should be read in conjunction with Chapter 12 (Separate businesses).

2ND SECTION: YOU AND YOUR BUSINESS

Chapter 7: Management of your business

This chapter is about the management and supervision of your *firm* or *in-house practice*.

Everyone has a role to play in the efficient running of a business, although of course that role will depend on the individual's position within the organisation. However, over-arching responsibility for the management of the business in the broadest sense rests with the *manager(s)*. The *manager(s)* should determine what arrangements are appropriate to meet the outcomes. Factors to be taken into account will include the size and complexity of the business; the number, experience and qualifications of the *employees*; the number of offices; and the nature of the work undertaken.

Where you are using a third party to provide services that you could provide, (often described as "outsourcing"), this chapter sets out the outcomes you need to achieve.

The outcomes in this chapter show how the *Principles* apply in the context of the management of your business.

Outcomes

You must achieve these outcomes:

O(7.1)   you have a clear and effective governance structure and reporting lines;

O(7.2)   you have effective systems and controls in place to achieve and comply with all the *Principles*, rules and outcomes and other requirements of the Handbook, where applicable;

O(7.3)   you identify, monitor and manage risks to compliance with all the *Principles*, rules and outcomes and other requirements of the Handbook, if applicable to you, and take steps to address issues identified;

O(7.4)   you maintain systems and controls for monitoring the financial stability of your *firm* and risks to money and *assets* entrusted to you by *clients* and others, and you take steps to address issues identified;

O(7.5)   you comply with legislation applicable to your business, including anti-money laundering and data protection legislation;

O(7.6)   you train individuals working in the *firm* to maintain a level of competence appropriate to their work and level of responsibility;

O(7.7)   you comply with the statutory requirements for the direction and supervision of *reserved legal activities* and *immigration work*;

O(7.8)   you have a system for supervising *clients'* matters, to include the regular checking of the quality of work by suitably competent and experienced people;

O(7.9)   you do not outsource *reserved legal activities* to a *person* who is not authorised to conduct such activities;

O(7.10)   subject to Outcome 7.9, where you outsource *legal activities* or any operational functions that are critical to the delivery of any *legal activities*, you ensure such outsourcing:

(a)   does not adversely affect your ability to comply with, or the *SRA's* ability to monitor your compliance with, your obligations in the Handbook;

(b)   is subject to contractual arrangements that enable the *SRA* or its agent to obtain information from, inspect the records (including electronic records) of, or enter the premises of, the third party, in relation to the outsourced activities or functions;

(c)   does not alter your obligations towards your *clients*; and

(d)   does not cause you to breach the conditions with which you must comply in order to be authorised and to remain so;

O(7.11)   you identify, monitor and manage the compliance of your *overseas practices* with the SRA Overseas Rules;

O(7.12)   you identify, monitor and manage all risks to your business which may arise from your *connected practices*;

O(7.13)   you assess and purchase the level of professional indemnity insurance cover that is appropriate for your current and past practice, taking into account potential levels of claim by your *clients* and others and any alternative arrangements you or your *client* may make.

Indicative behaviours

Acting in the following way(s) may tend to show that you have achieved these outcomes and therefore complied with the *Principles*:

IB(7.1)   safekeeping of documents and *assets* entrusted to the *firm*;

IB(7.2)   controlling budgets, expenditure and cash flow;

IB(7.3)   identifying and monitoring financial, operational and business continuity risks including *complaints*, credit risks and exposure, claims under legislation relating to matters such as data protection, IT failures and abuses, and damage to offices;

IB(7.4)   making arrangements for the continuation of your *firm* in the event of absences and emergencies, for example holiday or sick leave, with the minimum interruption to *clients'* business;

IB(7.5)   you maintain systems and controls for managing the risks posed by any financial inter-dependence which exists with your *connected practices*;

IB(7.6) you take appropriate action to control the use of your brand by any body or individual outside of England and Wales which is not an *overseas practice*.

In-house practice

Outcomes 7.5 and 7.7 apply to your *in-house practice*.

Outcomes 7.1 to 7.3, and 7.6 and 7.8 to 7.10 apply to you if you have management responsibilities.

Notes

(i) All of the chapters in the Code will be relevant to the management of your business, in particular those which require you to have systems and controls in place.

(ii) This chapter should also be read with the *SRA Authorisation Rules*, the SRA Financial Services (Conduct of Business) Rules 2001 and the *SRA Indemnity Insurance Rules*.

Chapter 8: Publicity

This chapter is about the manner in which you publicise your *firm* or *in-house practice* or any other businesses. The overriding concern is that *publicity* is not misleading and is sufficiently informative to ensure that *clients* and others can make informed choices.

In your *publicity*, you must comply with statutory requirements and have regard to voluntary codes.

The outcomes in this chapter show how the *Principles* apply in the context of *publicity*.

Outcomes

You must achieve these outcomes:

O(8.1) your *publicity* in relation to your *firm* or *in-house practice* or for any other business is accurate and not misleading, and is not likely to diminish the trust the public places in you and in the provision of legal services;

O(8.2) your *publicity* relating to charges is clearly expressed and identifies whether VAT and *disbursements* are included;

O(8.3) you do not make unsolicited approaches in person or by telephone to *members of the public* in order to publicise your *firm* or *in-house practice* or another business;

O(8.4) *clients* and the public have appropriate information about you, your *firm* and how you are regulated;

O(8.5) your letterhead, website and e-mails show the words "authorised and regulated by the Solicitors Regulation Authority" and either the *firm's* registered name and number if it is an *LLP* or *company* or, if the *firm* is a *partnership* or a *recognised sole practice*, the name under which it is licensed/authorised by the *SRA* and the number allocated to it by the *SRA*.

Indicative behaviours

Acting in the following way(s) may tend to show that you have achieved these outcomes and therefore complied with the *Principles*:

IB(8.1)   where you conduct other regulated activities your *publicity* discloses the manner in which you are regulated in relation to those activities;

IB(8.2)   where your *firm* is an *MDP*, any *publicity* in relation to that *practice* makes clear which services are regulated legal services and which are not;

IB(8.3)   any *publicity* intended for a jurisdiction outside England and Wales complies with the *Principles*, voluntary codes and the rules in force in that jurisdiction concerning *publicity*;

IB(8.4)   where you and another business jointly market services, the nature of the services provided by each business is clear.

Acting in the following way(s) may tend to show that you have not achieved these outcomes and therefore not complied with the *Principles*:

IB(8.5)   approaching people in the street, at ports of entry, in hospital or at the scene of an accident; including approaching people to conduct a survey which involves collecting contact details of potential *clients*, or otherwise promotes your *firm* or *in-house practice*;

IB(8.6)   allowing any other *person* to conduct *publicity* for your *firm* or *in-house practice* in a way that would breach the *Principles*;

IB(8.7)   advertising an estimated fee which is pitched at an unrealistically low level;

IB(8.8)   describing overheads of your *firm* (such a normal postage, telephone calls and charges arising in respect of *client* due diligence under the Money Laundering Regulations 2007) as *disbursements* in your advertisements;

IB(8.9)   advertising an estimated or fixed fee without making it clear that additional charges may be payable, if that is the case;

IB(8.10)   using a name or description of your *firm* or *in-house practice* that includes the word "solicitor(s)" if none of the *managers* are *solicitors*;

IB(8.11)   advertising your *firm* or *in-house practice* in a way that suggests that services provided by another business are provided by your *firm* or *in-house practice*;

IB(8.12)   producing misleading information concerning the professional status of any *manager* or *employee* of your *firm* or *in-house practice*.

In-house practice

Outcomes 8.1 to 8.4 apply to your *in-house practice* unless it is clear from the context that the outcome is not relevant in your particular circumstances.

Notes

(i) This chapter should be read in conjunction with Chapters 1 and 9.

Chapter 9: Fee sharing and referrals

This chapter is about protecting *clients'* interests where you have *arrangements* with third parties who introduce business to you and/or with whom you share your fees. The relationship between *clients* and *firms* should be built on trust, and any such *arrangement* should not jeopardise that trust by, for example, compromising your independence or professional judgement.

The outcomes in this chapter show how the *Principles* apply in the context of fee sharing and *referrals*.

Outcomes

You must achieve these outcomes:

O(9.1) your independence and your professional judgement are not prejudiced by virtue of any *arrangement* with another *person*;

O(9.2) your *clients'* interests are protected regardless of the interests of an *introducer* or *fee sharer* or your interest in receiving *referrals*;

O(9.3) *clients* are in a position to make informed decisions about how to pursue their matter;

O(9.4) *clients* are informed of any financial or other interest which an *introducer* has in referring the *client* to you;

O(9.5) *clients* are informed of any fee sharing *arrangement* that is relevant to their matter;

O(9.6) you do not make payments to an *introducer* in respect of *clients* who are the subject of criminal proceedings or who have the benefit of public funding;

O(9.7) where you enter into a financial *arrangement* with an *introducer* you ensure that the agreement is in writing;

O(9.8) you do not *pay* a *prohibited referral fee*.

Indicative behaviours

Acting in the following way(s) may tend to show that you have achieved these outcomes and therefore complied with the *Principles*:

IB(9.1)   only entering into *arrangements* with reputable third parties and monitoring the outcome of those *arrangements* to ensure that *clients* are treated fairly;

IB(9.2)   in any case where a *client* has entered into, or is proposing to enter into, an *arrangement* with an *introducer* in connection with their matter, which is not in their best interests, advising the *client* that this is the case;

IB(9.3)   terminating any *arrangement* with an *introducer* or *fee sharer* which is causing you to breach the *Principles* or any requirements of the Code;

IB(9.4)   being satisfied that any *client* referred by an *introducer* has not been acquired as a result of marketing or other activities which, if done by a *person* regulated by the *SRA*, would be contrary to the *Principles* or any requirements of the Code;

IB(9.5)   drawing the *client's* attention to any payments you make, or other consideration you provide, in connection with any *referral*;

IB(9.6)   where information needs to be given to a *client*, ensuring the information is clear and in writing or in a form appropriate to the *client's* needs;

IB(9.7)   having effective systems in place for assessing whether any *arrangement* complies with statutory and regulatory requirements;

IB(9.8)   ensuring that any *payments* you make for services, such as marketing, do not amount to the *payment* of *prohibited referral fees*;

IB(9.9)   retaining records and management information to enable you to demonstrate that any *payments* you make are not *prohibited referral fees*.

Acting in the following way(s) may tend to show that you have not achieved these outcomes and therefore not complied with the *Principles*:

IB(9.10)   entering into any type of business relationship with a third party, such as an unauthorised *partnership*, which places you in breach of the *SRA Authorisation Rules* or any other regulatory requirements in the Handbook;

IB(9.11)   allowing an *introducer* or *fee sharer* to influence the advice you give to *clients*;

IB(9.12)   accepting *referrals* where you have reason to believe that *clients* have been pressurised or misled into instructing you.

In-house practice

Outcomes 9.1 to 9.3 apply to your *in-house practice*.

Outcomes 9.4 to 9.8 apply unless it is clear from the context that the outcome is not relevant to your particular circumstances.

Notes

(i)   This chapter should be read in conjunction with:

    (a)   Chapter 1 (Client care)

    (b)   Chapter 4 (Confidentiality and disclosure)

    (c)   Chapter 8 (Publicity)

    (d)   The *SRA Authorisation Rules*

    (e)   The *SRA European Cross-Border Practice Rules*

3RD SECTION: YOU AND YOUR REGULATOR

Chapter 10: You and your regulator

This chapter is about co-operation with your regulators and ombudsmen, primarily the *SRA* and the *Legal Ombudsman.*

The information which we request from you will help us understand any risks to *clients*, and the public interest more generally.

The outcomes in this chapter show how the *Principles* apply in the context of you and your regulator.

Outcomes

You must achieve these outcomes:

O(10.1)   you ensure that you comply with all the reporting and notification requirements in the Handbook that apply to you;

O(10.2)   you provide the *SRA* with information to enable the *SRA* to decide upon any application you make, such as for a practising certificate, registration, recognition or a licence and whether any conditions should apply;

O(10.3)   you notify the *SRA* promptly of any material changes to relevant information about you including serious financial difficulty, action taken against you by another regulator and serious failure to comply with or achieve the *Principles*, rules, outcomes and other requirements of the Handbook;

O(10.4)   you report to the *SRA* promptly, serious misconduct by any person or *firm* authorised by the *SRA*, or any *employee, manager* or *owner* of any such *firm* (taking into account, where necessary, your duty of confidentiality to your *client*);

O(10.5)   you ensure that the *SRA* is in a position to assess whether any persons requiring prior approval are fit and proper at the point of approval and remain so;

O(10.6)   you co-operate fully with the *SRA* and the *Legal Ombudsman* at all times including in relation to any investigation about a *claim for redress* against you;

O(10.7) you do not attempt to prevent anyone from providing information to the *SRA* or the *Legal Ombudsman*;

O(10.8) you comply promptly with any written notice from the *SRA*;

O(10.9) pursuant to a notice under Outcome 10.8, you:

    (a) produce for inspection by the *SRA documents* held by you, or held under your control;

    (b) provide all information and explanations requested; and

    (c) comply with all requests from the *SRA* as to the form in which you produce any *documents* you hold electronically, and for photocopies of any *documents* to take away;

in connection with your *practice* or in connection with any trust of which you are, or formerly were, a trustee;

O(10.10) you provide any necessary permissions for information to be given, so as to enable the *SRA* to:

    (a) prepare a report on any *documents* produced; and

    (b) seek verification from *clients*, staff and the banks, building societies or other financial institutions used by you;

O(10.11) when required by the *SRA* in relation to a matter specified by the *SRA*, you:

    (a) act promptly to investigate whether any *person* may have a *claim for redress* against you;

    (b) provide the *SRA* with a report on the outcome of such an investigation, identifying *persons* who may have such a claim;

    (c) notify *persons* that they may have a right of redress against you, providing them with information as to the nature of the possible claim, about the *firm's complaints* procedure and about the *Legal Ombudsman*; and

    (d) ensure, where you have identified a *person* who may have a *claim for redress*, that the matter is dealt with under the *firm's complaints* procedure as if that *person* had made a *complaint*;

O(10.12) you do not attempt to abrogate to any third party your regulatory responsibilities in the Handbook, including the role of Compliance Officer for Legal Practice (*COLP*) or Compliance Officer for Finance and Administration (*COFA*);

O(10.13) once you are aware that your *firm* will cease to *practise*, you effect the orderly and transparent wind-down of activities, including informing the *SRA* before the *firm* closes.

Indicative behaviours

Acting in the following way(s) may tend to show that you have achieved these outcomes and therefore complied with the *Principles*:

IB(10.1)   actively monitoring your achievement of the outcomes in order to improve standards and identify non-achievement of the outcomes;

IB(10.2)   actively monitoring your financial stability and viability in order to identify and mitigate any risks to the public;

IB(10.3)   notifying the *SRA* promptly of any indicators of serious financial difficulty, such as inability to pay your professional indemnity insurance premium, or rent or salaries, or breach of bank covenants;

IB(10.4)   notifying the *SRA* promptly when you become aware that your business may not be financially viable to continue trading as a going concern, for example because of difficult trading conditions, poor cash flow, increasing overheads, loss of *managers* or *employees* and/or loss of sources of revenue;

IB(10.5)   notifying the *SRA* of any serious issues identified as a result of monitoring referred to in IB10.1 and IB10.2 above, and producing a plan for remedying issues that have been identified;

IB(10.6)   responding appropriately to any serious issues identified concerning competence and fitness and propriety of your *employees*, *managers* and *owners*;

IB(10.7)   reporting disciplinary action taken against you by another regulator;

IB(10.8)   informing the *SRA* promptly when you become aware of a significant change to your *firm*, for example:

  (a) key personnel, such as a *manager*, *COLP* or *COFA*, joining or leaving the *firm*;

  (b) a merger with, or an acquisition by or of, another *firm*;

IB(10.9)   having appropriate arrangements for the orderly transfer of *clients'* property to another *authorised body* if your *firm* closes;

IB(10.10)   having a "whistle-blowing" policy.

Acting in the following way(s) may tend to show that you have not achieved these outcomes and therefore not complied with the *Principles*:

IB(10.11)   entering into an agreement which would attempt to preclude the *SRA* or the *Legal Ombudsman* from investigating any actual or potential *complaint* or allegation of professional misconduct;

IB(10.12) unless you can properly allege malice, issuing defamation proceedings in respect of a *complaint* to the *SRA*.

In-house practice

The outcomes in this chapter apply to your *in-house practice*.

> *Notes*
>
> (i) A notice under this chapter is deemed to be duly served:
>
> > (a) on the date on which it is delivered to or left at your last notified *practising* address;
> >
> > (b) on the date on which it is sent electronically to your e-mail or fax address; or
> >
> > (c) seven days after it has been sent by post or document exchange to your last notified *practising* address.
>
> (ii) The outcomes in this chapter should be considered in conjunction with the following:
>
> > (a) Chapter 7 (Management of your business) – requirements for risk management procedures; and
> >
> > (b) note (xv) to Rule 8 of the *SRA Authorisation Rules*.

4TH SECTION: YOU AND OTHERS

Chapter 11: Relations with third parties

This chapter is about ensuring you do not take unfair advantage of those you deal with and that you act in a manner which promotes the proper operation of the legal system.

This includes your conduct in relation to *undertakings*; there is no obligation to give or receive an *undertaking* on behalf of a *client* but, if you do, you must ensure that you achieve the outcomes listed in this chapter.

The conduct requirements in this area extend beyond professional and business matters. They apply in any circumstances in which you may use your professional title to advance your personal interests.

The outcomes in this chapter show how the *Principles* apply in the context of your relations with third parties.

Outcomes

You must achieve these outcomes:

O(11.1) you do not take unfair advantage of third parties in either your professional or personal capacity;

O(11.2) you perform all *undertakings* given by you within an agreed timescale or within a reasonable amount of time;

O(11.3)   where you act for a seller of land, you inform all buyers immediately of the seller's intention to deal with more than one buyer;

O(11.4)   you properly administer oaths, affirmations or declarations where you are authorised to do so.

Indicative behaviours

Acting in the following way(s) may tend to show that you have achieved these outcomes and therefore complied with the *Principles*:

IB(11.1)   providing sufficient time and information to enable the costs in any matter to be agreed;

IB(11.2)   returning documents or money sent subject to an express condition if you are unable to comply with that condition;

IB(11.3)   returning documents or money on demand if they are sent on condition that they are held to the sender's order;

IB(11.4)   ensuring that you do not communicate with another party when you are aware that the other party has retained a *lawyer* in a matter, except:

    (a)   to request the name and address of the other party's *lawyer*; or

    (b)   the other party's *lawyer* consents to you communicating with the *client*; or

    (c)   where there are exceptional circumstances;

IB(11.5)   maintaining an effective system which records when *undertakings* have been given and when they have been discharged;

IB(11.6)   where an *undertaking* is given which is dependent upon the happening of a future event and it becomes apparent the future event will not occur, notifying the recipient of this.

Acting in the following way(s) may tend to show that you have not achieved these outcomes and therefore not complied with the *Principles*:

IB(11.7)   taking unfair advantage of an opposing party's lack of legal knowledge where they have not instructed a *lawyer*;

IB(11.8)   demanding anything for yourself or on behalf of your *client*, that is not legally recoverable, such as when you are instructed to collect a simple debt, demanding from the debtor the cost of the letter of claim since it cannot be said at that stage that such a cost is legally recoverable;

IB(11.9)   using your professional status or qualification to take unfair advantage of another *person* in order to advance your personal interests;

IB(11.10)   taking unfair advantage of a public office held by you, or a member of your family, or a member of your *firm* or their family.

In-house practice

The outcomes in this chapter apply to your *in-house practice*.

> *Notes*
>
> (i)   This chapter should be read in conjunction with Chapter 7 (Management of your business) in relation to the system you will need to have in place to control *undertakings*.

Chapter 12: Separate businesses

This chapter deals with your obligations when you have links to a *separate business* that is not authorised by the *SRA* or another *approved regulator*.

You can be a manager or employee of a *separate business*. However, you cannot *practise* as a *solicitor*, *REL* or *RFL* in a separate business except as permitted by Rule 4 (In-house practice) of the *SRA Practice Framework Rules* (see also Rules 1–3).

Clients of a *separate business* will not have the same regulatory protections as clients of an *authorised body* and it is important that this is clear to clients of the *separate business* particularly where they are being referred from the *authorised body* or cases are being divided with the *authorised body*.

Outcomes

You must achieve these outcomes:

O(12.1)   you ensure, and have safeguards in place to ensure, that *clients* are clear about the extent to which the services that you and the *separate business* offer are regulated;

O(12.2)   you do not represent, directly or indirectly, the *separate business* as being regulated by the *SRA* or any of its services being regulated by the *SRA*;

O(12.3)   the *separate business* does not carry on:

    (a)   reserved legal activities; or

    (b)   *immigration work* unless that work is regulated by the Office of the Immigration Services Commissioner;

O(12.4)   you only

    (a)   refer, recommend or introduce a *client* to the *separate business*;

    (b)   put your *client* and the *separate business* in touch with each other; or

(c) divide, or allow to be divided, a client's matter between you and the *separate business*,

where the *client* has given informed consent.

In-house practice

The outcomes in this chapter apply to your *in-house practice*.

5TH SECTION: APPLICATION, WAIVERS AND INTERPRETATION

Chapter 13: Application and waivers provisions

The SRA Code of Conduct applies to you in the following circumstances (and "you" must be construed accordingly):

Application of the SRA Code of Conduct in England and Wales

13.1   Subject to paragraphs 13.2 and 13.7 to 13.11 below and any other provisions in this Code, this Code applies to you, in relation to your activities carried out from an office in England and Wales, if you are:

(a) a *solicitor*, *REL* (subject to paragraph 13.12) or *RFL*, and you are *practising* as such, whether or not the entity through which you *practise* is subject to this Code;

(b) a *solicitor*, *REL* or *RFL* who is:

  (i)   a *manager*, *employee* or *owner* of a body which should be a *recognised body*, but has not been recognised by the *SRA*;

  (ii) a *manager*, *employee* or *owner* of a body that is a *manager* or *owner* of a body that should be a *recognised body*, but has not been recognised by the *SRA*;

  (iii) an *employee* in the *practice* of a *sole practitioner* which should be a *recognised sole practice*, but has not been recognised by the *SRA*;

  (iv) an *owner* of an *authorised body* or a body which should be a *recognised body* but has not been recognised by the *SRA*, even if you undertake no work for the body's *clients*; or

  (v)   a *manager* or *employee* of an *authorised non-SRA firm*, or a *manager* of a body which is a *manager* of an *authorised non-SRA firm*, when doing work of a sort authorised by the *SRA*, for that firm;

(c) an *authorised body*, or a body which should be a *recognised body* but has not been recognised by the *SRA*;

(d) any other person who is a *manager* or *employee* of an *authorised body*, or of a body which should be a *recognised body* but has not been recognised by the *SRA*;

(e) any other person who is an *employee* in the *practice* of a *sole practitioner* whose practice should be a *recognised sole practice*, but has not been recognised by the *SRA*;

and "you" includes "your" as appropriate.

13.2   Chapters 10, 12, 13, 14 and 15 of the Code apply to you if you are a *solicitor*, *REL* or *RFL* and you are:

(a) *practising* as a *manager* or *employee* of an *authorised non-SRA firm* when doing work of a sort authorised by the *authorised non-SRA firm's approved regulator*; or

(b) an *owner* of an *authorised non-SRA firm* even if you undertake no work for the body's *clients*.

Application of the SRA Code of Conduct in relation to practice from an office outside England and Wales

13.3   [Deleted]

13.4   [Deleted]

13.5   [Deleted]

13.6   [Deleted]

Application of the SRA Code of Conduct outside practice

13.7   In relation to activities which fall outside *practice*, whether undertaken as a *lawyer* or in some other business or private capacity, the following apply to you if you are a *solicitor*, or *REL*:

(a)   Outcome 11.1; and

(b)   Outcome 11.2.

General Provisions

13.8   The extent to which you are expected to implement the requirements of the Code will depend on your role in the *firm*, or your way of *practising*. For example, those who are managing the business will be expected to have more influence on how the *firm* or business is run than those *practising* in-house but not managing a legal department, or those *practising* as *employees* of a *firm*.

13.9   You must deliver all outcomes which are relevant to you and your situation.

13.10   Where in accordance with this chapter, the requirements of the Code apply to a *licensed body*, this Code applies to the *regulated activities* carried on by the body.

13.11   Where the *licensed body* is an *MDP*, the Code applies to the body, any *solicitor*, *REL* or *RFL* who is a *manager*, *employee* or *owner* of the body and any other person who is a *manager* or *employee* of the body as follows:

(a)   in relation to any *regulated activities*; and

(b)   in relation to any other *non-reserved legal activities*:

  (i)   outcomes 1.7, 1.9 to 1.11 and 10.6 apply to the body; and

  (ii)   outcomes 1.7, 1.9 to 1.11, chapters 4, 10, 11 and 13 to 15, apply to a *solicitor*, *REL* or *RFL* who is a *manager*, *employee* or *owner* of the body.

13.12   This Code applies to an *REL practising* as a *manager*, *employee*, *member* or *interest holder*, of an *Exempt European Practice* to the same extent that it applies to *In-house practice*.

Waivers

In any particular case or cases the *SRA* Board shall have the power, in exceptional circumstances, to waive in writing the provisions of these outcomes for a particular purpose or purposes expressed in such waiver, to place conditions on and to revoke such a waiver.

Chapter 13A: Practice Overseas

13A.1   If you are an individual or body *practising overseas*, the Code does not apply to you, but you must comply with the SRA Overseas Rules.

13A.2   However, if the following circumstances apply then you must comply with the provisions of the Code that are applicable to you as set out in 13A.3 to 13.A.6 below:

(a)   a body practising from an office outside England and Wales, only if you are required to be an *authorised body* as a result of the nature of your practice and you have been authorised by the *SRA* accordingly;

(b)   a *manager* of such a body; or

(c)   an individual engaged in *temporary practice overseas*;

(d)   a *regulated individual practising overseas* who is providing *reserved legal activities* to clients in England and Wales on an occasional basis, in accordance with rule 2(e)(i) of the *SRA Overseas Rules*.

13A.3   The following provisions of the Code apply:

(a)   chapter 3 (conflicts of interests);

(b)   chapter 4 (confidentiality and disclosure);

(c)   chapter 5 (your client and the court), to the extent that your practice relates to litigation or advocacy conducted before a court, tribunal or enquiry in England and Wales or a British court martial;

(d) outcomes 6.1 to 6.3 (your client and introductions to third parties);

(e) chapter 7 (management of your business);

(f) outcomes 8.1 and 8.4 (publicity);

(g) outcomes 9.1 to 9.7 (fee sharing and referrals), except where they conflict with the *SRA European Cross-Border Practice Rules*, in which case the latter will prevail;

(h) chapter 10 (you and your regulator);

(i) chapter 11 (relations with third parties), except that Outcome 11.3 only applies if the land in question is situated in England and Wales; and

(j) chapter 12 (separate businesses).

13A.4 In addition, you must meet the following outcomes:

O(13A.1) you properly account to your *clients* for any *financial benefit* you receive as a result of your instructions unless it is the prevailing custom of your local jurisdiction to deal with *financial benefits* in a different way;

O(13A.2) *clients* have the benefit of insurance or other indemnity in relation to professional liabilities which takes account of:

(a) the nature and extent of the risks you incur in your practice overseas;

(b) the local conditions in the jurisdiction in which you are *practising*; and

(c) the terms upon which insurance is available;

and you have not attempted to exclude liability below the minimum level required for practice in the local jurisdiction;

O(13A.3) you do not enter into unlawful contingency fee arrangements;

O(13A.4) you do not discriminate unlawfully according to the jurisdiction in which you are practising; and

O(13A.5) publicity intended for a jurisdiction outside England and Wales must comply with any applicable law or rules regarding lawyers' publicity in the jurisdiction in which your office is based and the jurisdiction for which the publicity is intended.

13A.5 you must be aware of the local laws and regulations governing your practice in an overseas jurisdiction;

13A.6 if compliance with any outcome in the Code would result in your breaching local laws or regulations you may disregard that outcome to the extent necessary to comply with that local law or regulation.

Chapter 14: Interpretation

14.1 The SRA Handbook Glossary 2012 shall apply and, unless the context otherwise requires:

(a) all italicised terms shall be defined; and

(b) all terms shall be interpreted,

in accordance with the *Glossary*.

Chapter 15: Transitional provisions

15.1 [Deleted]

15.2 [Deleted]

15.3 [Deleted]

15.4 [Deleted]

[D] Accounts Rules

SRA Accounts Rules 2011

PREAMBLE

Authority: made by the Solicitors Regulation Authority Board under sections 32, 33A, 34, 37, 79 and 80 of the Solicitors Act 1974, section 9 of the Administration of Justice Act 1985, section 83(5)(h) of, and paragraph 20 of Schedule 11 to, the Legal Services Act 2007 with the approval of the Legal Services Board;

date: 6 October 2011;

replacing: the Solicitors' Accounts Rules 1998;

regulating: the accounts of solicitors and their employees, registered European lawyers and their employees, registered foreign lawyers, recognised bodies and their managers and employees, and licensed bodies and their managers and employees, in respect of practice in England and Wales.

For the definition of words in italics see rule 2 – Interpretation.

INTRODUCTION

The Principles set out in the Handbook apply to all aspects of practice, including the handling of client money. Those which are particularly relevant to these rules are that you must:

- protect client money and assets;

- act with integrity;

- behave in a way that maintains the trust the public places in you and in the provision of legal services;

- comply with your legal and regulatory obligations and deal with your regulators and ombudsmen in an open, timely and co-operative manner; and

- run your business or carry out your role in the business effectively and in accordance with proper governance and sound financial and risk management principles.

The desired outcomes which apply to these rules are that:

- client money is safe;

- clients and the public have confidence that client money held by firms will be safe;

- firms are managed in such a way, and with appropriate systems and procedures in place, so as to safeguard client money;

- client accounts are used for appropriate purposes only; and

- the SRA is aware of issues in a firm relevant to the protection of client money.

Underlying principles which are specific to the accounts rules are set out in rule 1 below.

These rules apply to all those who carry on or work in a firm and to the firm itself (see rules 4 and 5). In relation to a multi-disciplinary practice, the rules apply only in respect of those activities for which the practice is regulated by the SRA, and are concerned only with money handled by the practice which relates to those regulated activities.

PART 1: GENERAL

Rule 1: The overarching objective and underlying principles

1.1   The purpose of these rules is to keep *client money* safe. This aim must always be borne in mind in the application of these rules.

1.2   *You* must comply with the Principles set out in the Handbook, and the outcomes in Chapter 7 of the *SRA Code of Conduct* in relation to the effective financial management of the *firm*, and in particular must:

(a)   keep other people's money separate from money belonging to *you* or *your firm*;

(b)   keep other people's money safely in a *bank* or *building society* account identifiable as a *client account* (except when the rules specifically provide otherwise);

(c)   use each *client's* money for that *client's* matters only;

(d)   use money held as *trustee* of a *trust* for the purposes of that *trust* only;

(e)   establish and maintain proper accounting systems, and proper internal controls over those systems, to ensure compliance with the rules;

(f)   keep proper accounting records to show accurately the position with regard to the money held for each *client* and *trust*;

(g)   account for *interest* on other people's money in accordance with the rules;

(h)   co-operate with the *SRA* in checking compliance with the rules; and

(i)   deliver annual accountants' reports as required by the rules.

Rule 2: Interpretation

2.1   The guidance notes do not form part of the rules.

2.2   The SRA Handbook Glossary 2012 shall apply and, unless the context otherwise requires:

(a)   all italicised terms shall be defined; and

(b)   all terms shall be interpreted,

in accordance with the *Glossary*.

2.3   References to the Legal Aid Agency are to be read, where appropriate, as including the Legal Services Commission.

Guidance notes

(i)   The effect of the definition of "you" is that the rules apply equally to all those who carry on or work in a firm and to the firm itself. See also rule 4 (persons governed by the rules) and rule 5 (persons exempt from the rules).

(ii)   The general definition of "office account" is wide. However, rule 17.1(b) (receipt and transfer of costs) and rule 19.1(b) and 19.2(b) (payments from the Legal Aid Agency) specify that certain money is to be placed in an office account at a bank or building society. Out-of-scope money can be held in an office account (which could be an account regulated by another regulator); it must not be held in a client account.

(iii)   For a flowchart summarising the effect of the rules, see Appendix 1. For more details of the treatment of different types of money, see the chart "Special situations – what applies" at Appendix 2. These two appendices do not form part of the rules but are included to help solicitors and their staff find their way about the rules.

Rule 3: Geographical scope

3.1   Parts 1 to 6 of these rules apply to practice carried on from an office in England and Wales. Part 7 of these rules applies to the practice of an *REL* from an office in England and Wales of an *Exempt European Practice*.

Rule 4: Persons governed by the rules

4.1   Save as provided in rule 4.2 below, Parts 1 to 6 of these rules apply to *you*.

4.2   In relation to an *MDP*, the rules apply to *you* only in respect of your *regulated activities*.

4.3   Part 6 of the rules (accountants' reports) also applies to reporting accountants.

4.4   If *you* have held or received *client money*, but no longer do so, whether or not *you* continue in practice, *you* continue to be bound by some of the rules.

Guidance notes

(i)   "You" is defined in the Glossary. All employees of a recognised body or licensed body are directly subject to the rules, following changes made by the Legal Services Act 2007. All employees in a recognised sole practice are also directly subject to the rules under section 34A of the Solicitors Act 1974. Non-compliance by any member of staff will also lead to the principals being in breach of the rules – see rule 6. Misconduct by an employee can also lead to an order of the SRA or the Solicitors Disciplinary Tribunal under section 43 of the Solicitors Act 1974 imposing restrictions on his or her employment.

(ii)   Rules which continue to apply to you where you no longer hold client money include:

    (a) rule 7 (duty to remedy breaches);

    (b) rule 17.2 and 17.8, rule 29.15 to 29.24 and rule 30 (retention of records);

    (c) rule 31 (production of documents, information and explanations);

    (d) Part 6 (accountants' reports), and in particular rule 32A and rule 33.5 (delivery of final report), and rule 35.2.

(iii)   The rules do not cover trusteeships carried on in a purely personal capacity outside any legal practice. It will normally be clear from the terms of the appointment whether you are being appointed in a purely personal capacity or in your professional capacity. If you are charging for the work, it is clearly being done in a professional capacity. Use of professional stationery may also indicate that the work is being done in a professional capacity.

(iv)   A solicitor who wishes to retire from private practice will need to make a decision about any professional trusteeship. There are three possibilities:

    (a) continue to act as a professional trustee (as evidenced by, for instance, charging for work done, or by continuing to use the title "solicitor" in connection with the trust). In this case, the solicitor must continue to hold a practising certificate, and money subject to the trust must continue to be dealt with in accordance with the rules.

    (b) continue to act as trustee, but in a purely personal capacity. In this case, the solicitor must stop charging for the work, and must not be held out as a solicitor (unless this is qualified by words such as "non-practising" or "retired") in connection with the trust.

    (c) cease to be a trustee.

(v)   A licensed body may undertake a range of services, comprising both "traditional" legal services and other, related, services of a non-legal nature, for example, where a solicitor, estate agent and surveyor set up in practice together. Where a licensed body practises in this way (an MDP), only some of the services it provides (reserved and other legal activities, and other activities which are subject to one or more conditions on the body's licence) are within the regulatory reach of the SRA. Other, "non-legal", activities of the licensed body may be regulated by another regulator, and some activities may not fall within the regulatory ambit of any regulator.

Rule 5: Persons exempt from the rules

5.1   The rules do not apply to *you* when:

    (a) practising as an employee of:

        (i)   a *local authority*;

        (ii) *statutory undertakers*;

(iii) a body whose accounts are audited by the Comptroller and Auditor General;

(iv) the Duchy of Lancaster;

(v) the Duchy of Cornwall; or

(vi) the Church Commissioners; or

(b) practising as the Solicitor of the City of London; or

(c) carrying out the functions of:

(i) a coroner or other judicial office; or

(ii) a sheriff or under-sheriff; or

(d) practising as a *manager* or employee of an *authorised non-SRA firm*, and acting within the scope of that *firm's* authorisation to practise.

Guidance note

(i) A person practising as a manager or employee of an authorised non-SRA firm is exempt from the Accounts Rules when acting within the scope of the firm's authorisation. Thus if a solicitor is a partner or employee in a firm authorised by the Council for Licensed Conveyancers, the rules will not apply to any money received by the solicitor in connection with conveyancing work. However if the solicitor does in-house litigation work – say collecting money owed to the firm – the Accounts Rules will apply to any money received by the solicitor in that context. This is because, whilst in-house litigation work is within the scope of the solicitor's authorisation as an individual, it is outside the scope of authorisation of the firm.

Rule 6: Principals' responsibility for compliance

6.1 All the *principals* in a *firm* must ensure compliance with the rules by the *principals* themselves and by everyone employed in the *firm*. This duty also extends to the *directors* of a *recognised body* or *licensed body* which is a *company*, or to the members of a *recognised body* or *licensed body* which is an *LLP*. It also extends to the COFA of a *firm* (whether a *manager* or non-*manager*).

Guidance note

(i) Rule 8.5(d) of the SRA Authorisation Rules requires all firms to have a COFA. The appointment of a COFA satisfies the requirement under section 92 of the Legal Services Act 2007 for a licensed body to appoint a Head of Finance and Administration. Under rule 6 of the accounts rules, the COFA must ensure compliance with the accounts rules. This obligation is in addition to, not instead of, the duty of all the principals to ensure compliance (the COFA may be subject to this duty both as COFA and as a principal). Under rule 8.5(e) of the SRA Authorisation Rules, the COFA of a licensed body must report any breaches, and the COFA of a recognised body must report material breaches, of the accounts rules to the SRA as soon as reasonably practicable. The COFA of a recognised sole practice has a duty to report material breaches under Rule 8.5(e) of the SRA Authorisation Rules. All

COFAs must record any breaches and make those records available to the SRA on request. (See also outcomes 10.3 and 10.4 of Chapter 10 of the SRA Code of Conduct in relation to the general duty to report serious financial difficulty or serious misconduct.)

Rule 7: Duty to remedy breaches

7.1   Any breach of the rules must be remedied promptly upon discovery. This includes the replacement of any money improperly withheld or withdrawn from a *client account*.

7.2   In a private practice, the duty to remedy breaches rests not only on the person causing the breach, but also on all the *principals* in the *firm*. This duty extends to replacing missing *client money* from the *principals'* own resources, even if the money has been misappropriated by an employee or another *principal*, and whether or not a claim is subsequently made on the *firm's* insurance or the Compensation Fund.

Rule 8: Liquidators, trustees in bankruptcy, Court of Protection deputies and trustees of occupational pension schemes

8.1   If in the course of practice *you* act as:

    (a)   a liquidator,

    (b)   a trustee in bankruptcy,

    (c)   a *Court of Protection deputy*, or

    (d)   a trustee of an occupational pension scheme which is subject to section 47(1)(a) of the Pensions Act 1995 (appointment of an auditor) and section 49(1) (separate bank account) and regulations under section 49(2)(b) (books and records),

you must comply with:

    (i)   the appropriate statutory rules or regulations;

    (ii)   the Principles referred to, and the underlying principles set out, in rule 1; and

    (iii) the requirements of rule 8.2 to 8.4 below;

and will then be deemed to have satisfactorily complied with the Accounts Rules.

8.2   In respect of any records kept under the appropriate statutory rules, there must also be compliance with:

    (a)   rule 29.15 – bills and notifications of costs;

    (b)   rule 29.17(c) – retention of records;

    (c)   rule 29.20 – centrally kept records;

    (d)   rule 31 – production of documents, information and explanations; and

    (e)   rule 43A.1 – reporting accountant to check compliance.

8.3   If a liquidator or trustee in bankruptcy uses any of the *firm's client accounts* for holding money pending transfer to the Insolvency Services Account or to a local bank account authorised by the Secretary of State, he or she must comply with the Accounts Rules in all respects whilst the money is held in the *client account*.

8.4   If the appropriate statutory rules or regulations do not govern the holding or receipt of *client money* in a particular situation (for example, money below a certain limit), *you* must comply with the Accounts Rules in all respects in relation to that money.

Guidance notes

(i)   The Insolvency Regulations 1994 (S.I. 1994 no. 2507) regulate liquidators and trustees in bankruptcy.

(ii)   The Court of Protection Rules 2007 (S.I. 2007 no. 1744 (L.12)) regulate Court of Protection deputies.

(iii)   Money held or received by liquidators, trustees in bankruptcy, Court of Protection deputies and trustees of occupational pension schemes is client money but, because of the statutory rules and rule 8.1, it will not normally be kept in a client account. If for any reason it is held in a client account, the Accounts Rules apply to that money for the time it is so held (see rule 8.3 and 8.4).

Rule 9: Joint accounts

9.1   If, when acting in a *client's* matter, *you* hold or receive money jointly with the *client*, another practice or another third party, the rules in general do not apply, but the following must be complied with:

(a)   rule 29.11 – statements from banks, building societies and other financial institutions;

(b)   rule 29.15 – bills and notifications of costs;

(c)   rule 29.17(b)(ii) – retention of statements and passbooks;

(d)   rule 29.21 – centrally kept records;

(e)   rule 31 – production of documents, information and explanations; and

(f)   rule 43A.1 – reporting accountant to check compliance.

A joint account is not a *client account* but money held in a joint account is *client money*.

Operation of the joint account by you only

9.2   If the joint account is operated only by *you*, *you* must ensure that *you* receive the statements from the *bank*, *building society* or other financial institution in accordance with rule 29.11, and have possession of any passbooks.

Shared operation of the joint account

9.3   If *you* share the operation of the joint account with the *client*, another practice or another third party, *you* must:

(a)   ensure that *you* receive the statements or duplicate statements from the *bank*, *building society* or other financial institution in accordance with rule 29.11, and retain them in accordance with rule 29.17(b)(ii); and

(b)   ensure that *you* either have possession of any passbooks, or take copies of the passbook entries before handing any passbook to the other signatory, and retain them in accordance with rule 29.17(b)(ii).

Operation of the joint account by the other account holder

9.4   If the joint account is operated solely by the other account holder, *you* must ensure that *you* receive the statements or duplicate statements from the *bank*, *building society* or other financial institution in accordance with rule 29.11, and retain them in accordance with rule 29.17(b)(ii).

Rule 10: Operation of a client's own account

10.1   If, in the course of practice, *you* operate a *client's* own account as signatory (for example, as donee under a power of attorney), the rules in general do not apply, but the following must be complied with:

(a)   rule 30.1 to 30.4 – accounting records for clients' own accounts;

(b)   rule 31 – production of documents, information and explanations; and

(c)   rule 43A.1 – reporting accountant to check compliance.

Operation by you only

10.2   If the account is operated by *you* only, *you* must ensure that *you* receive the statements from the *bank*, *building society* or other financial institution in accordance with rule 30, and have possession of any passbooks.

Shared operation of the account

10.3   If *you* share the operation of the account with the *client* or a co-attorney outside *your firm*, *you* must:

(a)   ensure that *you* receive the statements or duplicate statements from the *bank*, *building society* or other financial institution and retain them in accordance with rule 30.1 to 30.4; and

(b)   ensure that *you* either have possession of any passbooks, or take copies of the passbook entries before handing any passbook to the *client* or co-attorney, and retain them in accordance with rule 30.1 to 30.4.

Operation of the account for a limited purpose

10.4   If *you* are given authority (whether as attorney or otherwise) to operate the account for a limited purpose only, such as the taking up of a share rights issue during the *client's* temporary absence, *you* need not receive statements or possess passbooks, provided that *you* retain details of all cheques drawn or paid in, and retain copies of all passbook entries, relating to the transaction, and retain them in accordance with rule 30.1 to 30.3.

Application

10.5   This rule applies only to private practice. It does not cover money held or received by a donee of a power of attorney acting in a purely personal capacity outside any legal practice (see rule 4, guidance notes (iii)–(iv)).

10.6   A "*client's* own account" covers all accounts in a *client's* own name, whether opened by the *client* himself or herself, or by *you* on the *client's* instructions under rule 15.1(b). A "*client's* own account" also includes an account opened in the name of a person designated by the *client* under rule 15.1(b).

Guidance notes

(i)   Money held in a client's own account (under a power of attorney or otherwise) is not "client money" for the purpose of the rules because it is not "held or received" by you. If you close the account and receive the closing balance, this becomes client money subject to all the rules.

(ii)   Merely paying money into a client's own account, or helping the client to complete forms in relation to such an account, is not "operating" the account.

(iii)   If as executor you operate the deceased's account (whether before or after the grant of probate), you will be subject to the limited requirements of rule 10. If the account is subsequently transferred into your name, or a new account is opened in your name, you will have "held or received" client money and are then subject to all the rules.

Rule 11: Firm's rights not affected

11.1   Nothing in these rules deprives *you* of any recourse or right, whether by way of lien, set off, counterclaim, charge or otherwise, against money standing to the credit of a *client account*.

Rule 12: Categories of money

12.1   These rules do not apply to *out-of-scope money*, save to the limited extent specified in the rules. All other money held or received in the course of practice falls into one or other of the following categories:

(a)   "client money" – money held or received for a *client* or as *trustee*, and all other money which is not *office money*; or

    (b) "office money" – money which belongs to *you* or *your firm*.

12.2   "Client money" includes money held or received:

    (a) as *trustee*;

    (b) as agent, bailee, stakeholder, or as the donee of a power of attorney, or as a liquidator, trustee in bankruptcy, *Court of Protection deputy* or trustee of an occupational pension scheme;

    (c) for payment of unpaid *professional disbursements*;

    (d) for payment of stamp duty land tax, Land Registry registration fees, telegraphic transfer fees and court fees (but see also guidance note (i));

    (e) as a payment on account of *costs* generally;

    (f) as a financial benefit paid in respect of a *client*, unless the *client* has given *you* prior authority to retain it (see Chapter 1, outcome 1.15 and indicative behaviour 1.20 of the *SRA Code of Conduct*);

    (g) jointly with another person outside the *firm*.

12.3   Money held to the sender's order is *client money*.

    (a) If money is accepted on such terms, it must be held in a *client account*.

    (b) However, a cheque or draft sent to *you* on terms that the cheque or draft (as opposed to the money) is held to the sender's order must not be presented for payment without the sender's consent.

    (c) The recipient is always subject to a professional obligation to return the money, or the cheque or draft, to the sender on demand.

12.4   An advance to a *client* which is paid into a *client account* under rule 14.2(b) becomes *client money*.

12.5   A cheque in respect of damages and *costs*, made payable to the *client* but paid into a *client account* under rule 14.2(e), becomes *client money*.

12.6   Endorsing a cheque or draft over to a *client* or employer in the course of practice amounts to receiving *client money*. Even if no other *client money* is held or received, *you* must comply with some provisions of the rules, e.g.:

    (a) rule 7 (duty to remedy breaches);

    (b) rule 29 (accounting records for client accounts, etc.);

    (c) rule 31 (production of documents, information and explanations);

    (d) rule 32A (obtaining and delivery of accountants' reports).

12.7   "Office money" includes:

(a) money held or received in connection with running the *firm*; for example, PAYE, or VAT on the *firm's fees*;

(b) *interest* on *general client accounts*; the *bank* or *building society* should be instructed to credit such *interest* to the *office account* – but see also rule 14.2(d);

(c) payments received in respect of:

   (i) *fees* due to the *firm* against a bill or written notification of *costs* incurred, which has been given or sent in accordance with rule 17.2;

   (ii) *disbursements* already paid by the *firm*;

   (iii) *disbursements* incurred but not yet paid by the *firm*, but excluding unpaid *professional disbursements*;

   (iv) money paid for or towards an *agreed fee*;

(d) money held in a *client account* and earmarked for *costs* under rule 17.3;

(e) money held or received from the Legal Aid Agency as a *regular payment* (see rule 19.2).

12.8   If a *firm* conducts a personal or office transaction – for instance, conveyancing – for a *principal* (or for a number of *principals*), money held or received on behalf of the *principal(s)* is *office money*. However, other circumstances may mean that the money is *client money*, for example:

(a) If the *firm* also acts for a lender, money held or received on behalf of the lender is *client money*.

(b) If the *firm* acts for a *principal* and, for example, his or her spouse jointly (assuming the spouse is not a *partner* in the practice), money received on their joint behalf is *client money*.

(c) If the *firm* acts for an assistant *solicitor*, consultant or non-solicitor employee, or (if it is a *company*) a *director*, or (if it is an *LLP*) a member, he or she is regarded as a *client* of the *firm*, and money received for him or her is *client money* – even if he or she conducts the matter personally.

Guidance notes

(i)   Money held or received for payment of stamp duty land tax, Land Registry registration fees, telegraphic transfer fees and court fees is not office money because you have not incurred an obligation to HMRC, the Land Registry, the bank or the court to pay the duty or fee; (on the other hand, if you have already paid the duty or fee out of your own resources, or have received the service on credit, or the bank's charge for a telegraphic transfer forms part of your profit costs, payment subsequently received from the client will be office money);

(ii)   Money held:

(a) by liquidators, trustees in bankruptcy, Court of Protection deputies and trustees of occupational pension schemes;

(b) jointly with another person outside the practice (for example, with a lay trustee, or with another firm);

is client money, subject to a limited application of the rules – see rules 8 and 9. The donee of a power of attorney, who operates the donor's own account, is also subject to a limited application of the rules (see rule 10), although money kept in the donor's own account is not "client money" because it is not "held or received" by the donee.

(iii) If the SRA intervenes in a practice, money from the practice is held or received by the SRA's intervention agent subject to a trust under Schedule 1 paragraph 7(1) of the Solicitors Act 1974, and is therefore client money. The same provision requires the agent to pay the money into a client account.

(iv) Money held or received in the course of employment when practising in one of the capacities listed in rule 5 (persons exempt from the rules) is not "client money" for the purpose of the rules, because the rules do not apply at all.

(v) The receipt of out-of-scope money of an MDP which is mixed with other types of money is dealt with in rules 17 and 18.

(vi) See Appendices 1 and 2 (which do not form part of the rules) for a summary of the effect of the rules and the treatment of different types of money.

PART 2: CLIENT MONEY AND OPERATION OF A CLIENT ACCOUNT

Rule 13: Client accounts

13.1 If *you* hold or receive *client money*, *you* must keep one or more *client accounts* (unless all the *client money* is always dealt with outside any *client account* in accordance with rule 8, rule 9, rule 15 or rule 16).

13.2 A "client account" is an account of a practice kept at a *bank* or *building society* for holding *client money*, in accordance with the requirements of this part of the rules.

13.3 The *client account(s)* of:

(a) a *sole practitioner* must be in the name under which the *sole practitioner* is recognised by the *SRA*, whether that is the *sole practitioner's* own name or the *firm* name;

(b) a *partnership* must be in the name under which the *partnership* is recognised by the *SRA*;

(c) an incorporated practice must be in the company name, or the name of the *LLP*, as registered at Companies House;

(d) in-house *solicitors* or *RELs* must be in the name of the current *principal solicitor/REL* or *solicitors/RELs*;

(e) *trustees*, where all the *trustees* of a *trust* are *managers* and/or employees of the same *recognised body* or *licensed body*, must be either in the name of the *recognised body/licensed body* or in the name of the *trustee(s)*;

(f) *trustees*, where all the *trustees* of a *trust* are the *sole practitioner* and/or his or her employees, must be either in the name under which the *sole practitioner* is recognised by the *SRA* or in the name of the *trustee(s)*;

and the name of the account must also include the word "client" in full (an abbreviation is not acceptable).

13.4 A *client account* must be:

(a) a *bank* account at a branch (or a *bank's* head office) in England and Wales; or

(b) a *building society* account at a branch (or a society's head office) in England and Wales.

13.5 There are two types of *client account*:

(a) a "separate designated client account", which is an account for money relating to a single *client*, other person or *trust*, and which includes in its title, in addition to the requirements of rule 13.3 above, a reference to the identity of the *client*, other person or *trust*; and

(b) a "general client account", which is any other *client account*.

13.6 [Deleted]

13.7 The *clients* of a *licensed body* must be informed at the outset of the retainer, or during the course of the retainer as appropriate, if the *licensed body* is (or becomes) owned by a *bank* or *building society* and its *client account* is held at that *bank* or *building society* (or another *bank* or *building society* in the same group).

13.8 Money held in a *client account* must be immediately available, even at the sacrifice of *interest*, unless the *client* otherwise instructs, or the circumstances clearly indicate otherwise.

Guidance notes

(i)   In the case of in-house practice, any client account should include the names of all solicitors or registered European lawyers held out on the notepaper as principals. The names of other employees who are solicitors or registered European lawyers may also be included if so desired.

(ii)   Compliance with rule 13.1 to 13.4 ensures that clients, as well as the bank or building society, have the protection afforded by section 85 of the Solicitors Act 1974 or article 4 of the Legal Services Act 2007 (Designation as a Licensing Authority) (No. 2) Order 2011 as appropriate.

Rule 14: Use of a client account

14.1   *Client money* must *without delay* be paid into a *client account*, and must be held in a *client account*, except when the rules provide to the contrary (see rules 8, 9, 15, 16, 17 and 19).

14.2   Only *client money* may be paid into or held in a *client account*, except:

(a)   an amount of the *firm's* own money required to open or maintain the account;

(b)   an advance from the *firm* to fund a payment on behalf of a *client* or *trust* in excess of funds held for that *client* or *trust*; the sum becomes *client money* on payment into the account (for *interest* on *client money*, see rule 22.2(c));

(c)   money to replace any sum which for any reason has been drawn from the account in breach of rule 20; the replacement money becomes *client money* on payment into the account;

(d)   *interest* which is paid into a *client account* to enable payment from the *client account* of all money owed to the *client*; and

(e)   a cheque in respect of damages and *costs*, made payable to the *client*, which is paid into the *client account* pursuant to the *Society's* Conditional Fee Agreement; the sum becomes *client money* on payment into the account (but see rule 17.1(e) for the transfer of the *costs* element from *client account*);

and except when the rules provide to the contrary (see guidance note (ii) below).

14.3   *Client money* must be returned to the *client* (or other person on whose behalf the money is held) promptly, as soon as there is no longer any proper reason to retain those funds. Payments received after *you* have already accounted to the *client*, for example by way of a refund, must be paid to the *client* promptly.

14.4   *You* must promptly inform a *client* (or other person on whose behalf the money is held) in writing of the amount of any *client money* retained at the end of a matter (or the substantial conclusion of a matter), and the reason for that retention. *You* must inform the *client* (or other person) in writing at least once every twelve months thereafter of the amount of *client money* still held and the reason for the retention, for as long as *you* continue to hold that money.

14.5   *You* must not provide banking facilities through a *client account*. Payments into, and transfers or withdrawals from, a *client account* must be in respect of instructions relating to an underlying transaction (and the funds arising therefrom) or to a service forming part of *your* normal regulated activities.

Guidance notes

(i)   Exceptions to rule 14.1 (client money must be paid into a client account) can be found in:

(a) rule 8 – liquidators, trustees in bankruptcy, Court of Protection deputies and trustees of occupational pension schemes;

(b) rule 9 – joint accounts;

(c) rule 15 – client's instructions;

(d) rule 16 – cash paid straight to client, beneficiary or third party;

  (A) cheque endorsed to client, beneficiary or third party;

  (B) money withheld from client account on the SRA's authority;

  (C) money withheld from client account in accordance with a trustee's powers;

(e) rule 17.1(b) – receipt and transfer of costs;

(f) rule 19.1 – payments by the Legal Aid Agency.

(ii) Rule 14.2(a) to (e) provides for exceptions to the principle that only client money may be paid into a client account. Additional exceptions can be found in:

(a) rule 17.1(c) – receipt and transfer of costs;

(b) rule 18.2(b) – receipt of mixed payments;

(c) rule 19.2(c)(ii) – transfer to client account of a sum for unpaid professional disbursements, where regular payments are received from the Legal Aid Agency.

(iii) Only a nominal sum will be required to open or maintain an account. In practice, banks will usually open (and, if instructed, keep open) accounts with nil balances.

(iv) If client money is invested in the purchase of assets other than money – such as stocks or shares – it ceases to be client money, because it is no longer money held by the firm. If the investment is subsequently sold, the money received is, again, client money. The records kept under rule 29 will need to include entries to show the purchase or sale of investments.

(v) Rule 14.5 reflects decisions of the Solicitors Disciplinary Tribunal that it is not a proper part of a solicitor's everyday business or practice to operate a banking facility for third parties, whether they are clients of the firm or not. It should be noted that any exemption under the Financial Services and Markets Act 2000 is likely to be lost if a deposit is taken in circumstances which do not form part of your practice. It should also be borne in mind that there are criminal sanctions against assisting money launderers.

(vi) As with rule 7 (Duty to remedy breaches), "promptly" in rule 14.3 and 14.4 is not defined but should be given its natural meaning in the particular circumstances. Accounting to a client for any surplus funds will often fall naturally at the end of a matter. Other retainers may be more protracted and, even when the principal work has been completed, funds may still be needed, for example, to cover outstanding work in a conveyancing transaction or to meet a tax liability. (See also paragraphs 4.8 and 4.9 of the Guidelines for accounting procedures and systems at Appendix 3.)

(vii) There may be some instances when, during the course of a retainer, the specific purpose for which particular funds were paid no longer exists, for example, the need to instruct counsel or a medical expert. Rule 14.3 is concerned with returning funds to clients at the end of a matter (or the substantial conclusion of a matter) and is not intended to apply to ongoing retainers. However, in order to act in the best interests of your client, you may need to take instructions in such circumstances to ascertain, for instance, whether the money should be returned to the client or retained to cover the general funding or other aspects of the case.

(viii) See rule 20.1(j)–(k) for withdrawals from a client account when the rightful owner of funds cannot be traced. The obligation to report regularly under rule 14.4 ceases to apply if you are no longer able to trace the client, at which point rule 20.1(j) or (k) would apply.

Rule 15: Client money withheld from client account on client's instructions

15.1 *Client money* may be:

- (a) held by *you* outside a *client account* by, for example, retaining it in the *firm's* safe in the form of cash, or placing it in an account in the *firm's* name which is not a *client account*, such as an account outside England and Wales; or

- (b) paid into an account at a *bank*, *building society* or other financial institution opened in the name of the *client* or of a person designated by the *client*;

but only if the *client* instructs *you* to that effect for the *client's* own convenience, and only if the instructions are given in writing, or are given by other means and confirmed by *you* to the *client* in writing.

15.2 It is improper to seek blanket agreements, through standard terms of business or otherwise, to hold *client money* outside a *client account*.

15.3 If a *client* instructs *you* to hold part only of a payment in accordance with rule 15.1(a) or (b), the entire payment must first be placed in a *client account*, before transferring the relevant part out and dealing with it in accordance with the *client's* instructions.

15.4 A payment on account of *costs* received from a person who is funding all or part of *your fees* may be withheld from a *client account* on the instructions of that person given in accordance with rule 15.1.

Guidance notes

(i) Money withheld from a client account under rule 15.1(a) remains client money, and all the record-keeping provisions of rule 29 will apply.

(ii)   Once money has been paid into an account set up under rule 15.1(b), it ceases to be client money. Until that time, the money is client money and, under rule 29, a record is required of your receipt of the money, and its payment into the account in the name of the client or designated person. If you can operate the account, rule 10 (operating a client's own account) and rule 30 (accounting records for clients' own accounts) will apply. In the absence of instructions to the contrary, rule 14.1 requires any money withdrawn to be paid into a client account.

(iii)   Rule 29.17(d) requires clients' instructions under rule 15.1 to be kept for at least six years.

Rule 16: Other client money withheld from a client account

16.1   The following categories of *client money* may be withheld from a *client account*:

(a) cash received and *without delay* paid in cash in the ordinary course of business to the *client* or, on the *client's* behalf, to a third party, or paid in cash in the execution of a *trust* to a beneficiary or third party;

(b) a cheque or draft received and endorsed over in the ordinary course of business to the *client* or, on the *client's* behalf, to a third party, or *without delay* endorsed over in the execution of a *trust* to a beneficiary or third party;

(c) money withheld from a *client account* on instructions under rule 15;

(d) money which, in accordance with a *trustee's* powers, is paid into or retained in an account of the *trustee* which is not a *client account* (for example, an account outside England and Wales), or properly retained in cash in the performance of the *trustee's* duties;

(e) unpaid *professional disbursements* included in a payment of *costs* dealt with under rule 17.1(b);

(f) in respect of payments from the Legal Aid Agency:

(i) advance payments from the Legal Aid Agency withheld from *client account* (see rule 19.1(a)); and

(ii) unpaid *professional disbursements* included in a payment of *costs* from the Legal Aid Agency (see rule 19.1(b)); and

(g) money withheld from a *client account* on the written authorisation of the SRA. The *SRA* may impose a condition that the money is paid to a charity which gives an indemnity against any legitimate claim subsequently made for the sum received.

Guidance notes

(i)   If money is withheld from a client account under rule 16.1(a) or (b), rule 29 requires records to be kept of the receipt of the money and the payment out.

(ii)   If money is withheld from a client account under rule 16.1(d), rule 29 requires a record to be kept of the receipt of the money, and requires the inclusion of the money in the monthly reconciliations. (Money held by a trustee jointly with another party is subject only to the limited requirements of rule 9.)

(iii)   It makes no difference, for the purpose of the rules, whether an endorsement is effected by signature in the normal way or by some other arrangement with the bank.

(iv)   The circumstances in which authorisation would be given under rule 16.1(g) must be extremely rare. Applications for authorisation should be made to the Professional Ethics Guidance Team.

Rule 17: Receipt and transfer of costs

17.1   When *you* receive money paid in full or part settlement of *your* bill (or other notification of *costs*) *you* **must follow one of the following five options:**

(a)   **determine the composition of the payment without delay, and deal with the money accordingly:**

  (i)   if the sum comprises *office money* and/or *out-of-scope money* only, it must be placed in an *office account*;

  (ii)   if the sum comprises only *client money*, the entire sum must be placed in a *client account*;

  (iii) if the sum includes both *office money* and *client money*, or *client money* and *out-of-scope money*, or *client money*, *out-of-scope money* and *office money*, *you* must follow rule 18 (receipt of mixed payments); or

(b)   **ascertain that the payment comprises only *office money* and/or *out-of-scope money*, and/or *client money* in the form of *professional disbursements* incurred but not yet paid, and deal with the payment as follows:**

  (i)   place the entire sum in an *office account* at a *bank* or *building society* branch (or head office) in England and Wales; and

  (ii)   by the end of the second working day following receipt, either pay any unpaid *professional disbursement*, or transfer a sum for its settlement to a *client account*; **or**

(c)   **pay the entire sum into a *client account* (regardless of its composition), and transfer any *office money* and/or *out-of-scope money* out of the *client account* within 14 days of receipt; or**

(d)   **on receipt of *costs* from the Legal Aid Agency, follow the option in rule 19.1(b); or**

(e)   **in relation to a cheque paid into a *client account* under rule 14.2(e), transfer the *costs* element out of the *client account* within 14 days of receipt.**

17.2   If *you* properly require payment of *your fees* from money held for a *client* or *trust* in a *client account*, *you* must first give or send a bill of *costs*, or other written notification of the *costs* incurred, to the *client* or the paying party.

17.3   Once *you* have complied with rule 17.2 above, the money earmarked for *costs* becomes *office money* and must be transferred out of the *client account* within 14 days.

17.4   A payment on account of *costs* generally in respect of those activities for which the practice is regulated by the *SRA* is *client money*, and must be held in a *client account* until *you* have complied with rule 17.2 above. (For an exception in the case of legal aid payments, see rule 19.1(a). See also rule 18 on dealing with mixed payments of *client money* and/or *out-of-scope money* when part of a payment on account of *costs* relates to activities not regulated by the *SRA*.)

17.5   A payment for an *agreed fee* must be paid into an *office account*. An "agreed fee" is one that is fixed – not a *fee* that can be varied upwards, nor a *fee* that is dependent on the transaction being completed. An *agreed fee* must be evidenced in writing.

17.6   *You* will not be in breach of rule 17 as a result of a misdirected electronic payment or other direct transfer from a *client* or paying third party, provided:

  (a)   appropriate systems are in place to ensure compliance;

  (b)   appropriate instructions were given to the *client* or paying third party;

  (c)   the *client's* or paying third party's mistake is remedied promptly upon discovery; and

  (d)   appropriate steps are taken to avoid future errors by the *client* or paying third party.

17.7   *Costs* transferred out of a *client account* in accordance with rule 17.2 and 17.3 must be specific sums relating to the bill or other written notification of *costs*, and covered by the amount held for the particular *client* or *trust*. Round sum withdrawals on account of *costs* are a breach of the rules.

17.8   In the case of a *trust* of which the only *trustee(s)* are within the *firm*, the paying party will be the *trustee(s)* themselves. *You* must keep the original bill or notification of *costs* on the file, in addition to complying with rule 29.15 (central record or file of copy bills, etc.).

17.9   Undrawn *costs* must not remain in a *client account* as a "cushion" against any future errors which could result in a shortage on that account, and cannot be regarded as available to set off against any general shortage on *client account*.

Guidance notes

  (i)   This note lists types of disbursement and how they are categorised:

    (a)   Money received for paid disbursements is office money.

(b) Money received for unpaid professional disbursements is client money.

(c) Money received for other unpaid disbursements for which you have incurred a liability to the payee (for example, travel agents' charges, taxi fares, courier charges or Land Registry search fees, payable on credit) is office money.

(d) Money received for disbursements anticipated but not yet incurred is a payment on account, and is therefore client money.

(ii)   The option in rule 17.1(a) allows you to place all payments in the correct account in the first instance. The option in rule 17.1(b) allows the prompt banking into an office account of an invoice payment when the only uncertainty is whether or not the payment includes some client money in the form of unpaid professional disbursements. The option in rule 17.1(c) allows the prompt banking into a client account of any invoice payment in advance of determining whether the payment is a mixture of office and client money (of whatever description), or client money and out-of-scope money, or client money, out-of-scope money and office money, or is only office money and/or out-of-scope money.

(iii)   If you are not in a position to comply with the requirements of rule 17.1(b), you cannot take advantage of that option.

(iv)   The option in rule 17.1(b) cannot be used if the money received includes a payment on account – for example, a payment for a professional disbursement anticipated but not yet incurred.

(v)   In order to be able to use the option in rule 17.1(b) for electronic payments or other direct transfers from clients, you may choose to establish a system whereby clients are given an office account number for payment of costs. The system must be capable of ensuring that, when invoices are sent to the client, no request is made for any client money, with the sole exception of money for professional disbursements already incurred but not yet paid.

(vi)   Rule 17.1(c) allows clients to be given a single account number for making direct payments by electronic or other means – under this option, it has to be a client account.

(vii)   "Properly" in rule 17.2 implies that the work has actually been done, whether at the end of the matter or at an interim stage, and that you are entitled to appropriate the money for costs. For example, the costs set out in a completion statement in a conveyancing transaction will become due on completion and should be transferred out of the client account within 14 days of completion in accordance with rule 17.3. The requirement to transfer costs out of the client account within a set time is intended to prevent costs being left on client account to conceal a shortage.

(viii)   Money is "earmarked" for costs under rule 17.2 and 17.3 when you decide to use funds already held in client account to settle your bill. If you wish to obtain the client's prior approval, you will need to agree the amount to be taken with your client before issuing the bill to avoid the possibility of failing to meet the 14 day time limit for making the transfer out of client account. If you wish to retain the funds, for example, as money on account of costs on another matter, you will need to ask the client to send the full amount in settlement of the bill. If, when submitting a bill, you fail to indicate whether you intend to take your costs from client account, or expect the client to make a payment, you will be regarded as having "earmarked" your costs.

(ix)   An amendment to section 69 of the Solicitors Act 1974 by the Legal Services Act 2007 permits a solicitor or recognised body to sue on a bill which has been signed electronically and which the client has agreed can be delivered electronically.

(x)   The rules do not require a bill of costs for an agreed fee, although your VAT position may mean that in practice a bill is needed. If there is no bill, the written evidence of the agreement must be filed as a written notification of costs under rule 29.15(b).

(xi)   The bill of an MDP may be in respect of costs for work of the SRA-regulated part of the practice, and also for work that falls outside the scope of SRA regulation. Money received in respect of the non-SRA regulated work, including money for disbursements, is out-of-scope money and must be dealt with in accordance with rule 17.

(xii)   See Chapter 1, indicative behaviour 1.21 of the SRA Code of Conduct in relation to ensuring that disbursements included in a bill reflect the actual amount spent or to be spent.

Rule 18: Receipt of mixed payments

18.1   A "mixed payment" is one which includes *client money* as well as *office money* and/or *out-of-scope money*.

18.2   A *mixed payment* must either:

(a)   be split between a *client account* and *office account* as appropriate; or

(b)   be placed *without delay* in a *client account*.

18.3   If the entire payment is placed in a *client account*, all *office money* and/or *out-of-scope money* must be transferred out of the *client account* within 14 days of receipt.

Guidance notes

(i)   See rule 17.1(b) and (c) for additional ways of dealing with (among other things) mixed payments received in response to a bill or other notification of costs.

(ii) See rule 19.1(b) for (among other things) mixed payments received from the Legal Aid Agency.

(iii) Some out-of-scope money may be subject to the rules of other regulators which may require an earlier withdrawal from the client account operated under these rules.

Rule 19: Treatment of payments to legal aid practitioners

Payments from the Legal Aid Agency

19.1 Two special dispensations apply to payments (other than *regular payments*) from the Legal Aid Agency:

(a) An advance payment, which may include *client money*, may be placed in an *office account*, provided the Legal Aid Agency instructs in writing that this may be done.

(b) A payment for *costs* (interim and/or final) may be paid into an *office account* at a *bank* or *building society* branch (or head office) in England and Wales, regardless of whether it consists wholly of *office money*, or is mixed with *client money* in the form of:

(i) advance payments for *fees* or *disbursements*; or

(ii) money for unpaid *professional disbursements*;

provided all money for payment of *disbursements* is transferred to a *client account* (or the *disbursements* paid) within 14 days of receipt.

19.2 The following provisions apply to *regular payments* from the Legal Aid Agency:

(a) "Regular payments" (which are *office money*) are:

(i) standard monthly payments paid by the Legal Aid Agency under the civil legal aid contracting arrangements;

(ii) standard monthly payments paid by the Legal Aid Agency under the criminal legal aid contracting arrangements; and

(iii) any other payments for work done or to be done received from the Legal Aid Agency under an arrangement for payments on a regular basis.

(b) *Regular payments* must be paid into an *office account* at a *bank* or *building society* branch (or head office) in England and Wales.

(c) *You* must within 28 days of submitting a report to the Legal Aid Agency, notifying completion of a matter, either:

(i) pay any unpaid *professional disbursement(s)*, or

(ii) transfer to a *client account* a sum equivalent to the amount of any unpaid *professional disbursement(s)*, relating to that matter.

(d) In cases where the Legal Aid Agency permits *you* to submit reports at various stages during a matter rather than only at the end of a matter, the requirement in rule 19.2(c) above applies to any unpaid *professional disbursement(s)* included in each report so submitted.

Payments from a third party

19.3   If the Legal Aid Agency has paid any *costs* to *you* or a previously nominated *firm* in a matter (advice and assistance or legal help *costs*, advance payments or interim *costs*), or has paid *professional disbursements* direct, and *costs* are subsequently settled by a third party:

(a) The entire third party payment must be paid into a *client account*.

(b) A sum representing the payments made by the Legal Aid Agency must be retained in the *client account*.

(c) Any balance belonging to *you* must be transferred to an *office account* within 14 days of *your* sending a report to the Legal Aid Agency containing details of the third party payment.

(d) The sum retained in the *client account* as representing payments made by the Legal Aid Agency must be:

   (i)   **either** recorded in the individual *client's* ledger account, and identified as the Legal Aid Agency's money;

   (ii) **or** recorded in a ledger account in the Legal Aid Agency's name, and identified by reference to the *client* or matter;

   and kept in the *client account* until notification from the Legal Aid Agency that it has recouped an equivalent sum from subsequent payments due to *you*. The retained sum must be transferred to an *office account* within 14 days of notification.

19.4   Any part of a third party payment relating to unpaid *professional disbursements* or outstanding *costs* of the *client's* previous *firm* is *client money*, and must be kept in a *client account* until *you* pay the *professional disbursement* or outstanding *costs*.

Guidance notes

(i)   This rule deals with matters which specifically affect legal aid practitioners. It should not be read in isolation from the remainder of the rules which apply to everyone, including legal aid practitioners.

(ii)   In cases carried out under public funding certificates, firms can apply for advance payments ("Payments on Account" under the Standard Civil Contract). The Legal Aid Agency has agreed that these payments may be placed in office account.

(iii)   Rule 19.1(b) deals with the specific problems of legal aid practitioners by allowing a mixed or indeterminate payment of costs (or even a payment consisting entirely of unpaid professional disbursements) to be paid into an office account, which for the purpose of rule 19.1(b) must be an account at a bank or building society. However, it is always open to you to comply with rule 17.1(a) to (c), which are the options for everyone for the receipt of costs. For regular payments, see guidance notes (v)–(vii) below.

(iv)   Firms are required by the Legal Aid Agency to report promptly to the Legal Aid Agency on receipt of costs from a third party. It is advisable to keep a copy of the report on the file as proof of compliance with the Legal Aid Agency's requirements, as well as to demonstrate compliance with the rule.

(v)   Rule 19.2(c) permits a firm, which is required to transfer an amount to cover unpaid professional disbursements into a client account, to make the transfer from its own resources if the regular payments are insufficient.

(vi)   The 28 day time limit for paying, or transferring an amount to a client account for, unpaid professional disbursements is for the purposes of these rules only. An earlier deadline may be imposed by contract with the Legal Aid Agency or with counsel, agents or experts. On the other hand, you may have agreed to pay later than 28 days from the submission of the report notifying completion of a matter, in which case rule 19.2(c) will require a transfer of the appropriate amount to a client account (but not payment) within 28 days.

(vii)   For the appropriate accounting records for regular payments, see rule 29.7.

Rule 20: Withdrawals from a client account

20.1   *Client money* may only be withdrawn from a *client account* when it is:

(a)   properly required for a payment to or on behalf of the *client* (or other person on whose behalf the money is being held);

(b)   properly required for a payment in the execution of a particular *trust*, including the purchase of an investment (other than money) in accordance with the *trustee's* powers;

(c)   properly required for payment of a *disbursement* on behalf of the *client* or *trust*;

(d)   properly required in full or partial reimbursement of money spent by *you* on behalf of the *client* or *trust*;

(e)   transferred to another *client account*;

(f)   withdrawn on the *client's* instructions, provided the instructions are for the *client's* convenience and are given in writing, or are given by other means and confirmed by *you* to the *client* in writing;

(g)   transferred to an account other than a *client account* (such as an account outside England and Wales), or retained in cash, by a *trustee* in the proper performance of his or her duties;

(h) a refund to *you* of an advance no longer required to fund a payment on behalf of a *client* or *trust* (see rule 14.2(b));

(i) money which has been paid into the account in breach of the rules (for example, money paid into the wrong *separate designated client account*) – see rule 20.5 below;

(j) money not covered by (a) to (i) above, where *you* comply with the conditions set out in rule 20.2; or

(k) money not covered by (a) to (i) above, withdrawn from the account on the written authorisation of the *SRA*. The *SRA* may impose a condition that *you* pay the money to a charity which gives an indemnity against any legitimate claim subsequently made for the sum received.

20.2   A withdrawal of *client money* under rule 20.1(j) above may be made only where the amount held does not exceed £500 in relation to any one individual *client* or *trust* matter and *you*:

(a) establish the identity of the owner of the money, or make reasonable attempts to do so;

(b) make adequate attempts to ascertain the proper destination of the money, and to return it to the rightful owner, unless the reasonable costs of doing so are likely to be excessive in relation to the amount held;

(c) pay the funds to a charity;

(d) record the steps taken in accordance with rule 20.2(a)–(c) above and retain those records, together with all relevant documentation (including receipts from the charity), in accordance with rule 29.16 and 29.17(a); and

(e) keep a central register in accordance with rule 29.22.

20.3   *Office money* may only be withdrawn from a *client account* when it is:

(a) money properly paid into the account to open or maintain it under rule 14.2(a);

(b) properly required for payment of *your costs* under rule 17.2 and 17.3;

(c) the whole or part of a payment into a *client account* under rule 17.1(c);

(d) part of a *mixed payment* placed in a *client account* under rule 18.2(b); or

(e) money which has been paid into a *client account* in breach of the rules (for example, *interest* wrongly credited to a *general client account*) – see rule 20.5 below.

20.4   *Out-of-scope money* must be withdrawn from a *client account* in accordance with rules 17.1(a), 17.1(c) and 18 as appropriate.

20.5 Money which has been paid into a *client account* in breach of the rules must be withdrawn from the *client account* promptly upon discovery.

20.6 Money withdrawn in relation to a particular *client* or *trust* from a *general client account* must not exceed the money held on behalf of that *client* or *trust* in all *your general client accounts* (except as provided in rule 20.7 below).

20.7 *You* may make a payment in respect of a particular *client* or *trust* out of a *general client account*, even if no money (or insufficient money) is held for that *client* or *trust* in *your general client account(s)*, provided:

(a) sufficient money is held for that *client* or *trust* in a *separate designated client account*; and

(b) the appropriate transfer from the *separate designated client account* to a *general client account* is made immediately.

20.8 Money held for a *client* or *trust* in a *separate designated client account* must not be used for payments for another *client* or *trust*.

20.9 A *client account* must not be overdrawn, except in the following circumstances:

(a) A *separate designated client account* operated in *your* capacity as *trustee* can be overdrawn if *you* make payments on behalf of the *trust* (for example, inheritance tax) before realising sufficient assets to cover the payments.

(b) If a *sole practitioner* dies and his or her *client accounts* are frozen, overdrawn *client accounts* can be operated in accordance with the rules to the extent of the money held in the frozen accounts.

Guidance notes

(i) Withdrawals in favour of firm, and for payment of disbursements

(a) Disbursements to be paid direct from a client account, or already paid out of your own money, can be withdrawn under rule 20.1(c) or (d) in advance of preparing a bill of costs. Money to be withdrawn from a client account for the payment of costs (fees and disbursements) under rule 17.2 and 17.3 becomes office money and is dealt with under rule 20.3(b).

(b) Money is "spent" under rule 20.1(d) at the time when you despatch a cheque, unless the cheque is to be held to your order. Money is also regarded as "spent" by the use of a credit account, so that, for example, search fees, taxi fares and courier charges incurred in this way may be transferred to your office account.

(c) See rule 21.4 for the way in which a withdrawal from a client account in your favour must be effected.

(ii) Cheques payable to banks, building societies, etc.

(a) In order to protect client money against misappropriation when cheques are made payable to banks, building societies or other large institutions, it is strongly recommended that you add the name and number of the account after the payee's name.

(iii)   Drawing against uncleared cheques

(a)   You should use discretion in drawing against a cheque received from or on behalf of a client before it has been cleared. If the cheque is not met, other clients' money will have been used to make the payment in breach of the rules (see rule 7 (duty to remedy breaches)). You may be able to avoid a breach of the rules by instructing the bank or building society to charge all unpaid credits to your office or personal account.

(iv)   Non-receipt of electronic payments

(a)   If you withdraw money from a general client account on the strength of information that an electronic payment is on its way, but the electronic payment does not arrive, you will have used other clients' money in breach of the rules. See also rule 7 (duty to remedy breaches).

(v)   Withdrawals on instructions

(a)   One of the reasons why a client might authorise a withdrawal under rule 20.1(f) might be to have the money transferred to a type of account other than a client account. If so, the requirements of rule 15 must be complied with.

(vi)   Withdrawals where the rightful owner cannot be traced, on the SRA's authorisation and without SRA authorisation

(a)   Applications for authorisation under rule 20.1(k) should be made to the Professional Ethics Guidance Team, who can advise on the criteria which must normally be met for authorisation to be given. You may under rule 20.1(j) pay to a charity sums of £500 or less per client or trust matter without the SRA's authorisation, provided the safeguards set out in rule 20.2 are followed.

(b)   You will need to apply to the SRA, whatever the amount involved, if the money to be withdrawn is not to be paid to a charity. This situation might arise, for example, if you have been unable to deliver a bill of costs because the client has become untraceable and so cannot make a transfer from client account to office account in accordance with rule 17.2–17.3.

(c)   After a practice has been wound up, surplus balances are sometimes discovered in an old client account. This money remains subject to rule 20 and rule 21. An application can be made to the SRA under rule 20.1(k).

Rule 21: Method of and authority for withdrawals from client account

21.1   A withdrawal from a *client account* may be made only after a specific authority in respect of that withdrawal has been signed by an appropriate person or persons in accordance with the *firm's* procedures for signing on *client account*. An authority for withdrawals from *client account* may be signed electronically, subject to appropriate safeguards and controls.

21.2   *Firms* must put in place appropriate systems and procedures governing withdrawals from *client account*, including who should be permitted by the *firm* to sign on *client account*. A non-*manager* owner or a non-employee owner of a *licensed body* is not an appropriate person to be a signatory on *client account* and must not be permitted by the *firm* to act in this way.

21.3   There is no need to comply with rule 21.1 above when transferring money from one *general client account* to another *general client account* at the same *bank* or *building society*.

21.4   A withdrawal from a *client account* in *your* favour must be either by way of a cheque, or by way of a transfer to the *office account* or to *your* personal account. The withdrawal must not be made in cash.

Guidance notes

(i)   A firm should select suitable people to authorise withdrawals from the client account. Firms will wish to consider whether any employee should be able to sign on client account, and whether signing rights should be given to all managers of the practice or limited to those managers directly involved in providing legal services. Someone who has no day-to-day involvement in the business of the practice is unlikely to be regarded as a suitable signatory because of the lack of proximity to client matters. An appropriate understanding of the requirements of the rules is essential – see paragraph 4.2 of the Guidelines for accounting procedures and systems at Appendix 3.

(ii)   Instructions to the bank or building society to withdraw money from a client account (rule 21.1) may be given over the telephone, provided a specific authority has been signed in accordance with this rule before the instructions are given. It is of paramount importance that there are appropriate in-built safeguards, such as passwords, to give the greatest protection possible for client money. Suitable safeguards will also be needed for practices which operate a CHAPS terminal or other form of electronic instruction for payment.

(iii)   In the case of a withdrawal by cheque, the specific authority (rule 21.1) is usually a signature on the cheque itself. Signing a blank cheque is not a specific authority.

(iv)   A withdrawal from a client account by way of a private loan from one client to another can only be made if the provisions of rule 27.2 are complied with.

(v)   If, in your capacity as trustee, you instruct an outside administrator to run, or continue to run, on a day-to-day basis, the business or property portfolio of an estate or trust, you will not need to comply with rule 21.1, provided all cheques are retained in accordance with rule 29.18. (See also rule 29, guidance note (ii)(d).)

(vi) You may set up a "direct debit" system of payment for Land Registry application fees on either the office account or a client account. If a direct debit payment is to be taken from a client account for the payment of Land Registry application fees, a signature, which complies with the firm's systems and procedures set up under rule 21, on the application for registration will constitute the specific authority required by rule 21.1. As with any other payment method, care must be taken to ensure that sufficient uncommitted funds are held in the client account for the particular client before signing the authority. You should also bear in mind that should the Land Registry take an incorrect amount in error from a firm's client account (for example, a duplicate payment), the firm will be in breach of the rules if other clients' money has been used as a result.

(vii) If you fail to specify the correct Land Registry fee on the application for registration (either by specifying a lesser amount than that actually due, or failing to specify any fee at all), you will be in breach of rule 21.1 if the Land Registry takes a sum from your client account greater than that specified on the application, without a specific authority for the revised sum being in place as required by rule 21. In order that you can comply with the rules, the Land Registry will need to contact you before taking the revised amount, so that the necessary authority may be signed prior to the revised amount being taken.

(viii) Where the Land Registry contacts you by telephone, and you wish to authorise an immediate payment by direct debit over the telephone, you will first need to check that there is sufficient money held in client account for the client and, if there is, that it is not committed to some other purpose.

(ix) The specific authority required by rule 21.1 can be signed after the telephone call has ended but must be signed before the additional payment (or correct full payment) is taken by the Land Registry. It is advisable to sign the authority promptly and, in any event, on the same day as the telephone instruction is given to the Land Registry to take the additional (or correct full) amount. If you decide to fund any extra amount from the office account, the transfer of office money to the client account would need to be made, preferably on the same day but, in any event, before the direct debit is taken. Your internal procedures would need to make it clear how to deal with such situations; for example, who should be consulted before a direct debit for an amount other than that specified on the application can be authorised, and the mechanism for ensuring the new authority is signed by a person permitted by the firm to sign on client account.

(x) You may decide to set up a direct debit system of payment on the office account because, for example, you do not wish to allow the Land Registry to have access to the firm's client account. Provided you are in funds, a transfer from the client account to the office account may be made under rule 20.1(d) to reimburse you as soon as the direct debit has been taken.

(xi)   Variable "direct debit" payments to the Land Registry, as described in guidance notes (vi)–(x) above, are not direct debits in the usual sense as each payment is authorised and confirmed individually. A traditional direct debit or standing order should not be set up on a client account because of the need for a specific authority for each withdrawal.

PART 3: INTEREST

Rule 22: When interest must be paid

22.1   When *you* hold money in a *client account* for a *client*, or for a person funding all or part of *your fees*, or for a *trust*, *you* must account to the *client* or that person or *trust* for *interest* when it is fair and reasonable to do so in all the circumstances. (This also applies if money should have been held in a *client account* but was not. It also applies to money held in an account in accordance with rule 15.1(a) (or which should have been held in such an account), or rule 16.1(d).)

22.2   *You* are not required to pay *interest*:

(a)   on money held for the payment of a *professional disbursement*, once counsel etc. has requested a delay in settlement;

(b)   on money held for the Legal Aid Agency;

(c)   on an advance from *you* under rule 14.2(b) to fund a payment on behalf of the *client* or *trust* in excess of funds held for that *client* or *trust*; or

(d)   if there is an agreement to contract out of the provisions of this rule under rule 25.

22.3   *You* must have a written policy on the payment of *interest*, which seeks to provide a fair outcome. The terms of the policy must be drawn to the attention of the *client* at the outset of a retainer, unless it is inappropriate to do so in the circumstances.

Guidance notes

(i)   Requirement to pay interest

(a)   Money is normally held for a client as a necessary, but incidental, part of the retainer, to facilitate the carrying out of the client's instructions. The main purpose of the rules is to keep that money safe and available for the purpose for which it was provided. The rules also seek to provide for the payment of a fair sum of interest, when appropriate, which is unlikely to be as high as that obtainable by the client depositing those funds.

(b)   An outcomes-focused approach has been adopted in this area, allowing firms the flexibility to set their own interest policies in order to achieve a fair outcome for both the client and the firm.

(c)   In addition to your obligation under rule 22.3, it is good practice to explain your interest arrangements to clients. These will usually be based on client money being held in an instant access account to facilitate a transaction.

Clients are unlikely to receive as much interest as might have been obtained had they held and invested the money themselves. A failure to explain the firm's policy on interest may lead to unrealistic expectations and, possibly, a complaint to the Legal Ombudsman.

(d) The Legal Services Act 2007 has abolished the distinction in the Solicitors Act 1974 between interest earned on client money held in a general client account or a separate designated client account, meaning that interest earned on the latter type of account is, in theory, to be accounted for like interest on any other client money on a "fair and reasonable" basis. In practice, however, a firm which wishes to retain any part of the interest earned on client money will need to hold that money in a general client account and continue to have interest paid to the office account (see rule 12.7(b)). The tax regime still treats interest arising on money held in a separate designated client account as belonging to the client, and requires banks to deduct tax at source from that interest (subject to the tax status of the individual client) and credit the interest to the separate designated client account. This makes it impracticable for firms to retain any part of the interest earned on a separate designated client account.

(e) Some firms may wish to apply a de minimis by reference to the amount held and period for which it was held, for example, providing that no interest is payable if the amount calculated on the balance held is £20 or less. Any de minimis will need to be set at a reasonable level and regularly reviewed in the light of current interest rates.

(f) It is likely to be appropriate for firms to account for all interest earned in some circumstances, for example, where substantial sums of money are held for lengthy periods of time.

(g) If sums of money are held in relation to separate matters for the same client, it is normally appropriate to treat the money relating to the different matters separately but there may be cases when the matters are so closely related that they ought to be considered together, for example, when you are acting for a client in connection with numerous debt collection matters. Similarly, it may be fair and reasonable in the circumstances to aggregate sums of money held intermittently during the course of acting for a client.

(h) There is no requirement to pay interest on money held on instructions under rule 15.1(a) in a manner which attracts no interest.

(i) Accounts opened in the client's name under rule 15.1(b) (whether operated by you or not) are not subject to rule 22, as the money is not held by you. All interest earned belongs to the client. The same applies to any account in the client's own name operated by you as signatory under rule 10.

(ii) Interest policy (rule 22.3)

(a) It is important that your clients should be aware of the terms of your interest policy. This should normally be covered at the outset of a retainer, although it may be unnecessary where you have acted for the client previously. It is open to you and your client to agree that interest will be dealt with in a different way (see rule 25).

(iii)   Unpresented cheques

(a)   A client may fail to present a cheque to his or her bank for payment. Whether or not it is reasonable to recalculate the amount due will depend on all the circumstances of the case. A reasonable charge may be made for any extra work carried out if you are legally entitled to make such a charge.

(iv)   Liquidators, trustees in bankruptcy, Court of Protection deputies and trustees of occupational pension schemes

(a)   Under rule 8, Part 3 of the rules does not normally apply to liquidators, etc. You must comply with the appropriate statutory rules and regulations, and rule 8.3 and 8.4 as appropriate.

(v)   Joint accounts

(a)   Under rule 9, Part 3 of the rules does not apply to joint accounts. If you hold money jointly with a client, interest earned on the account will be for the benefit of the client unless otherwise agreed. If money is held jointly with another practice, the allocation of interest earned will depend on the agreement reached.

(vi)   Failure to pay interest

(a)   A client, including one of joint clients, or a person funding all or part of your fees, may complain to the Legal Ombudsman if he or she believes that interest was due and has not been paid, or that the amount paid was insufficient. It is advisable for the client (or other person) to try to resolve the matter with you before approaching the Legal Ombudsman.

Rule 23: Amount of interest

23.1   The *interest* paid must be a fair and reasonable sum calculated over the whole period for which the money is held.

Guidance notes

(i)   You will usually account to the client for interest at the conclusion of the client's matter, but might in some cases consider it appropriate to account to the client at intervals throughout.

(ii)   The sum paid by way of interest need not necessarily reflect the highest rate of interest obtainable but it is unlikely to be appropriate to look only at the lowest rate of interest obtainable. A firm's policy on the calculation of interest will need to take into account factors such as:

(a)   the amount held;

(b)   the length of time for which cleared funds were held;

(c)   the need for instant access to the funds;

(d)   the rate of interest payable on the amount held in an instant access account at the bank or building society where the client account is kept;

(e)   the practice of the bank or building society where the client account is kept in relation to how often interest is compounded.

(iii)   A firm needs to have regard to the effect of the overall banking arrangements negotiated between it and the bank, on interest rates payable on individual balances. A fair sum of interest is unlikely to be achieved by applying interest rates which are set at an artificially low level to reflect, for example, more favourable terms in relation to the firm's office account.

(iv)   A firm might decide to apply a fixed rate of interest by reference, for example, to the base rate. In setting that rate, the firm would need to consider (and regularly review) the level of interest it actually receives on its client accounts, but also take into account its overall banking arrangements so far as they affect the rates received.

(v)   When looking at the period over which interest must be calculated, it will usually be unnecessary to check on actual clearance dates. When money is received by cheque and paid out by cheque, the normal clearance periods will usually cancel each other out, so that it will be satisfactory to look at the period between the dates when the incoming cheque is banked and the outgoing cheque is drawn.

(vi)   Different considerations apply when payments in and out are not both made by cheque. So, for example, the relevant periods would normally be:

(a)   from the date when you receive incoming money in cash until the date when the outgoing cheque is sent;

(b)   from the date when an incoming telegraphic transfer begins to earn interest until the date when the outgoing cheque is sent;

(c)   from the date when an incoming cheque or banker's draft is or would normally be cleared until the date when the outgoing telegraphic transfer is made or banker's draft is obtained.

(vii)   Rule 13.8 requires that money held in a client account must be immediately available, even at the sacrifice of interest, unless the client otherwise instructs, or the circumstances clearly indicate otherwise. The need for access can be taken into account in assessing the appropriate rate for calculating interest to be paid.

(viii)   For failure to pay a sufficient sum by way of interest, see guidance note (vi)(a) to rule 22.

Rule 24: Interest on stakeholder money

24.1   When *you* hold money as stakeholder, *you* must pay *interest* on the basis set out in rule 22 to the person to whom the stake is paid, unless the parties have contracted out of this provision (see rule 25.3).

Rule 25: Contracting out

25.1   In appropriate circumstances *you* and *your client* may by a written agreement come to a different arrangement as to the matters dealt with in rule 22 (payment of interest).

25.2   *You* must act fairly towards *your clients* when entering into an agreement to depart from the *interest* provisions, including providing sufficient information at the outset to enable them to give informed consent.

25.3   When acting as stakeholder *you* may, by a written agreement with *your* own *client* and the other party to the transaction, come to a different arrangement as to the matters dealt with in rule 22.

Guidance notes

(i)   Whether it is appropriate to contract out depends on all the circumstances, for example, the size of the sum involved or the nature, status or bargaining position of the client. It might, for instance, be appropriate to contract out by standard terms of business if the client is a substantial commercial entity and the interest involved is modest in relation to the size of the transaction. The larger the sum of interest involved, the more there would be an onus on you to show that a client who had accepted a contracting out provision was properly informed and had been treated fairly.

(ii)   Contracting out which on the face of it appears to be against the client's interests is permissible where the client has given informed consent. For example, some clients may wish to contract out for reasons related to their tax position or to comply with their religious beliefs.

(iii)   A firm which decides not to receive or pay interest, due to the religious beliefs of its principals, will need to ensure that clients are informed at the outset, so that they can choose to instruct another firm if the lack of interest is an issue for them.

(iv)   Another example of contracting out is when the client stipulates, and the firm agrees, that all interest earned should be paid to the client despite the terms of the firm's interest policy.

(v)   In principle, you are entitled to make a reasonable charge to the client for acting as stakeholder in the client's matter.

(vi)   Alternatively, it may be appropriate to include a special provision in the contract that you retain the interest on the deposit to cover your charges for acting as stakeholder. This is only acceptable if it will provide a fair and reasonable payment for the work and risk involved in holding a stake. The contract could stipulate a maximum charge, with any interest earned above that figure being paid to the recipient of the stake.

(vii)   Any right to charge the client, or to stipulate for a charge which may fall on the client, would be excluded by, for instance, a prior agreement with the client for a fixed fee for the client's matter, or for an estimated fee which cannot be varied upwards in the absence of special circumstances. It is therefore not normal practice for a stakeholder in conveyancing transactions to receive a separate payment for holding the stake.

(viii)   A stakeholder who seeks an agreement to exclude the operation of rule 24 should be particularly careful not to take unfair advantage either of the client, or of the other party if unrepresented.

PART 4: ACCOUNTING SYSTEMS AND RECORDS

Rule 26: Guidelines for accounting procedures and systems

26.1   The *SRA* may from time to time publish guidelines for accounting procedures and systems to assist *you* to comply with Parts 1 to 4 of the rules, and *you* may be required to justify any departure from the guidelines.

Guidance notes

(i)   The current guidelines appear at Appendix 3.

Rule 27: Restrictions on transfers between clients

27.1   A paper transfer of money held in a *general client account* from the ledger of one *client* to the ledger of another *client* may only be made if:

  (a) it would have been permissible to withdraw that sum from the account under rule 20.1; and

  (b) it would have been permissible to pay that sum into the account under rule 14;

(but there is no requirement in the case of a paper transfer for a written authority under rule 21.1).

27.2   No sum in respect of a *private loan* from one *client* to another can be paid out of funds held for the lender either:

  (a) by a payment from one *client account* to another;

  (b) by a paper transfer from the ledger of the lender to that of the borrower; or

  (c) to the borrower directly,

except with the prior written authority of both *clients*.

27.3   If a *private loan* is to be made by (or to) joint *clients*, the consent of each *client* must be obtained.

Rule 28: Executor, trustee or nominee companies

28.1   If *your firm* owns all the shares in a *recognised body* or a *licensed body* which is an executor, trustee or nominee company, *your firm* and the *recognised body* or *licensed body* must not operate shared *client accounts*, but may:

(a)   use one set of accounting records for money held, received or paid by the *firm* and the *recognised body* or *licensed body*; and/or

(b)   deliver a single accountant's report for both the *firm* and the *recognised body* or *licensed body*.

28.2   If such a *recognised body* or *licensed body* as nominee receives a dividend cheque made out to the *recognised body* or *licensed body*, and forwards the cheque, either endorsed or subject to equivalent instructions, to the share-owner's *bank* or *building society*, etc., the *recognised body* or *licensed body* will have received (and paid) *client money*. One way of complying with rule 29 (accounting records) is to keep a copy of the letter to the share-owner's *bank* or *building society*, etc., on the file, and, in accordance with rule 29.23, to keep another copy in a central book of such letters. (See also rule 29.17(f) (retention of records for six years)).

Rule 29: Accounting records for client accounts, etc.

Accounting records which must be kept

29.1   *You* must at all times keep accounting records properly written up to show *your* dealings with:

(a)   *client money* received, held or paid by *you*; including *client money* held outside a *client account* under rule 15.1(a) or rule 16.1(d); and

(b)   any *office money* relating to any *client* or *trust* matter.

29.2   All dealings with *client money* must be appropriately recorded:

(a)   in a client cash account or in a record of sums transferred from one client ledger account to another; and

(b)   on the client side of a separate client ledger account for each *client* (or other person, or *trust*).

No other entries may be made in these records.

29.3   If *separate designated client accounts* are used:

(a)   a combined cash account must be kept in order to show the total amount held in *separate designated client accounts*; and

(b)   a record of the amount held for each *client* (or other person, or *trust*) must be made either in a deposit column of a client ledger account, or on the client side of a client ledger account kept specifically for a *separate designated client account*, for each *client* (or other person, or *trust*).

29.4   All dealings with *office money* relating to any *client* matter, or to any *trust* matter, must be appropriately recorded in an office cash account and on the office side of the appropriate client ledger account.

29.5   A cheque or draft received on behalf of a *client* and endorsed over, not passing through a *client account*, must be recorded in the books of account as a receipt and payment on behalf of the *client*. The same applies to cash received and not deposited in a *client account* but paid out to or on behalf of a *client*.

29.6   Money which has been paid into a *client account* under rule 17.1(c) (receipt of costs), or rule 18.2(b) (mixed money), and for the time being remains in a *client account*, is to be treated as *client money*; it must be appropriately identified and recorded on the client side of the client ledger account.

29.7   Money which has been paid into an *office account* under rule 17.1(b) (receipt of costs), rule 19.1(a) (advance payments from the Legal Aid Agency), or rule 19.1(b) (payment of costs from the Legal Aid Agency), and for the time being remains in an *office account* without breaching the rules, is to be treated as *office money*. Money paid into an *office account* under rule 19.2(b) (regular payments) is *office money*. All these payments must be appropriately identified and recorded on the office side of the client ledger account for the individual *client* or for the Legal Aid Agency.

29.8   *Client money* in a currency other than sterling must be held in a separate account for the appropriate currency, and *you* must keep separate books of account for that currency.

Current balance

29.9   The current balance on each client ledger account must always be shown, or be readily ascertainable, from the records kept in accordance with rule 29.2 and 29.3 above.

Acting for both lender and borrower

29.10   When acting for both lender and borrower on a mortgage advance, separate client ledger accounts for both *clients* need not be opened, provided that:

(a)   the funds belonging to each *client* are clearly identifiable; and

(b)   the lender is an institutional lender which provides mortgages on standard terms in the normal course of its activities.

Statements from banks, building societies and other financial institutions

29.11   *You* must, at least every 5 weeks:

    (a) obtain hard copy statements (or duplicate statements permitted in lieu of the originals by rule 9.3 or 9.4 from *banks*, *building societies* or other financial institutions, or

    (b) obtain and save in the *firm's* accounting records, in a format which cannot be altered, an electronic version of the *bank's*, *building society's* or other financial institution's on-line record,

in respect of:

    (i)   any *general client account* or *separate designated client account*;

    (ii) any joint account held under rule 9;

    (iii) any account which is not a *client account* but in which *you* hold *client money* under rule 15.1(a) or rule 16.1(d); and

    (iv) any *office account* maintained in relation to the *firm*;

and each statement or electronic version must begin at the end of the previous statement.

This provision does not apply in respect of passbook-operated accounts, nor in respect of the *office accounts* of an *MDP* operated solely for activities not subject to *SRA* regulation.

Reconciliations

29.12   *You* must, at least once every five weeks:

    (a) compare the balance on the client cash account(s) with the balances shown on the statements and passbooks (after allowing for all unpresented items) of all *general client accounts* and *separate designated client accounts*, and of any account which is not a *client account* but in which *you* hold *client money* under rule 15.1(a) or rule 16.1(d), and any *client money* held by *you* in cash; and

    (b) as at the same date prepare a listing of all the balances shown by the client ledger accounts of the liabilities to *clients* (and other persons, and *trusts*) and compare the total of those balances with the balance on the client cash account; and also

    (c) prepare a reconciliation statement; this statement must show the cause of the difference, if any, shown by each of the above comparisons.

29.13   Reconciliations must be carried out as they fall due, or at the latest by the due date for the next reconciliation. In the case of a *separate designated client account* operated with a passbook, there is no need to ask the *bank*, *building society* or other financial institution for confirmation of the balance held. In the case of other *separate designated client accounts*, *you* must either obtain statements at least monthly or written confirmation of the balance direct from the *bank*, *building society* or other financial institution. There is no requirement to check that *interest* has been credited since the last statement, or the last entry in the passbook.

29.14   All shortages must be shown. In making the comparisons under rule 29.12(a) and (b), *you* must not, therefore, use credits of one *client* against debits of another when checking total client liabilities.

Bills and notifications of costs

29.15   *You* must keep readily accessible a central record or file of copies of:

(a)   all bills given or sent by *you* (other than those relating entirely to activities not regulated by the *SRA*); and

(b)   all other written notifications of *costs* given or sent by *you* (other than those relating entirely to activities not regulated by the *SRA*).

Withdrawals under rule 20.1(j)

29.16   If *you* withdraw *client money* under rule 20.1(j) *you* must keep a record of the steps taken in accordance with rule 20.2(a)–(c), together with all relevant documentation (including receipts from the charity).

Retention of records

29.17   *You* must retain for at least six years from the date of the last entry:

(a)   all documents or other records required by rule 29.1 to 29.10, 29.12, and 29.15 to 29.16 above;

(b)   all statements required by rule 29.11(a) above and passbooks, as printed and issued by the *bank*, *building society* or other financial institution; and/or all on-line records obtained and saved in electronic form under rule 29.11(b) above, for:

(i)   any *general client account* or *separate designated client account*;

(ii)   any joint account held under rule 9;

(iii)   any account which is not a *client account* but in which *you* hold *client money* under rule 15.1(a) or rule 16.1(d); and

(iv)   any *office account* maintained in relation to the practice, but not the *office accounts* of an *MDP* operated solely for activities not subject to *SRA* regulation;

(c)   any records kept under rule 8 (liquidators, trustees in bankruptcy, Court of Protection deputies and trustees of occupational pension schemes) including, as printed or otherwise issued, any statements, passbooks and other accounting records originating outside *your* office;

(d)   any written instructions to withhold *client money* from a *client account* (or a copy of *your* confirmation of oral instructions) in accordance with rule 15;

(e)   any central registers kept under rule 29.19 to 29.22 below; and

(f) any copy letters kept centrally under rule 28.2 (dividend cheques endorsed over by nominee company).

29.18 *You* must retain for at least two years:

(a) originals or copies of all authorities, other than cheques, for the withdrawal of money from a *client account*; and

(b) all original paid cheques (or digital images of the front and back of all original paid cheques), unless there is a written arrangement with the *bank*, *building society* or other financial institution that:

   (i) it will retain the original cheques on *your* behalf for that period; or

   (ii) in the event of destruction of any original cheques, it will retain digital images of the front and back of those cheques on *your* behalf for that period and will, on demand by *you*, *your* reporting accountant or the *SRA*, produce copies of the digital images accompanied, when requested, by a certificate of verification signed by an authorised officer.

(c) The requirement to keep paid cheques under rule 29.18(b) above extends to all cheques drawn on a *client account*, or on an account in which *client money* is held outside a *client account* under rule 15.1(a) or rule 16.1(d).

(d) Microfilmed copies of paid cheques are not acceptable for the purposes of rule 29.18(b) above. If a *bank*, *building society* or other financial institution is able to provide microfilmed copies only, *you* must obtain the original paid cheques from the *bank* etc. and retain them for at least two years.

Centrally kept records for certain accounts, etc.

29.19 Statements and passbooks for *client money* held outside a *client account* under rule 15.1(a) or rule 16.1(d) must be kept together centrally, or *you* must maintain a central register of these accounts.

29.20 Any records kept under rule 8 (liquidators, trustees in bankruptcy, Court of Protection deputies and trustees of occupational pension schemes) must be kept together centrally, or *you* must maintain a central register of the appointments.

29.21 The statements, passbooks, duplicate statements and copies of passbook entries relating to any joint account held under rule 9 must be kept together centrally, or *you* must maintain a central register of all joint accounts.

29.22 A central register of all withdrawals made under rule 20.1(j) must be kept, detailing the name of the *client*, other person or *trust* on whose behalf the money is held (if known), the amount, the name of the recipient charity and the date of the payment.

29.23 If a nominee company follows the option in rule 28.2 (keeping instruction letters for dividend payments), a central book must be kept of all instruction letters to the share-owner's *bank* or *building society*, etc.

Computerisation

29.24 Records required by this rule may be kept on a computerised system, apart from the following documents, which must be retained as printed or otherwise issued:

(a) original statements and passbooks retained under rule 29.17(b) above;

(b) original statements, passbooks and other accounting records retained under rule 29.17(c) above; and

(c) original cheques and original hard copy authorities retained under rule 29.18 above.

There is no obligation to keep a hard copy of computerised records. However, if no hard copy is kept, the information recorded must be capable of being reproduced reasonably quickly in printed form for at least six years, or for at least two years in the case of digital images of paid cheques retained under rule 29.18 above.

Suspense ledger accounts

29.25 Suspense client ledger accounts may be used only when *you* can justify their use; for instance, for temporary use on receipt of an unidentified payment, if time is needed to establish the nature of the payment or the identity of the *client*.

Guidance notes

(i) It is strongly recommended that accounting records are written up at least weekly, even in the smallest practice, and daily in the case of larger firms.

(ii) Rule 29.1 to 29.10 (general record-keeping requirements) and rule 29.12 (reconciliations) do not apply to:

(a) liquidators, trustees in bankruptcy, Court of Protection deputies and trustees of occupational pension schemes operating in accordance with statutory rules or regulations under rule 8.1(i);

(b) joint accounts operated under rule 9;

(c) a client's own account operated under rule 10; the record-keeping requirements for this type of account are set out in rule 30;

(d) you in your capacity as a trustee when you instruct an outside administrator to run, or continue to run, on a day-to-day basis, the business or property portfolio of an estate or trust, provided the administrator keeps and retains appropriate accounting records, which are available for inspection by the SRA in accordance with rule 31. (See also guidance note (v) to rule 21.)

(iii) A cheque made payable to a client, which is forwarded to the client by you, is not client money and falls outside the rules, although it is advisable to record the action taken. See rule 14.2(e) for the treatment of a damages cheque, made payable to the client, which you pay into a client account under the Law Society's Conditional Fee Agreement.

(iv)   Some accounting systems do not retain a record of past daily balances. This does not put you in breach of rule 29.9.

(v)   "Clearly identifiable" in rule 29.10 means that by looking at the ledger account the nature and owner of the mortgage advance are unambiguously stated. For example, if a mortgage advance of £100,000 is received from the ABC Building Society, the entry should be recorded as "£100,000, mortgage advance, ABC Building Society". It is not enough to state that the money was received from the ABC Building Society without specifying the nature of the payment, or vice versa.

(vi)   Although you do not open a separate ledger account for the lender, the mortgage advance credited to that account belongs to the lender, not to the borrower, until completion takes place. Improper removal of these mortgage funds from a client account would be a breach of rule 20.

(vii)   Section 67 of the Solicitors Act 1974 permits a solicitor or recognised body to include on a bill of costs any disbursements which have been properly incurred but not paid before delivery of the bill, subject to those disbursements being described on the bill as unpaid.

(viii)   Rule 29.17(d) – retention of client's instructions to withhold money from a client account – does not require records to be kept centrally; however this may be prudent, to avoid losing the instructions if the file is passed to the client.

(ix)   You may enter into an arrangement whereby the bank keeps digital images of paid cheques in place of the originals. The bank should take an electronic image of the front and back of each cheque in black and white and agree to hold such images, and to make printed copies available on request, for at least two years. Alternatively, you may take and keep your own digital images of paid cheques.

(x)   Certificates of verification in relation to digital images of cheques may on occasion be required by the SRA when exercising its investigative and enforcement powers. The reporting accountant will not need to ask for a certificate of verification but will be able to rely on the printed copy of the digital image as if it were the original.

(xi)   These rules require an MDP to keep accounting records only in respect of those activities for which it is regulated by the SRA. Where an MDP acts for a client in a matter which includes activities regulated by the SRA, and activities outside the SRA's regulatory reach, the accounting records should record the MDP's dealings in respect of the SRA-regulated part of the client's matter. It may also be necessary to include in those records dealings with out-of-scope money where that money has been handled in connection with, or relates to, the SRA-regulated part of the transaction. An MDP is not required to maintain records in respect of client matters which relate entirely to activities not regulated by the SRA.

Rule 30: Accounting records for clients' own accounts

30.1   When *you* operate a *client's* own account as signatory under rule 10, *you* must retain, for at least six years from the date of the last entry, the statements or passbooks as printed and issued by the *bank*, *building society* or other financial institution, and/or the duplicate statements, copies of passbook entries and cheque details permitted in lieu of the originals by rule 10.3 or 10.4; and any central register kept under rule 30.2 below.

30.2   *You* must either keep these records together centrally, or maintain a central register of the accounts operated under rule 10.

30.3   If *you* use on-line records made available by the *bank*, *building society* or other financial institution, *you* must save an electronic version in the *firm's* accounting records in a format which cannot be altered. There is no obligation to keep a hard copy but the information recorded must be capable of being reproduced reasonably quickly in printed form for at least six years.

30.4   If, when *you* cease to operate the account, the *client* requests the original statements or passbooks, *you* must take photocopies and keep them in lieu of the originals.

30.5   This rule applies only to private practice.

PART 5: MONITORING AND INVESTIGATION BY THE SRA

Rule 31: Production of documents, information and explanations

31.1   *You* must at the time and place fixed by the *SRA* produce to any person appointed by the *SRA* any records, papers, *client* and *trust* matter files, financial accounts and other documents, and any other information, necessary to enable preparation of a report on compliance with the rules.

31.2   A requirement for production under rule 31.1 above must be in writing, and left at or sent by post or document exchange to the most recent address held by the *SRA's* Information Directorate, or sent electronically to the *firm's* e-mail or fax address, or delivered by the *SRA's* appointee. A notice under this rule is deemed to be duly served:

   (a)   on the date on which it is delivered to or left at *your* address;

   (b)   on the date on which it is sent electronically to *your* e-mail or fax address; or

   (c)   48 hours (excluding Saturdays, Sundays and Bank Holidays) after it has been sent by post or document exchange.

31.3   Material kept electronically must be produced in the form required by the *SRA's* appointee.

31.4   The *SRA's* appointee is entitled to seek verification from *clients* and staff, and from the *banks*, *building societies* and other financial institutions used by *you*. *You* must, if necessary, provide written permission for the information to be given.

31.5   The *SRA's* appointee is not entitled to take original documents away but must be provided with photocopies on request.

31.6   *You* must be prepared to explain and justify any departures from the Guidelines for accounting procedures and systems published by the *SRA* (see rule 26).

31.7   Any report made by the *SRA's* appointee may, if appropriate, be sent to the Crown Prosecution Service or the Serious Fraud Office and/or used in proceedings before the Solicitors Disciplinary Tribunal. In the case of an *REL* or *RFL*, the report may also be sent to the competent authority in that lawyer's home state or states. In the case of a *solicitor* who is established in another state under the *Establishment Directive*, the report may also be sent to the competent authority in the host state. The report may also be sent to any of the accountancy bodies set out in rule 34.1(a) and/or taken into account by the *SRA* in relation to a possible disqualification of a reporting accountant under rule 34.3.

31.8   Without prejudice to rule 31.1 above, *you* must produce documents relating to any account kept by *you* at a *bank* or with a *building society*:

(a) in connection with *your* practice; or

(b) in connection with any *trust* of which *you* are or formerly were a *trustee*,

for inspection by a person appointed by the *SRA* for the purpose of preparing a report on compliance with the rules or on whether the account has been used for or in connection with a breach of any of the Principles or other SRA Handbook requirements made or issued by the *SRA*. Rules 31.2–31.7 above apply in relation to this paragraph in the same way as to rule 31.1.

Guidance notes

(i)   The SRA's powers override any confidence or privilege between you and the client.

(ii)   The SRA's monitoring and investigation powers are exercised by Forensic Investigations.

(iii)   The SRA will normally give a brief statement of the reasons for its investigations and inspections but not if the SRA considers that there is a risk that disclosure could:

(a) breach any duty of confidentiality;

(b) disclose, or risk disclosure of, a confidential source of information;

(c) significantly increase the risk that those under investigation may destroy evidence, seek to influence witnesses, default, or abscond; or

(d) otherwise prejudice or frustrate an investigation or other regulatory action.

PART 6: ACCOUNTANTS' REPORTS

Rule 32: Delivery of accountants' reports

[Deleted]

Rule 32A: Obtaining and delivery of accountants' reports

32A.1   Subject to rule 32A.1A, if *you* have, at any time during an *accounting period*, held or received *client money*, or operated a *client's* own account as signatory, *you* must:

- (a) obtain an accountant's report for that *accounting period* within six months of the end of the *accounting period*; and
- (b) if the report has been qualified, deliver it to the SRA within six months of the end of the *accounting period*.

This duty extends to the *directors* of a *company*, or the members of an *LLP*, which is subject to this rule.

32A.1A   Subject to rule 32A.2, you are not required to obtain or deliver an accountant's report if:

- (a) all of the *client money* held or received during an *accounting period* is money held or received from the Legal Aid Agency or in the circumstances set out in rule 19.3; or
- (b) in the *accounting period*, the statement or passbook balance of client money you have held or received does not exceed:
  - (i) an average of £10,000; and
  - (ii) a maximum of £250,000,

  or the equivalent in foreign currency.

32A.1B   In rule 32A.1A above:

- (a) a "statement or passbook balance" is the total balance obtained at least once every five weeks, from a bank, building society or other institution of all *general client accounts* and *separate designated client accounts*, and accounts that are not *client accounts* but are holding *client money*, when carrying out reconciliations in accordance with rules 29.11 to 29.14; and
- (b) an average "statement or passbook balance" is the total of all statement or passbook balances obtained in any *accounting period* divided by the number of such balances in that period.

32A.2   Notwithstanding the provisions of rules 32A.1 and 32A.1A, the *SRA* may require you to obtain or deliver an accountant's report at any time in circumstances other than those set out in rules 32A.1 and in the circumstances set out in rule 32A.1A if the *SRA* has reason to believe that it is in the public interest to do so.

Guidance notes

(i)   A qualified accountant's report is a report prepared in accordance with rule 32A.1(a) where the reporting accountant forms the judgement that these rules have not been complied with such that the safety of client money is at risk. The form of the report is dealt with in rule 44. See also the SRA's "Guidance to Reporting Accountants and firms on planning and completion of the annual Accountants' Reports, under Rule 32A of the SRA Accounts Rules 2011".

(ii)   To qualify for the exemption in rule 32A.1A(b), you are required to assess at the end of the accounting period if the average (at least five weekly) balance of client money you have held or received is or less than, or equal to £10,000 and that the maximum aggregated total of client money held or received is less than, or equal to £250,000 (or the equivalent in foreign currency). Both thresholds need to be satisfied for the exemption to apply. If you do satisfy the criteria you will be exempted from the requirement of obtaining an annual accountant's report for that accounting period. We expect that firms will inevitably move in and out of the thresholds from year to year and it is your obligation to satisfy yourself, and if required the SRA, that you have properly applied the exemptions. You should ensure you keep full records of your decisions in this regard. For the avoidance of any doubt if you or your firm is exempted from the obligation to obtain an accountant's report under rule 32A.1A, all of the other sections of these rules will continue to apply to you in full.

(iii)   Examples of situations under rule 32A.2 include:

(a)   when no report has been obtained or delivered but the SRA has reason to believe that a report should have been obtained or delivered, for example, because you have failed to deliver a qualified report to the SRA or where you have failed to obtain a report because you have improperly applied one of the exemptions in rule 32A.1A;

(b)   when a report has been delivered but the SRA has reason to believe that it may be inaccurate;

(c)   when your conduct gives the SRA reason to believe that it would be appropriate to require you to obtain or deliver a report earlier than would otherwise have been the case (for instance three months after the end of the accounting period);

(d)   when your conduct gives the SRA reason to believe that it would be appropriate to require the obtaining and delivery of a report, whether or not qualified that an exemption would otherwise apply, or the more frequent obtaining and delivery of reports (for instance every six months);

(e)   when the SRA has reason to believe that the regulatory risk justifies the imposition on a category of firm of a requirement to obtain and deliver reports earlier or at more frequent intervals;

(f) when a condition on a solicitor's practising certificate requires earlier delivery of reports or the obtaining and delivery of reports at more frequent intervals.

(iv) The requirement in rule 32A for a registered foreign lawyer to deliver an accountant's report applies only to a registered foreign lawyer practising in one of the ways set out in paragraph (vi)(C) of the definition of "you" in the Glossary.

(v) When client money is held or received by an unincorporated practice, the principals in the practice will have held or received client money. A salaried partner whose name appears in the list of partners on a firm's letterhead, even if the name appears under a separate heading of "salaried partners" or "associate partners", is a principal.

(vi) In the case of an incorporated practice, it is the company or LLP (i.e. the recognised body or licensed body) which will have held or received client money. The recognised body/licensed body and its directors (in the case of a company) or members (in the case of an LLP) will have the duty to obtain the accountant's report and to deliver any such report to the SRA if it is qualified, although the directors or members will not usually have held client money.

(vii) Assistant solicitors, consultants and other employees do not normally hold client money. An assistant solicitor or consultant might be a signatory for a firm's client account, but this does not constitute holding or receiving client money. If a client or third party hands cash to an assistant solicitor, consultant or other employee, it is the sole principal or the partners (rather than the assistant solicitor, consultant or other employee) who are regarded as having received and held the money. In the case of an incorporated practice, whether a company or an LLP, it would be the recognised body or licensed body itself which would be regarded as having held or received the money.

(viii) If, exceptionally, an assistant solicitor, consultant or other employee has a client account (as a trustee), or operates a client's own account as signatory, the assistant solicitor, consultant or other employee will have to obtain and deliver an accountant's report unless the exemptions in rule 32A.1A apply. The assistant solicitor, consultant or other employee can be included in the report of the practice, but will need to ensure that his or her name is added, and an explanation given.

(ix) Rule 32A does not apply to a solicitor or registered European lawyer, employed as an in-house lawyer by a non-solicitor employer, who operates the account of the employer or a related body of the employer.

(x) In exceptional circumstances, a waiver of the obligation to obtain a report may sometimes be granted. Applications should be made to the SRA.

(xi) If a firm owns all the shares in a recognised body or licensed body which is an executor, trustee or nominee company, the firm and the recognised body/licensed body may obtain a single accountant's report (see rule 28.1(b)).

Rule 33: Accounting periods

The norm

33.1   An "accounting period" means the period for which *your* accounts are ordinarily made up, except that it must:

(a)   begin at the end of the previous *accounting period*; and

(b)   cover twelve months.

Rules 33.2 to 33.5 below set out exceptions.

First and resumed reports

33.2   If *you* are under a duty to obtain *your* first report, the *accounting period* must begin:

(a)   on the date when *you* first held or received *client money* (or operated a *client's* own account as signatory); or

(b)   at the end of the last *accounting period* in which an exemption under rule 32A.1A applied.

33.3   If *you* are under a duty to obtain *your* first report after a break, the *accounting period* must begin:

(a)   on the date when *you*, for the first time after the break, held or received *client money* (or operated a *client's* own account as signatory); or

(b)   at the end of the last *accounting period* in which an exemption under rule 32A.1A applied

and may cover less than twelve months.

Change of accounting period

33.4   If *you* change the period for which *your* accounts are made up (for example, on a merger, or simply for convenience), the *accounting period* immediately preceding the change may be shorter than twelve months, or longer than twelve months up to a maximum of 18 months, provided that the *accounting period* shall not be changed to a period longer than twelve months unless the *SRA* receives written notice of the change before expiry of the deadline for delivery of the accountant's report which would have been expected on the basis of *your* old *accounting period*.

Final reports

33.5   If *you* for any reason stop holding or receiving *client money* (and operating any *client's* own account as signatory), *you* must obtain and deliver a final report to the *SRA*. The *accounting period* must end on the date upon which *you* stopped holding or receiving *client money* (and operating any *client's* own account as signatory), and may cover less than twelve months.

Guidance notes

(i)   You must obtain and deliver a final report to the SRA when you cease to hold client money. This applies regardless of whether you would otherwise have been exempted from the requirement to obtain an annual accountant's report on the basis you meet the criteria set out in Rule 32A.1A above and irrespective of whether the report is qualified or unqualified.

(ii)   For a person who did not previously hold or receive client money, etc., and has become a principal in the firm, the report for the firm will represent, from the date of joining, that person's first report for the purpose of rule 33.2. For a person who was a principal in the firm and, on leaving, stops holding or receiving client money, etc., the report for the firm will represent, up to the date of leaving, that person's final report for the purpose of rule 33.5 above.

(iii)   When a partnership splits up, it is usually appropriate for the books to be made up as at the date of dissolution, and for an accountant's report to be delivered within six months of that date. If, however, the old partnership continues to hold or receive client money, etc., in connection with outstanding matters, accountant's reports will continue to be required for those matters; the books should then be made up on completion of the last of those matters and a report delivered within six months of that date. The same would be true for a sole practitioner winding up matters on retirement.

(iv)   When a practice is being wound up, you may be left with money which is unattributable, or belongs to a client who cannot be traced. It may be appropriate to apply to the SRA for authority to withdraw this money from the client account – see rule 20.1(k) and guidance note (vi)(a) to rule 20.

Rule 34: Qualifications for making a report

34.1   A report must be prepared and signed by an accountant:

(a)   **who is a member of:**

  (i)   the Institute of Chartered Accountants in England and Wales;

  (ii)   the Institute of Chartered Accountants of Scotland;

  (iii)   the Association of Chartered Certified Accountants;

  (iv)   the Institute of Chartered Accountants in Ireland; or

  (v)   the Association of Authorised Public Accountants; **and**

(b)   **who is also:**

  (i)   an individual who is a registered auditor within the terms of section 1239 of the Companies Act 2006; or

  (ii)   an employee of such an individual; or

  (iii)   a *partner* in or employee of a *partnership* which is a registered auditor within the terms of section 1239 of the Companies Act 2006; or

(iv) a director or employee of a company which is a registered auditor within the terms of section 1239 of the Companies Act 2006; or

(v) a member or employee of an *LLP* which is a registered auditor within the terms of section 1239 of the Companies Act 2006.

34.2 An accountant is not qualified to make a report if:

(a) at any time between the beginning of the *accounting period* to which the report relates, and the completion of the report:

(i) he or she was a *partner* or employee, or an officer or employee (in the case of a company), or a member or employee (in the case of an *LLP*) in the *firm* to which the report relates; or

(ii) he or she was employed by the same *non-solicitor employer* as the *solicitor* or *REL* for whom the report is being made; or

(iii) he or she was a *partner* or employee, or an officer or employee (in the case of a company), or a member or employee (in the case of an *LLP*) in an accountancy practice which had an ownership interest in, or was part of the group structure of, the *licensed body* to which the report relates; or

(b) he or she has been disqualified under rule 34.3 below and notice of disqualification has been given under rule 34.4 (and has not subsequently been withdrawn).

34.3 The *SRA* may disqualify an accountant from making any accountant's report if:

(a) the accountant has been found guilty by his or her professional body of professional misconduct or discreditable conduct; or

(b) the *SRA* is satisfied that *you* have not complied with the rules in respect of matters which the accountant has negligently failed to specify in a report.

In coming to a decision, the *SRA* will take into account any representations made by the accountant or his or her professional body.

34.4 Written notice of disqualification must be left at or sent by recorded delivery to the address of the accountant shown on an accountant's report or in the records of the accountant's professional body. If sent through the post, receipt will be deemed 48 hours (excluding Saturdays, Sundays and Bank Holidays) after posting.

34.5 An accountant's disqualification may be notified to any *firm* likely to be affected and may be printed in the *Society's* Gazette or other publication.

Guidance note

(i) It is not a breach of the rules for you to retain an outside accountant to write up the books of account and to instruct the same accountant to prepare the accountant's report. However, both you and the accountant will have to be satisfied that these circumstances do not affect his or her independence in preparing the report.

Rule 35: Reporting accountant's rights and duties – letter of engagement

35.1 *You* must ensure that the reporting accountant's rights and duties are stated in a letter of engagement incorporating the following terms:

"In accordance with rule 35 of the SRA Accounts Rules 2011, you are instructed as follows:

(a) I/this firm/this company/this limited liability partnership recognises that, if during the course of preparing an accountant's report:

(i)   you discover evidence of fraud or theft in relation to money

(A)   held by a solicitor (or registered European lawyer, or registered foreign lawyer, or recognised body, or licensed body, or employee of a solicitor or registered European lawyer, or manager or employee of a recognised body or licensed body) for a client or any other person (including money held on trust), or

(B)   held in an account of a client, or an account of another person, which is operated by a solicitor (or registered European lawyer, registered foreign lawyer, recognised body, licensed body, employee of a solicitor or registered European lawyer, or manager or employee of a recognised body or licensed body); or

(ii)   you obtain information which you have reasonable cause to believe is likely to be of material significance in determining whether a solicitor (or registered European lawyer, or registered foreign lawyer, or recognised body, or licensed body, or employee of a solicitor or registered European lawyer, or manager or employee of a recognised body or licensed body) is a fit and proper person

(A)   to hold money for clients or other persons (including money held on trust), or

(B)   to operate an account of a client or an account of another person,

(iii)   you discover a failure by the firm to submit a qualified accountant's report to the Solicitors Regulation Authority, as required by these rules,

you must immediately give a report of the matter to the Solicitors Regulation Authority in accordance with section 34(9) of the Solicitors Act 1974 or article 3(1) of the Legal Services Act 2007 (Designation as a Licensing Authority) (No. 2) Order 2011 as appropriate;

(b) you may, and are encouraged to, make that report without prior reference to me/this firm/this company/this limited liability partnership;

(c) you are to report directly to the Solicitors Regulation Authority should your appointment be terminated following the issue of, or indication of intention to issue, a qualified accountant's report, or following the raising of concerns prior to the preparation of an accountant's report;

(d) you are to deliver to me/this firm/this company/this limited liability partnership your report which you should also retain for at least six years from the date of its signature and to produce the copy to the Solicitors Regulation Authority on request;

(e) you are to retain these terms of engagement for at least six years after the termination of the retainer and to produce them to the Solicitors Regulation Authority on request; and

(f) following any direct report made to the Solicitors Regulation Authority under (a) or (c) above, you are to provide to the Solicitors Regulation Authority on request any further relevant information in your possession or in the possession of your firm.

To the extent necessary to enable you to comply with (a) to (f) above, I/we waive my/the firm's/the company's/the limited liability partnership's right of confidentiality. This waiver extends to any report made, document produced or information disclosed to the Solicitors Regulation Authority in good faith pursuant to these instructions, even though it may subsequently transpire that you were mistaken in your belief that there was cause for concern."

35.2 The letter of engagement and a copy must be signed by *you* and by the accountant. *You* must keep the copy of the signed letter of engagement for at least six years after the termination of the retainer and produce it to the *SRA* on request. Both *you* and the reporting accountant must also retain a copy of the accountant's report, whether qualified or not, for at least six years from the date of its signature and produce the copy to the *SRA* on request.

35.3 The specified terms may be included in a letter from the accountant to *you* setting out the terms of the engagement but the text must be adapted appropriately. The letter must be signed in duplicate by both parties, with *you* keeping the original and the accountant the copy.

Guidance note

(i) Any direct report by the accountant to the SRA under rule 35.1(a) or (c) should be made to the Fraud and Confidential Intelligence Bureau.

Rule 36: Change of accountant

36.1 On instructing an accountancy practice to replace that previously instructed to produce accountant's reports, *you* must immediately notify the *SRA* of the change and provide the name and business address of the new accountancy practice.

Rule 37: Place of examination

[Deleted]

Rule 38: Provision of details of bank accounts, etc.

38.1 The accountant must request, and *you* must provide, details of all accounts kept or operated by *you* in connection with *your* practice at any *bank*, *building society* or other financial institution at any time during the *accounting period* to which the report relates. This includes *client accounts*, *office accounts*, accounts which are not *client accounts* but which contain *client money*, and *clients'* own accounts operated by *you* as signatory.

Rule 39: Test procedures

[Deleted]

Rule 40: Departures from guidelines for accounting procedures and systems

[Deleted]

Rule 41: Matters outside the accountant's remit

[Deleted]

Rule 42: Privileged documents

[Deleted]

Rule 43: Completion of checklist

[Deleted]

Rule 43A: Work to be undertaken

43A.1 The accountant should exercise his or her professional judgement in determining the work required for the firm they are instructed to obtain the report on in order to assess risks to *client money* arising from compliance with these rules. This should cover the work that the accountant considers is appropriate to enable completion of the report required by the *SRA* at the date the report is commissioned (referred to in Rule 44 below).

Guidance notes

(i) The purpose of the accountant's report is to enable a proportionate degree of oversight by the SRA over risks to clients' funds. It may also help the firm identify any improvements in its control systems that are required. The form of the report that the accountant is required to complete is intended to provide assurance that client funds are properly safeguarded. If the accountant forms the judgement that these Rules have not been complied with such that the safety of client money is at risk, then the accountant is required to "qualify" the report and set out in the report details of the areas where risks have been identified. Rule 32A.1 sets out which firms are required to obtain a report but only qualified reports have to be delivered to the SRA within the time frame set out.

(ii)   The types of work that the accountant is required to undertake will depend on a number of factors including the size and complexity of the firm, the nature of the work undertaken, the number of transactions and amount of client funds held. The accountant may also want to consider the firm's existing systems and for example, the numbers and types of breaches of these Rules that the firm's COFA has recorded under his/her reporting obligations. Separate guidance as to the work that might be considered as part of a work programme has been issued by the SRA and will be updated from time to time; see the SRA's "Guidance to Reporting Accountants and firms on planning and completion of the annual Accountants' Reports, under Rule 32A of the SRA Accounts Rules 2011".

Rule 43B: Failure to provide documentation

43B.1   *You* must provide documentation to the accountant as required to enable completion of the accountant's report. When acting on a *client's* instructions, *you* will normally have the right on the grounds of privilege as between *solicitor* and *client* to decline to produce any document requested by the accountant for the purposes of his or her examination. A significant failure to provide documentation may result in the accountant deciding that they should qualify the report if they consider that as a result, they cannot properly prepare the report in accordance with these rules.

Guidance note

(i)   In a recognised body or licensed body with one or more managers who are not legally qualified, legal professional privilege may not attach to work which is neither done nor supervised by a legally qualified individual – see Legal Services Act 2007, section 190(3) to (7), and Schedule 22, paragraph 17.

Rule 44: Form of accountant's report

44.1   The accountant must complete and sign his or her report in the form published from time to time by the *SRA*.

Guidance notes

(i)   The current form of the accountant's report under rule 44 requires the accountant to confirm of he/she has found it necessary to qualify the report. If so, the report must be delivered to the SRA – see rule 32A.1(b) and guidance notes to that rule.

(ii)   Separate reports can be obtained for each principal in a partnership but most firms choose to obtain one report in the name of all the principals. In either case, the report must be delivered to the SRA if it is qualified – see rule 32A.1(b) and the guidance notes to that rule. For assistant solicitors, consultants and other employees, see rule 32A, guidance notes (vii) and (viii).

(iii)   An incorporated practice will obtain only one report, on behalf of the company and its directors, or on behalf of the LLP and its members – see rule 32A.1. The report must be delivered to the SRA if it is qualified – see rule 32A.1(b) and the guidance notes to that rule.

(iv) Although it may be agreed that the accountant will send a qualified report direct to the SRA, the responsibility for delivery is that of the firm. The form of report requires the accountant to confirm that a copy of the report (whether qualified or unqualified) has been sent to the COFA on behalf of the firm to which it relates. The COFA should ensure that the report is seen by each of the managers of the firm.

(v) For direct reporting by the accountant to the SRA in cases of concern, see rule 35 and guidance note (i) to that rule.

Rule 45: Firms with two or more places of business

45.1 If a *firm* has two or more offices:

(a) separate reports may be obtained in respect of the different offices; and

(b) separate *accounting periods* may be adopted for different offices, provided that:

(i) separate reports are obtained;

(ii) every office is covered by a report obtained within six months of the end of its *accounting period*; and

(iii) there are no gaps between the *accounting periods* covered by successive reports for any particular office or offices.

Rule 46: Waivers

46.1 The *SRA* may waive in writing in any particular case or cases any of the provisions of Part 6 of the rules, and may revoke any waiver.

Guidance note

(i) Applications for waivers should be made to the SRA. In appropriate cases, firms may be granted a waiver of the obligation to obtain an accountant's and in accordance with the SRA's current Waivers Policy.

PART 7: PRACTICE AS AN REL FROM AN OFFICE IN ENGLAND AND WALES OF AN EXEMPT EUROPEAN PRACTICE

Rule 47: Purpose of the overseas accounts provisions

[Deleted]

Rule 47A: Purpose of rules applying to RELs in Exempt European Practices

47A.1 The purpose of applying different accounts provisions to the practice of an *REL* from an office in England and Wales of an *Exempt European Practice* is to ensure similar protection for *client monies* but by way of rules which recognise that the body in which the *REL* is practising is not itself a regulated entity.

Rule 48: Application and Interpretation

48.1   Part 7 of these rules applies to your practice as an *REL* from an office in England and Wales of an *Exempt European Practice*.

48.2   The SRA Handbook Glossary 2012 shall apply and, unless the context otherwise requires:

(a)   all italicised terms shall be defined; and

(b)   all terms shall be interpreted,

in accordance with the *Glossary*.

Rule 49: Interest

[Deleted]

Rule 50: Accounts

[Deleted]

Rule 50A: Client money

50A.1   You must comply with this Part if you have held or received *client money*.

50A.2   In all dealings with *client money*, you must:

(a)   keep *client money* separate from money which is not *client money*;

(b)   on receipt, pay *client money* into a *client account* without undue delay and keep it there, unless the *client* has agreed otherwise, or it is paid directly to a third party in the execution of a *trust* under which it is held;

(c)   ensure by use of proper accounting systems and processes that *client money* is used for *client's* matters only and for the purposes for which it has been paid;

(d)   use money held as *trustee* of a *trust* for the purposes of that *trust* only;

(e)   establish and maintain proper accounting systems and proper internal controls over those systems to ensure compliance with these rules;

(f)   return *client money* to the person on whose behalf the money is held promptly, as soon as there is no longer any proper reason to retain those funds;

(g)   keep accounting records to show accurately the position with regard to the money held for each *client* and *trust* for a minimum period of six years;

(h)   Account for interest on *client money* in accordance with rule 22.

Rule 50B: Accountants' Reports

50B.1   You must obtain an accountant's report in respect of any period during which you or the *Exempt European Practice* from which you practice have held or received *client money* unless you fall within any of the exceptions contained in rule 32A.1A.

50B.2   You must comply with the rules in Part 6 in relation to any accountant's report that you are required to obtain under rule 50B.1.

Rule 51: Production of documents, information and explanations

51.1   You must promptly comply with:

(a) a written notice from the *SRA* that you must produce for inspection by the appointee of the *SRA* all documents held by you or held under your control and all information and explanations requested:

(i)   in connection with your practice; or

(ii) in connection with any *trust* of which you are, or formerly were, a *trustee*;

for the purpose of ascertaining whether any person subject to Part 7 of these rules is complying with or has complied with any provision of this Part of these rules, or on whether the account has been used for or in connection with a breach of any of the Principles or other SRA Handbook requirements made or issued by the *SRA*; and

(b) a notice given by the *SRA* in accordance with section 44B or 44BA of the *SA* or section 93 of the *LSA* for the provision of documents, information or explanations.

51.2   You must provide any necessary permissions for information to be given so as to enable the appointee of the *SRA* to:

(a) prepare a report on the documents produced under rule 51.1 above; and

(b) seek verification from clients, staff and the banks, building societies or other financial institutions used by you.

51.3   You must comply with all requests from the *SRA* or its appointee as to:

(a) the form in which you produce any documents you hold electronically; and

(b) photocopies of any documents to take away.

51.4   A notice under this rule is deemed to be duly served:

(a) on the date on which it is delivered to or left at your address;

(b) on the date on which it is sent electronically to your e-mail or fax address; or

(c) 48 hours (excluding Saturdays, Sundays and Bank Holidays) after it has been sent by post or document exchange to your last notified practising address.

Rule 52: Waivers

52.1   The *SRA* may waive in writing in any particular case or cases any of the provisions of Part 7 of the rules, may place conditions on, and may revoke, any waiver.

Guidance note

(i)   Applications for waivers should be made to the Professional Ethics Guidance Team. You will need to show that your circumstances are exceptional in order for a waiver to be granted.

PART 8:

[Deleted]

APPENDIX 1: FLOWCHART – EFFECT OF SRA ACCOUNTS RULES 2011

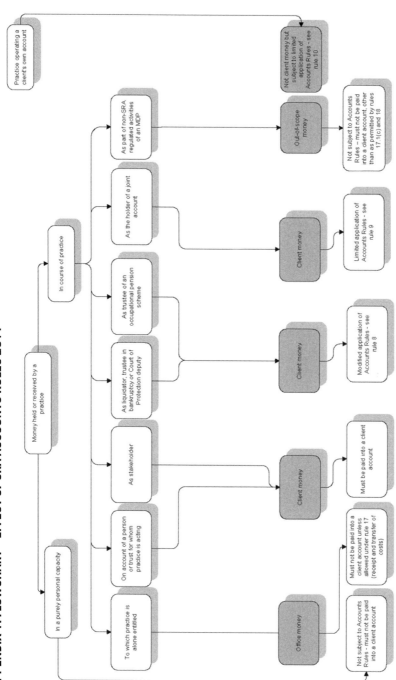

APPENDIX 2: SPECIAL SITUATIONS – WHAT APPLIES

	Is it client money?	Subject to reconciliations?	Keep books?	Retain statements?	Subject to accountant's report?	Produce records to SRA?	Interest?	Retain records generally?	Central records?	Subject to reporting accountant's comparisons?
1	R.15.1(a) a/cs in practice name (not client a/c)	Yes	Yes	Yes – r.29.1(a) and 29.2	Yes – r.29.17	Yes	Yes	Yes – r.22	Yes – r.29.17	Statements or register – r.29.19, bills – r.29.15	Yes – r.39.1(f)
2	R.15.1(b) a/cs in name of client – not operated by practice	No	No	No – record receipt and payment only	No	No	No	No – all interest earned for client – r.22, guidance note (i)(i)	No – except record of receipt and payment	Bills – r.29.15	No
3	R.15.1(b) a/cs in name of client – operated by practice	No	No	No – record receipt and payment only	Yes – r.30	Limited – r.39.1(n)	Yes – r.10	No – all interest earned for client – r.22, guidance note (i)(i)	No – except record of receipt and payment	Statements – r.30, Bills – r.29.15	No

	Is it client money?	Subject to reconciliations?	Keep books?	Retain statements?	Subject to accountant's report?	Produce records to SRA?	Interest?	Retain records generally?	Central records?	Subject to reporting accountant's comparisons?
4	Liquidators, trustees in bankruptcy and Court of Protection deputies	Yes – r.8	No – r.8	Modified – statutory records – r.8	Yes – r.8 and r.29.17(c)	Limited – r.39.1(l)	Yes – r.8	No – r.8 – comply with statutory rules (but see r.8.4 and r.22, guidance note (iv)(a))	Yes – modified r.29.17(c)	Yes – r.29.20 Bills – r.29.15	No – r.8
5	Trustees of occupational pension schemes	Yes – r.8	No – r.8	Modified – statutory records – r.8	Yes – r.8 and r.29.17(c)	Limited – r.39.1(l)	Yes – r.8	No – r.8 – comply with statutory rules (but see r.8.4 and r.22, guidance note (iv)(a))	Yes – modified r.29.17(c)	Yes – r.29.20 Bills – r.29.15	No – r.8

	Is it client money?	Subject to reconciliations?	Keep books?	Retain statements?	Subject to accountant's report?	Produce records to SRA?	Interest?	Retain records generally?	Central records?	Subject to reporting accountant's comparisons?
6 Joint accounts – r.9	Yes – r.9	No – r.9	No – r.9	Yes – r.9 and 29.17(b)(ii)	Limited – r.39.1(m)	Yes – r.9	No. For joint a/c with client, all interest to client (r.22, guidance note (v)(a)); for joint a/c with another practice or other third party, depends on agreement	No – r.9	Statements – r.29.21 Bills – r.29.15	No – r.9
7 Acting under power of attorney	Yes	Yes	Yes	Yes	Yes	Yes	Yes	Yes	Bills – r.29.15	Yes

	Is it client money?	Subject to reconciliations?	Keep books?	Retain statements?	Subject to accountant's report?	Produce records to SRA?	Interest?	Retain records generally?	Central records?	Subject to reporting accountant's comparisons?
8 Operating client's own a/c e.g. under power of attorney – r.10	No	No	No	Yes – r.30	Limited – r.39.1(n)	Yes – r.10	No – all interest earned for client (r.22, guidance note (i)(i))	No – r.10	Statements – r.30 Bills – r.29.15	No
9 Exempt persons under r.5	No	No	No	No	No	No	No	No	No	No
10 Non-SRA regulated activities of an MDP	No – out-of-scope money – r.12	No	No – but see guidance note (xi) to r.29	No	No	Yes – r.31 – only to extent needed to check rule compliance	No	No – but see guidance note (xi) to r.29	No	No

APPENDIX 3: SRA GUIDELINES – ACCOUNTING PROCEDURES AND SYSTEMS

1.   Introduction

1.1   These guidelines, published under rule 26 of the SRA Accounts Rules 2011, are intended to be a benchmark or broad statement of good practice requirements which should be present in an effective regime for the proper control of client money. They should therefore be of positive assistance to firms in establishing or reviewing appropriate procedures and systems. They do not override, or detract from the need to comply fully with, the Accounts Rules.

1.2   References to managers or firms in the guidelines are intended to include sole practitioners, recognised bodies and licensed bodies, and the managers of those bodies.

2.   General

2.1   Compliance with the Accounts Rules is the equal responsibility of all managers in a firm. This responsibility also extends to the Compliance Officer for Finance and Administration, whether or not a manager (see rule 6). They should establish policies and systems to ensure that the firm complies fully with the rules, including procedures for verifying that the controls are operating effectively. Responsibility for day to day supervision may be delegated to one or more managers to enable effective control to be exercised. Delegation of total responsibility to a cashier or book-keeper is not acceptable.

2.2   The firm should hold a copy of the current version of the Accounts Rules and/or have ready access to the current on-line version. The person who maintains the books of account must have a full knowledge of the requirements of the rules and the accounting requirements of firms.

2.3   Proper books of account should be maintained on the double-entry principle. They should be legible, up to date and contain narratives with the entries which identify and/or provide adequate information about the transaction. Entries should be made in chronological order and the current balance should be shown on client ledger accounts, or be readily ascertainable, in accordance with rule 29.9.

2.4   Ledger accounts for clients, other persons or trusts should include the name of the client or other person or trust and contain a heading which provides a description of the matter or transaction.

2.5   Manual systems for recording client money are capable of complying with these guidelines. A computer system, with suitable support procedures will, however, provide an efficient means of producing the accounts and associated control information.

2.6   When introducing new systems, care must be taken to ensure:

(1)   that balances transferred from the books of account of the old system are reconciled with the opening balances held on the new system before day to day operation commences;

(2) that the new system operates correctly before the old system is abandoned. This may require a period of parallel running of the old and new systems and the satisfactory reconciliation of the two sets of records before the old system ceases.

2.7   The firm should ensure that office account entries in relation to each client or trust matter are maintained up to date as well as the client account entries. Credit balances on office account in respect of client or trust matters should be fully investigated.

2.8   The firm should establish policies and operate systems for the payment of fair and reasonable interest to clients in accordance with rules 22 and 23.

3.   Receipt of client money

3.1   The firm should have procedures for identifying client money, including cash, when received in the firm, and for promptly recording the receipt of the money either in the books of account or a register for later posting to the client cash book and ledger accounts. The procedures should cover money received through the post, electronically or direct by fee earners or other personnel. They should also cover the safekeeping of money prior to payment to bank.

3.2   The firm should have a system which ensures that client money is paid promptly into a client account.

3.3   The firm should have a system for identifying money which should not be in a client account and for transferring it without delay.

3.4   The firm should determine a policy and operate a system for dealing with money which is a mixture of office money and client money, or client money and out-of-scope money, or client money, out-of-scope money and office money, in compliance with rules 17–19.

4.   Payments from client account

4.1   The firm should have clear procedures for ensuring that all withdrawals from client accounts are properly authorised. In particular, suitable persons should be named for the following purposes:

(1)   authorisation of internal payment vouchers;

(2)   signing client account cheques;

(3)   authorising telegraphic or electronic transfers.

No other personnel should be allowed to authorise or sign the documents.

4.2   The firm should establish clear procedures and systems for ensuring that persons permitted to authorise the withdrawal of client money from a client account have an appropriate understanding of the requirements of the rules, including rules 20 and 21 which set out when and how a withdrawal from client account may properly be made.

4.3 Persons nominated for the purpose of authorising internal payment vouchers should, for each payment, ensure there is supporting evidence showing clearly the reason for the payment, and the date of it. Similarly, persons signing cheques and authorising transfers should ensure there is a suitable voucher or other supporting evidence to support the payment.

4.4 The firm should have clear systems and procedures for authorising withdrawals from client accounts by electronic means, with appropriate safeguards and controls to ensure that all such withdrawals are properly authorised.

4.5 The firm should have a system for checking the balances on client ledger accounts to ensure no debit balances occur. Where payments are to be made other than out of cleared funds, clear policies and procedures must be in place to ensure that adequate risk assessment is applied.

N.B. If incoming payments are ultimately dishonoured, a debit balance will arise, in breach of the rules, and full replacement of the shortfall will be required under rule 7. See also rule 20, guidance notes (iii)(a) and (iv)(a).

4.6 The firm should establish systems for the transfer of costs from client account to office account in accordance with rule 17.2 and 17.3. Normally transfers should be made only on the basis of rendering a bill or written notification. The payment from the client account should be by way of a cheque or transfer in favour of the firm or sole principal – see rule 21.4.

4.7 The firm should establish policies and operate systems to control and record accurately any transfers between clients of the firm. Where these arise as a result of loans between clients, the written authority of both the lender and borrower must be obtained in accordance with rule 27.2.

4.8 The firm should establish policies and operate systems for the timely closure of files, and the prompt accounting for surplus balances in accordance with rule 14.3.

4.9 The firm should establish systems in accordance with rule 14.4 to keep clients (or other people on whose behalf money is held) regularly informed when funds are retained for a specified reason at the end of a matter or the substantial conclusion of a matter.

5.   Overall control of client accounts

5.1 The firm should maintain control of all its bank and building society accounts opened for the purpose of holding client money. In the case of a joint account, a suitable degree of control should be exercised.

5.2 Central records or central registers must be kept in respect of:

>   (1) accounts held for client money, which are not client accounts (rules 15.1(a), 16.1(d) and 29.19);

(2) practice as a liquidator, trustee in bankruptcy, Court of Protection deputy or trustee of an occupational pension scheme (rules 8 and 29.20);

(3) joint accounts (rules 9 and 29.21);

(4) dividend payments received by an executor, trustee or nominee company as nominee (rules 28.2 and 29.23); and

(5) clients' own accounts (rules 10, 15.1(b) and 30.3).

5.3   In addition, there should be a master list of all:

- general client accounts;

- separate designated client accounts;

- accounts held in respect of 5.2 above; and

- office accounts.

The master list should show the current status of each account; e.g. currently in operation or closed with date of closure.

5.4   The firm should operate a system to ensure that accurate reconciliations of the client accounts are carried out at least every five weeks. In particular it should ensure that:

(1) a full list of client ledger balances is produced. Any debit balances should be listed, fully investigated and rectified immediately. The total of any debit balances cannot be "netted off" against the total of credit balances;

(2) a full list of unpresented cheques is produced;

(3) a list of outstanding lodgements is produced;

(4) formal statements are produced reconciling the client account cash book balances, aggregate client ledger balances and the client bank accounts. All unresolved differences must be investigated and, where appropriate, corrective action taken;

(5) a manager or the Compliance Officer for Finance and Administration checks the reconciliation statement and any corrective action, and ensures that enquiries are made into any unusual or apparently unsatisfactory items or still unresolved matters.

5.5   The firm should have clear policies, systems and procedures to control access to computerised client accounts by determining the personnel who should have "write to" and "read only" access. Passwords should be held confidentially by designated personnel and changed regularly to maintain security. Access to the system should not unreasonably be restricted to a single person nor should more people than necessary be given access.

5.6   The firm should establish policies and systems for the retention of the accounting records to ensure:

- books of account, reconciliations, bills, bank statements and passbooks are kept for at least six years;

- paid cheques, digital images of paid cheques and other authorities for the withdrawal of money from a client account are kept for at least two years;

- other vouchers and internal expenditure authorisation documents relating directly to entries in the client account books are kept for at least two years.

5.7   The firm should ensure that unused client account cheques are stored securely to prevent unauthorised access. Blank cheques should not be pre-signed. Any cancelled cheques should be retained.

APPENDIX 4: REPORTING ACCOUNTANT'S CHECKLIST

[Any checks made in respect of the period [   ] to 5 October 2011 relate to compliance with the Solicitors' Accounts Rules 1998.]

The following items have been tested to satisfy the examination requirements under rules 38-40, with the results as indicated. Where the position has been found to be unsatisfactory as a result of these tests, further details have been reported in section 6 of this checklist or reported by separate appendix.

Name of practice

Results of test checks:

1. For all client money		Were any breaches discovered? (Tick the appropriate column.)		If "yes" should breaches be noted in the accountant's report?		Cross reference to audit file documentation
(a)	**Book-keeping system for every office:**	Yes	No	Yes	No	
(i)	The accounting records satisfactorily distinguish client money from all other money dealt with by the firm.					
(ii)	A separate ledger account is maintained for each client and trust (excepting section (I) below) and the particulars of all client money received, held or paid on account of each client and trust, including funds held on separate designated deposits, or elsewhere, are recorded.					
(iii)	The client ledgers for clients and trusts show a current balance at all times, or the current balance is readily ascertainable.					
(iv)	A record of all bills of costs and written notifications has been maintained, either in the form of a central record or a file of copies of such bills.					
(b)	**Postings to ledger accounts and casts:**	Yes	No	Yes	No	
(i)	Postings to ledger accounts for clients and trusts from records of receipts and payments are correct.					
(ii)	Casts of ledger accounts for clients and trusts and receipts and payments records are correct.					
(iii)	Postings have been recorded in chronological sequence with the date being that of the initiation of the transaction.					
(c)	**Receipts and payments of client money:**	Yes	No	Yes	No	
(i)	Sample receipts and payments of client money as shown in bank and building society statements have been compared with the firm's records of receipts and payments of client money, and are correct.					

For alternative formats, email info.services@sra.org.uk or telephone 0870 606 2555.

1. continued.....		Were any breaches discovered? (Tick the appropriate column.)		If "yes" should breaches be noted in the accountant,'s report?		Cross reference to audit file documentation.
(ii)	Sample paid cheques, or digital images of the front and back of sample paid cheques, have been obtained and details agreed to receipts and payment records.					
(d)	**System of recording costs and making transfers:**	Yes	No	Yes	No	
(i)	The firm's system of recording costs has been ascertained and is suitable.					
(ii)	Costs have been drawn only where required for or towards payment of the firm's costs where there has been sent to the client a bill of costs or other written notification of the amount of the costs.					
(e)	**Examination of documents for verification of transactions and entries in accounting records:**	Yes	No	Yes	No	
(i)	Make a test examination of a number of client and trust files.					
(ii)	All client and trust files requested for examination were made available.					
(iii)	The financial transactions as detailed on client and trust files and other documentation (including transfers from one ledger account to another) were valid and appropriately authorised in accordance with Parts 1 and 2 of the SRA Accounts Rules 2011 (AR).					
(iv)	The financial transactions evidenced by documents on the client and trust files were correctly recorded in the books of account in a manner complying with Part 4 AR.					
(f)	**Extraction of client ledger balances for clients and trusts:**	Yes	No	Yes	No	
(i)	The extraction of client ledger balances for clients and trusts has been checked for no fewer than two separate dates in the period subject to this report.					
(ii)	The total liabilities to clients and trusts as shown by such ledger accounts has been compared to the cash account balance(s) at each of the separate dates selected in (f)(i) above and agreed.					
(iii)	The cash account balance(s) at each of the dates selected has/have been reconciled to the balance(s) in client bank account and elsewhere as confirmed directly by the relevant banks and building societies.					
(g)	**Reconciliations:**	Yes	No	Yes	No	
(i)	During the accounting year under review, reconciliations have been carried out at least every five weeks.					
(ii)	Each reconciliation is in the form of a statement set out in a logical format which is likely to reveal any discrepancies.					
(iii)	Reconciliation statements have been retained.					
(iv)	On entries in an appropriate sample of reconciliation statements:	Yes	No	Yes	No	
	(A) All accounts containing client money have been included.					
	(B) All ledger account balances for clients and trusts as at the reconciliation date have been listed and totalled.					
	(C) No debit balances on ledger accounts for clients and trusts have been included in the total.					

1. continued.......		Were any breaches discovered? (Tick the appropriate column.)		If "yes" should breaches be noted in the accountant;'s report?		Cross reference to audit file documentation.
	(D) The cash account balance(s) for clients and trusts is/are correctly calculated by the accurate and up to date recording of transactions.					
	(E) The client bank account totals for clients and trusts are complete and correct being calculated by:					
	the closing balance **plus** an accurate and complete list of outstanding lodgements **less** an accurate and complete list of unpresented cheques.					
(v)	Each reconciliation selected under paragraph (iv) above has been achieved by the comparison and agreement **without adjusting or balancing entries** of:					
	total of ledger balances for clients and trusts;					
	total of cash account balances for clients and trusts;					
	total of client bank accounts.					
(vi)	In the event of debit balances existing on ledger accounts for clients and trusts, the firm has investigated promptly and corrected the position satisfactorily.					
(vii)	In the event of the reconciliations selected under paragraph (iv) above not being in agreement, the differences have been investigated and corrected promptly.					
(h)	**Payments of client money:**	Yes	No	Yes	No	
	Make a test examination of the ledger accounts for clients and trusts in order to ascertain whether payments have been made on any individual account in excess of money held on behalf of that client or trust.					
(i)	**Office accounts - client money:**	Yes	No	Yes	No	
(i)	Check such office ledger and cash account and bank and building society statements as the firm maintains with a view to ascertaining whether any client money has not been paid into a client account.					
(ii)	Investigate office ledger credit balances and ensure that such balances do not include client money incorrectly held in office account.					
(j)	**Client money not held in client account:**	Yes	No	Yes	No	
(i)	Have sums not held on client account been identified?					
(ii)	Has the reason for holding such sums outside client account been established?					
(iii)	Has a written client agreement been made if appropriate?					
(iv)	Are central records or a central register kept for client money held outside client account on the client's instructions?					
(k)	**Rule 27 - inter-client transfers:**	Yes	No	Yes	No	
	Make test checks of inter-client transfers to ensure that rule 27 has been complied with.					
(l)	**Rule 29.10 - acting for borrower and lender:**	Yes	No	Yes	No	
	Make a test examination of the client ledger accounts in order to ascertain whether rule 29.10 AR has been complied with, where the firm acts for both borrower and lender in a conveyancing transaction.					
(m)	**Rule 29.23 – executor, trustee or nominee companies:**	Yes	No	Yes	No	
	Is a central book of dividend instruction letters kept?					

1. continued.......	Were any breaches discovered? (Tick the appropriate column.)		If "yes" should breaches be noted in the accountant¡'s report?		Cross reference to audit file documentation.
(n) **Information and explanations:**	Yes	No	Yes	No	
All information and explanations required have been received and satisfactorily cleared.					

2. Liquidators, trustees in bankruptcy, Court of Protection deputies and trustees of occupational pension schemes (rule 8)	Were any breaches discovered? (Tick the appropriate column.)		If 'yes' should breaches be noted in the accountant's report?		Cross reference to audit file documentation
	Yes	No	Yes	No	
(a) A record of all bills of costs and written notifications has been maintained, either in the form of a central record or a file of copies of such bills or notifications.					
(b) Records kept under rule 8 including any statements, passbooks and other accounting records originating outside the firm's office have been retained.					
(c) Records kept under rule 8 are kept together centrally, or a central register is kept of the appointments.					

3. Joint accounts (rule 9)	Were any breaches discovered? (Tick the appropriate column.)		If 'yes' should breaches be noted in the accountant's report?		Cross reference to audit file documentation
	Yes	No	Yes	No	
(a) A record of all bills of costs and written notifications has been maintained, either in the form of a central record or a file of copies of such bills or notifications.					
(b) Statements and passbooks and/or duplicate statements or copies of passbook entries have been retained.					
(c) Statements, passbooks, duplicate statements and copies of passbook entries are kept together centrally, or a central register of all joint accounts is kept.					

4. Clients' own accounts (rule 10)	Were any breaches discovered? (Tick the appropriate column.)		If 'yes' should breaches be noted in the accountant's report?		Cross reference to audit file documentation
	Yes	No	Yes	No	
(a) Statements and passbooks and/or duplicate statements, copies of passbook entries and cheque details have been retained					
(b) Statements and passbooks and/or duplicate statements, copies of passbook entries and cheque details are kept together centrally, or a central register of clients' own accounts is kept.					

5.	SRA guidelines - accounting procedures and systems	Yes	No
	Discovery of substantial departures from the guidelines? *If "yes" please give details below.*		

6. Please give further details of unsatisfactory items below. (Please attach additional schedules as required.)

Signature	Date
Reporting Accountant	Print Name

APPENDIX 5: ACCOUNTANT'S REPORT FORM

AR1

Accountant's Report Form

An annual accountant's report is required under rule 32 of the SRA Accounts Rules 2011 (the Rules). For further information on the Rules and for clarification on whether or not the requirement to deliver an accountant's report applies to you, see our website at http://www.sra.org.uk/solicitors/handbook/accountsrules/content.page.

The accountant who prepares the report must be qualified under rule 34 of the Rules and is required to report on compliance with Parts 1, 2 and 4 of the Rules.

When a practice closes but the ceased practice continues to hold or receive client money during the process of dealing with outstanding costs and unattributable or unreturnable funds, the Rules, including the obligation to deliver accountant's reports, will continue to apply.

When a practice ceases to hold and/or receive client money (and/or to operate any client's own account as signatory), either on closure of the practice or for any other reason, the practice must deliver a final report within six months of ceasing to hold and/or receive client money (and/or to operate any client's own account as signatory), unless the SRA requires earlier delivery.

If you need any assistance completing this form please telephone the Contact Centre on 0370 606 2555 or email at contactcentre@sra.org.uk. Our lines are open from 08.00 to 18.00 Monday, Wednesday, Thursday, Friday and 09.30 to 18.00 Tuesday. Please note calls may be monitored/recorded for training purposes.

If you are calling from overseas please use +44 (0) 121 329 6800. Note that reports in respect of practice from an office outside England and Wales are submitted under Part 7 of the Rules. Specimen form **AR2** may be used for such reports.

Section one: Firm details

Insert here all names used by the firm or in-house practice from the offices covered by this report. This must include the registered name of a recognised body/licensed body which is an LLP or company, and the name under which a partnership or sole practitioner is recognised. It is assumed that all addresses used by the practice during the accounting period are covered by this report , except offices outside England and Wales (Refer to Part 7 of the Rules). All address(es) of the practice during the reporting period must be covered by an accountant's report.

Firm name(s) during the reporting period		Firm SRA no	
Report Period from		to	

Firm COFA(s) (if more than one) during the reporting period with dates of appointment		COFA's SRA no	
Dates of appointment (where appropriate)		to	

Is this a cease to hold report?		Yes ☐	No ☐

1

Have any consultants or employees held or received client money, or operated a client's own account as signatory, during the report period   Yes ☐   No ☐

If **'yes'** please set out the details on a separate sheet of paper if necessary

Section 2: Comparison dates

The results of the comparisons required under rule 39.1(f) of the SRA Accounts Rules 2011, at the dates selected by me/us were:

(a) at _____ *(insert date 1)*

   (i) Liabilities to clients and trusts (and other persons for whom client money is held) as shown by ledger accounts for client and trust matters. £ _____

   (ii) Cash held in client account, and client money held in any account other than a client account, after allowances for lodgments cleared after date and for outstanding cheques. £ _____

   (iii) Difference between (i) and (ii) (if any). £ _____

(b) at _____ *(insert date 2)*

   (i) Liabilities to clients and trusts (and other persons for whom client money is held) as shown by ledger accounts for client and trust matters. £ _____

   (ii) Cash held in client account, and client money held in any account other than a client account, after allowances for lodgments cleared after date and for outstanding cheques. £ _____

   (iii) Difference between (i) and (ii) (if any). £ _____

Notes:

The figure to be shown in 2(a)(i) and 2(b)(i) above is the total of credit balances, without adjustment for debit balances (unless capable of proper set off, i.e. being in respect of the same client), or for receipts and payments not capable of allocation to individual ledger accounts.

An explanation must be given for any significant difference shown at 2(a)(iii) or 2(b)(iii) - see rule 44 of the SRA Accounts Rules 2011. If appropriate, it would be helpful if the explanation is given here:

2

Section 3: Qualified report

Have you found it necessary to make this report 'Qualified'?   No [ ]   If 'No' proceed to section 5

Yes [ ]   If 'Yes' please complete the relevant boxes

(a) Please indicate in the space provided any matters (other than trivial breaches) in respect of which it appears to you that there has been a failure to comply with the provisions of Parts 1, 2 and 4 of the SRA Accounts Rules 2011 and, in the case of private practice only, any part of the period covered by this report for which the practice does not appear to have been covered in respect of its offices in England and Wales by the insurance/indemnity documents referred to in rule 39.1(p) of the SRA Accounts Rules 2011 *(continue on an additional sheet if necessary)*:

(b) Please indicate in the space provided any matters in respect of which you have been unable to satisfy yourself and the reasons for that inability, e.g. because a client's file is not available *(continue on an additional sheet if necessary)*.

Section 4: Accountant's details

The reporting accountant must be qualified in accordance with rule 34 of the SRA Accounts Rules 2011.

Name of accountant		Professional body	
		Accountant membership/ registration number	
Recognised Supervisory Body under which individual/firm is a registered auditor		Reference number of individual/firm audit registration(s)	
Firm name			
Firm address			
Email address			

3

Section 5: Declaration

1. In compliance with Part 6 of the SRA Accounts Rules 2011, I/we have examined to the extent required by rule 39 of those rules, the accounting records, files and other documents produced to me/us in respect of the above practice.

2. In so far as an opinion can be based on this limited examination, I am/we are satisfied that during the above mentioned period the practice has complied with the provisions of Parts 1, 2 and 4 of the SRA Accounts Rules 2011 except so far as concerns:

    (i)   certain trivial breaches due to clerical errors or mistakes in book-keeping, all of which were rectified on discovery and none of which, I am/we are satisfied, resulted in any loss to any client or trust; and/or
    (ii) any matters detailed in section 3 of this report.

3. In the case of private practice only, I/we certify that, in so far as can be ascertained from a limited examination of the insurance/indemnity documents produced to me/us, the practice was covered in respect of its offices in England and Wales for the period covered by this report by the insurance/indemnity documents referred to in rule 39.1(p) of the SRA Accounts Rules 2011, except as stated in section 3 of this report.

I/we have relied on the exception contained in rule 39.2 of the SRA Accounts Rules 2011.   Yes ☐   No ☐

Rule 39.2 of the SRA Accounts Rules 2011 states: "For the purposes of rule 39.1(f) above [extraction of balances] if you use a computerised or mechanised system of accounting which automatically produces an extraction of all client ledger balances, the accountant need not check all client ledger balances extracted on the list produced by the computer or machine against the individual records of client ledger accounts, provided the accountant:

    (a)   confirms that a satisfactory system of control is in operation and the accounting records are in balance;
    (b)   carries out a test check of the extraction against the individual records; and
    (c)   states in the report that he or she has relied on this exception."

In carrying out work in preparation of this report, I/we have discovered the following substantial departures from the SRA's current Guidelines for Accounting Procedures and Systems (*continue on an additional sheet if necessary*):

4

4.   I/we have completed and signed the 'Reporting accountant's checklist' and retained a copy. The original checklist has been sent to the firm's current COFA as set out in Section 1 of this report .

5.   I/we confirm that there are no circumstances which might affect my independence in preparing this report.

6.   A copy of this report has been sent to the firm's current COFA as set out in Section 1 of this report

Date	
Signature	
Name (Block Capitals)	

Please return this form via one of the options below:

Email: SRAAccountantsReports@sra.org.uk

Post: Authorisation – Accountant's Reports
Solicitors Regulation Authority
The Cube
199 Wharfside Street
Birmingham
B1 1RN

DX: DX 720293 Birmingham 47

The reporting accountant's checklist should be retained by the practice which is the subject of the report for at least three years, and not submitted to the Solicitors Regulation Authority with this report.

5

[E]   Authorisation and Practising Requirements

[E.0] Introduction to Authorisation and Practising Requirements

This section of the Handbook contains the following sets of rules:

- SRA Practice Framework Rules;

- SRA Authorisation Rules;

- SRA Practising Regulations;

- Solicitors Keeping of the Roll Regulations;

- SRA Training Regulations 2014 – Qualification and Training Provider Regulations;

- SRA Training Regulations 2011 Part 3 – CPD Regulations;

- SRA Admission Regulations;

- SRA Qualified Lawyers Transfer Scheme Regulations;

- SRA Higher Rights of Audience Regulations;

- SRA Quality Assurance Scheme for Advocates (Crime) Regulations; and

- SRA Suitability Test.

These rules must be read in conjunction with the Principles. The Principles underpin all aspects of practice, including applications for authorisation or approval by firms and individuals and achievement of training requirements.

The desired outcomes that apply to authorisation and training are that:

- clients and the general public remain confident that legal services provided by our regulated community will be delivered to the required standard and in a principled manner;

- firms and individuals provide the SRA with sufficient information to enable the SRA to make appropriate judgements concerning whether to authorise, or continue to authorise, any firm or person;

- only those individuals and firms who/that meet the SRA's criteria for authorisation (including the requirements to be suitable and capable of providing legal services to the required standard) are authorised;

- firms are managed in such a way, and with appropriate systems and controls, so as to protect the public and safeguard the reputation of the legal profession;

- solicitors, regardless of the route by which they qualify, have been educated and trained to a standard that clients, the public, the profession and the judiciary properly expect;

- providers of training are authorised and monitored to an appropriate standard;

- solicitors have demonstrated their competence to exercise rights of audience in the higher courts;

- solicitors have achieved the standard of competence required of advocates conducting criminal advocacy;

- solicitors demonstrate this competence through independent assessment;

- solicitors act so that clients, the judiciary and the wider public, have confidence that this has been demonstrated.

[E.1] SRA Practice Framework Rules 2011

Rules dated 17 June 2011 commencing on 6 October 2011

made by the Solicitors Regulation Authority Board, under sections 31, 79 and 80 of the Solicitors Act 1974, sections 9 and 9A of the Administration of Justice Act 1985 and section 83 and Schedule 11 to the Legal Services Act 2007, with the approval of the Legal Services Board under paragraph 19 of Schedule 4 to the Legal Services Act 2007.

INTRODUCTION

Part 1 of these rules sets out the types of business through which solicitors, RELs, RFLs and authorised bodies may practise. It restricts the types of business available in order to reflect statutory provisions and to ensure that clients and the public have the protections provided for by statute.

Part 2 permits authorised bodies, solicitors, RELs and RFLs to carry out certain types of work, including immigration work.

Part 3 governs the formation and practice requirements which must be satisfied by bodies and sole practitioners to be eligible for authorisation by the SRA, and is based on the requirements of sections 9 and 9A of the AJA and section 72 of the LSA.

Part 4 sets out certain requirements relating to compliance with these rules and the SRA's regulatory arrangements.

PART 1: FRAMEWORK OF PRACTICE

Rule 1: Solicitors

Practice from an office in England and Wales

1.1 You may *practise* as a *solicitor* from an office in England and Wales in the following ways only:

  (a) as a *sole practitioner* of a *recognised sole practice*;

  (b) as a *solicitor* exempted under Rule 10.2 from the obligation for the *solicitor's practice* to be a *recognised sole practice*;

  (c) as a *manager, employee, member* or *interest holder* of an *authorised body* provided that all work you do is:

  (i) of a sort the body is authorised by the *SRA* to carry out; or

  (ii) done for the body itself, or falls within Rule 4.1 to 4.11, and where this sub-paragraph applies, references in Rule 4 to *"employer"* shall be construed as referring to that body, accordingly;

(d) as a *manager, employee, member* or *interest holder* of an *authorised non-SRA firm*, provided that all work you do is:

   (i) *reserved legal activity* of a sort the firm is authorised by the firm's *approved regulator* to carry out or any other activity that is not precluded by the terms of your authorisation from the firm's *approved regulator*; or

   (ii) done for the firm itself, or falls within Rule 4.1 to 4.11, and where this sub-paragraph applies, references in Rule 4 to *"employer"* shall be construed as referring to that firm, accordingly;

(e) as the *employee* of another *person*, business or organisation, provided that you undertake work only for your *employer*, or as permitted by Rule 4 (In-house practice).

Practice from an office outside England and Wales

1.2   You may *practise* as a *solicitor* from an office outside England and Wales in the following ways only:

(a) as a *sole practitioner*;

(b) as the *employee* of a sole *principal* who is a *lawyer*;

(c) as a *manager, employee, member* or *interest holder* of an *authorised body* or of an *authorised non-SRA firm*, provided that if any of the body's *managers* or *interest holders* are non-lawyers and the office is in an *Establishment Directive state* other than the *UK*, the rules for local *lawyers* would permit a local *lawyer* to practise through a business of that composition and structure;

(d) as an *employee* of a business which is not required to be an *authorised body*, provided that it meets all the following conditions:

   (i) the business carries on the provision of legal advice or assistance, or representation in connection with the application of the law or resolution of legal disputes;

   (ii) a controlling majority of the *managers* and the *interest holders* are *lawyers* practising as such and/or *bodies corporate* in which *lawyers* practising as such constitute a controlling majority of the *managers* and *interest holders*;

   (iii) if any of the business's *managers* or *interest holders* are non-lawyers and any *manager* or *interest holder* is subject to the rules for local *lawyers*, the composition and structure of the business complies with those rules; and

   (iv) if any of the business's *managers* or *interest holders* are non-lawyers and the office is in an *Establishment Directive state*, the rules for local *lawyers* would permit a local *lawyer* to practise through a business of that composition and structure;

(e) as *manager*, *member* or *interest holder* of a business which is not required to be an *authorised body*, provided that it has no office in England and Wales, and that it meets all the conditions set out in sub-paragraph (d)(i) to (iv) above;

(f) as the *employee* of another *person*, business or organisation, provided that you undertake work only for your *employer*, or as permitted by Rule 4.22 to 4.25 (In-house practice overseas);

(g) as a *manager*, *employee*, *member* or *interest holder* of an *overseas practice*.

Guidance notes

(i)   See also Rules 10 (Sole practitioners), 13 (Eligibility criteria and fundamental requirements for recognised bodies and recognised sole practices), 14 (Eligibility criteria and fundamental requirements for licensed bodies), 15 (Formation, registered office and practising address), 16 (Composition of an authorised body) and 17 (Authorised bodies which are companies) below, Chapter 13 of the SRA Code of Conduct (Application and waivers provisions) and the SRA Practising Regulations.

(ii)   See Rule 4.3 below and the definition of "in-house practice" in the Glossary, in relation to in-house work that you carry out for clients which is outside of your firm's authorisation.

(iii)   A recognised body which is a company may not have a corporate director (this also applies to a licensed body). However, when permitted, a corporate body owner and/or manager of a recognised body will need to be a legally qualified body (see the Glossary).

(iv)   The rules do not prevent a solicitor establishing, for example, their own company for tax purposes (which is itself a recognised body) so that that company can be a corporate manager of another firm through which the solicitor practises.

Rule 2: RELs

Practice from an office in England and Wales

2.1   You may *practise* as an *REL* from an office in England and Wales in the following ways only:

(a) as a *sole practitioner* of a *recognised sole practice*;

(b) as an *REL* exempted under Rule 10.2 from the obligation for the *REL's* practice to be a *recognised sole practice*;

(c) as a *manager*, *employee*, *member* or *interest holder* of an *authorised body*, provided that all work you do is:

- (i) of a sort the firm is authorised by the *SRA* to carry out; or

- (ii) done for the body itself, or falls within Rule 4.1 to 4.11, and where this sub-paragraph applies, references in Rule 4 to *"employer"* shall be construed as referring to that body, accordingly;

- (d) as a *manager, employee, member* or *interest holder* of an *authorised non-SRA firm,* provided that all work you do is:

  - (i) *reserved legal activity* of a sort the firm is authorised by the firm's *approved regulator* to carry out or any other activity that is not precluded by the terms of your authorisation from the firm's *approved regulator;* or

  - (ii) done for the firm itself, or falls within Rule 4.1 to 4.11, and where this sub-paragraph applies, references in Rule 4 to *"employer"* shall be construed as referring to that firm, accordingly;

- (e) as the *employee* of another *person,* business or organisation, provided that you undertake work only for your *employer,* or as permitted by Rule 4 (In-house practice);

- (f) as a *manager, employee, member* or *interest holder* of an *Exempt European Practice,* provided that you meet the conditions set out under Rule 4.20(a), (b) and (c).

Practice from an office in Scotland or Northern Ireland

2.2   You may *practise* as an *REL* from an office in Scotland or Northern Ireland in the following ways only:

- (a) as a *sole practitioner;*

- (b) as the *employee* of a sole *principal* who is a *lawyer;*

- (c) as a *manager, employee, member* or *interest holder* of an *authorised body* or of an *authorised non-SRA firm;*

- (d) as an *employee* of a business which is not required to be an *authorised body,* provided that it meets all the following conditions:

  - (i) the business carries on the provision of legal advice or assistance, or representation in connection with the application of the law or resolution of legal disputes;

  - (ii) a controlling majority of the *managers* and the *interest holders* are *lawyers* practising as such and/or *bodies corporate* in which *lawyers* practising as such constitute a controlling majority of the *managers* and *interest holders;* and

  - (iii) if any of the business's *managers* or *interest holders* are non-lawyers, the professional rules governing a solicitor of that jurisdiction would allow such a solicitor to practise through a business of that composition and structure;

(e) as *manager*, *member* or *interest holder* of a business which is not required to be an *authorised body*, provided that it has no office in England and Wales or is an *Exempt European Practice*, and that it meets all the conditions set out in sub-paragraph (d)(i) to (iii) above and that you meet the conditions set out under Rule 4.20(a), (b) and (c);

(f) as the *employee* of another *person*, business or organisation, provided that you undertake work only for your *employer*, or as permitted by Rule 4.22 to 4.25 (In-house practice overseas);

(g) as a *manager*, *employee*, *member* or *interest holder* of an *overseas practice*.

Guidance notes

(i) The overseas provisions for an REL are the same as those for a solicitor practising overseas except that they apply only in Scotland and Northern Ireland. RELs are not subject to Rule 2 in relation to practice from an office outside the UK.

(ii) See Rule 4.3 and the definition of "in-house practice" in the Glossary, in relation to in-house work that you carry out for clients which is outside of your firm's authorisation.

(iii) A recognised body which is a company may not have a corporate director (this also applies to a licensed body). However, when permitted, a corporate body owner and/or manager of a recognised body will need to be a legally qualified body (see the Glossary).

(iv) The rules do not prevent an REL establishing, for example, their own company for tax purposes (which is itself a recognised body) so that that company can be a corporate manager of another firm through which the REL practises.

Rule 3: RFLs

Practice in the capacity of an RFL

3.1 Your *practice* as a *foreign lawyer* in the capacity of an *RFL* is confined to *practice* as:

(a) [Deleted]

(b) a *manager*, *employee*, *member* or *interest holder* of an *authorised body*, provided that all work you do is:

    (i) of a sort the body is authorised by the *SRA* to carry out; or

    (ii) done for the body itself, or falls within Rule 4.1 to 4.11, and where this sub-paragraph applies, references in Rule 4 to "*employer*" shall be construed as referring to that body, accordingly;

(c) a *manager*, *employee*, *member* or *interest holder* of an *authorised non-SRA firm*, provided that all work you do is:

(i)   *reserved legal activity* of a sort the firm is authorised by the firm's *approved regulator* to carry out or any other activity that is not precluded by the terms of your authorisation from the firm's *approved regulator*; or

(ii)   done for the firm itself, or falls within Rule 4.1 to 4.11, and where this sub-paragraph applies, references in Rule 4 to "*employer*" shall be construed as referring to that firm, accordingly.

Practice in another capacity than as an RFL

3.2   If you provide services as a *foreign lawyer* in any of the following ways in England and Wales or elsewhere, you will not be *practising* in the capacity of an *RFL* and you must not be held out or described in that context as an *RFL*, or as regulated by or registered with the *Society* or the *SRA*:

(a)   as a sole *principal*; or

(b)   as a *manager*, *member* or *interest holder* of any business or organisation other than an *authorised body* or an *authorised non-SRA firm*; or

(c)   as a *manager*, *member* or *interest holder* of a *body corporate* which is a *manager*, *member* or *interest holder* of any business or organisation other than an *authorised body* or an *authorised non-SRA firm*; or

(d)   as the *employee* of any business or organisation other than an *authorised body* or an *authorised non-SRA firm*.

3.3   If you have a *practice* under Rule 3.1 above, and another business under Rule 3.2 above, the latter is a *separate business* for the purpose of these rules and you must therefore comply with Chapter 12 (Separate businesses) of the *SRA Code of Conduct*.

Scope of practice

3.4   Whether or not you are *practising* in the capacity of an *RFL* you must not:

(a)   be held out in any way which suggests that you are, or are entitled to *practise* as, a *lawyer of England and Wales*;

(b)   undertake the following *reserved work* in England and Wales:

(i)   advocacy in open *court*;

(ii)   the conduct of *court* litigation;

(iii)   the administration of oaths and statutory declarations;

(c)   undertake advocacy in chambers in England and Wales, except under instructions given by a person qualified to supervise that *reserved work*;

(d)   undertake the following *reserved work* in England and Wales, except at the direction and under the supervision of a person qualified to supervise that *reserved work*:

(i)   the preparation of *court* documents;

(ii) the preparation of instruments and the lodging of documents relating to the transfer or charge of land;

(iii) the preparation of papers on which to found or oppose a grant of probate or a grant of letters of administration;

(iv) the preparation of trust deeds disposing of capital, unless you also are eligible to act as a *lawyer of England and Wales*;

(e) If you are not *practising* in the capacity of an *RFL* you must not carry out *immigration work* in the *UK* unless you are entitled to do so by virtue of being a qualified person within the meaning of section 84 of the Immigration and Asylum Act 1999, whether this is as a result of being entitled to do the work in your own right, doing so under supervision, or otherwise.

Guidance notes

(i)   A foreign lawyer must be registered with the SRA as an RFL to be a manager, member or interest holder of a recognised body, with the following exceptions:

(a) a foreign lawyer who is also qualified as a lawyer of England and Wales does not have to be an RFL;

(b) a member of an Establishment Directive profession – except that if the lawyer is not a national of an Establishment Directive state and will be based, or partly based, in England and Wales, he or she does have to be an RFL in order to be a manager, member or interest holder of a recognised body. See our website for additional guidance on RFLs and multi-national practice [**www.sra.org.uk/solicitors/code-of-conduct/guidance.page**].

(ii) There is no requirement to register as an RFL in order to be employed by a recognised body or recognised sole practice or to be a manager or interest holder of, or employed by, a licensed body but, if you are registered as an RFL, you will be subject to SRA regulation in this capacity when working for an SRA firm or an authorised non-SRA firm.

(iii) An RFL is subject to the same restrictions as a solicitor or REL in relation to practice from an office in England and Wales with two exceptions. Your registration as an RFL does not entitle you to practise:

(a) as an RFL sole practitioner; or

(b) as an in-house RFL (subject to note (iv) below).

(iv) Registration as an RFL is portable to the extent that it will enable you to be a manager, employee, member or interest holder of an authorised non-SRA firm, although your ability to work within such a firm will depend on the framework of practice requirements of the relevant approved regulator. You will be able to undertake work authorised by the firm's approved regulator (subject to any statutory limitations or requirements). Additionally you will be able to function as an in-house lawyer under Rule 4, doing other work for the employer, related bodies, work colleagues and pro bono clients under the SRA's rules.

(v) Your registration as an RFL will not be relevant in the role of interest holder or employee of a business in England and Wales which is not regulated by the SRA or one of the other approved regulators. The SRA does not regulate any practice you might have outside the framework established under the LSA, so there must be no implication in such a context that you are an RFL, or that you or the business are regulated by or registered with the SRA or the Society.

(vi) Where, in order to satisfy statutory requirements, there is a need for an RFL doing reserved work to be supervised or directed by someone in the firm, this can only be undertaken by a person of equivalent or higher status.

(vii) See the application provisions in 4.2 of the SRA Principles. Also see the provisions relating to practice from an office outside England and Wales in Chapter 13 of the SRA Code of Conduct.

(viii) See Rule 4.3 and the definition of "in-house practice" in the Glossary, in relation to in-house work that you carry out for clients which is outside of your firm's authorisation.

(ix) A recognised body which is a company may not have a corporate director (this also applies to a licensed body). However, when permitted, a corporate body owner and/or manager of a recognised body will need to be a legally qualified body (see the Glossary).

Rule 4: In-house practice

4.1 If you are a *solicitor*, *REL* or *RFL* conducting *in-house practice*:

  (a) you must not act for *clients* other than your *employer* except in the circumstances in 4.4 to 4.26 (all of which are subject to 4.1(b) and 4.2) and where you are able to act without compromising the *Principles* or your obligations under the *SRA Code of Conduct*;

  (b) nothing in this rule permits any *person* to conduct *reserved legal activities* in circumstances where to do so would require authorisation under the *LSA* and you must satisfy yourself that any such authorisation is in place before conducting any such activity.

4.1A If your *in-house practice* comprises:

  (a) employment in a body within England and Wales, rules 4.2 to 4.18 and 4.26 apply to you;

  (b) employment in a foreign law firm which is not an *overseas practice*, rules 4.19 to 4.21 apply to you; and

  (c) employment in a body overseas, including where you are *practising overseas*, rules 4.22 to 4.25 apply to you.

4.2   Indemnity

(a) In order to act for a *client* other than your *employer* under Rule 4.10, 4.14, 4.16 and 4.19, you must have professional indemnity insurance cover.

(b) In all other cases you must consider whether your *employer* has appropriate indemnity insurance or funds to meet any award made as a result of a claim in professional negligence against you, for which your *employer* might be vicariously liable. If not, you must inform the *client* in writing that you are not covered by the compulsory insurance scheme.

4.3   If you are a *solicitor, REL* or *RFL* in a *licensed body* or an *authorised non-SRA firm*, you must comply with this rule as if you were an *in-house solicitor* or *REL* when, as a *manager* or *employee*, you do work of a type which is outside the scope of the firm's authorisation in accordance with Rules 1, 2 or 3, either for the firm itself or within 4.4 to 4.6 (Work colleagues), 4.7 to 4.9 (Related bodies) or 4.10 to 4.11 (Pro bono work).

Work colleagues

4.4   Subject to Rule 4.5 below, you may act for a *person* who is, or was formerly:

(a) an *employee*, a *manager*, the company secretary, a board member or a trustee of your *employer*;

(b) an *employee*, a *manager*, the company secretary, a board member or a trustee of a *related body* of your *employer*; or

(c) a contributor to a programme or periodical publication, broadcast or published by your *employer* or by a *related body*, but only where the contributor is a defendant or potential defendant in a defamation case.

4.5   You may act under Rule 4.4 above only if:

(a) the matter relates to and arises out of the work of the *employee, manager*, company secretary, board member, trustee or contributor in that capacity;

(b) the matter does not relate to a claim arising as a result of a personal injury to the *employee, manager*, company secretary, board member, trustee or contributor;

(c) you are satisfied that the *employee, manager*, company secretary, board member, trustee or contributor does not wish to instruct some other *lawyer*; and

(d) no charge is made for your work unless those costs are recoverable from another source.

4.6   Where acting in a conveyancing transaction under Rule 4.4(a) or (b) above you may also act for a joint owner or joint buyer of the property and for a mortgagee.

Related bodies

4.7   You may act for:

(a)   your *employer's* holding, associated or subsidiary company;

(b)   a *partnership*, syndicate, LLP or company by way of joint venture in which your *employer* and others have an interest;

(c)   a trade association of which your *employer* is a member; or

(d)   a club, association, pension fund or other scheme operated for the benefit of *employees* of your *employer*.

4.8   If you are employed in local government, Rule 4.7(a) and (b) above do not apply.

4.9   For the purpose of Rule 4.10 to 4.14 references to your *employer* include *related bodies* of the *employer*, and "employment" and "employed" must be construed accordingly.

Pro bono work

4.10   You may, in the course of your *practice*, conduct work on a pro bono basis for a *client* other than your *employer* provided:

(a)   the work is covered by an indemnity reasonably equivalent to that required under the SRA Indemnity Insurance Rules;

(b)   either:

(i)   no fees are charged; or

(ii)   a conditional fee agreement is used and the only fees charged are those which you receive by way of costs from your *client's* opponent or other third party and all of which you pay to a *charity* under a fee sharing agreement; and

(c)   you do not undertake any *reserved legal activities*, unless the provision of relevant services to the public or a section of the public (with or without a view to profit) is not part of your employer's business.

4.11   Rule 4.10 above does not permit you to conduct work on a pro bono basis in conjunction with services provided by your *employer* under Rule 4.12 (Associations), Rule 4.13 (Insurers), Rule 4.14 (Commercial legal advice services) or Rule 4.19 to 4.21 (Foreign law firms).

Associations

4.12   If you are employed by an association you may act for a member of that association provided:

(a)   the membership of the association is limited to *persons* engaged or concerned in a particular trade, occupation or specialist activity or otherwise having a community of interest, such interest being a specialist interest;

(b) the association is one formed bona fide for the benefit of its members and not formed directly or indirectly for your benefit or primarily for securing assistance in legal proceedings;

(c) there is no charge to the member in non-contentious matters, and in contentious matters the association indemnifies the member in relation to your costs and disbursements insofar as they are not recoverable from any other source; and

(d) you act only in matters that relate to or arise out of the particular trade, occupation or specialist activity of the association or otherwise relate to the specialist community of interest, for which the association is formed.

Insurers

4.13   If you are employed by an insurer subrogated to the rights of an insured in respect of any matter you may act on behalf of the insurer in relation to that matter in the name of the insured, and also:

(a) act on behalf of the insured in relation to uninsured losses in respect of the matter;

(b) act in proceedings both for the insured and for a defendant covered by another insurer where the insurers have agreed an apportionment of liability; and/or

(c) act in the matter on behalf of the *employer* and another insurer in the joint prosecution of a claim.

Commercial legal advice services

4.14   If you are employed by a commercial organisation providing a telephone legal advice service you may advise *persons* making enquiries of that organisation, provided:

(a) the advice comprises telephone advice only, together with a follow up letter to the enquirer when necessary;

(b) you are satisfied that there is indemnity cover reasonably equivalent to that required under the SRA Indemnity Insurance Rules; and

(c) you do not undertake any *reserved legal activities*.

Local government

4.15   If you are employed in local government you may act:

(a) for another organisation or *person* to which or to whom the *employer* is statutorily empowered to provide legal services, subject to the conditions in (b) to (g) below;

(b) for a member or former member of the local authority, provided that:

  (i)   the matter relates to or arises out of the work of the member in that capacity;

  (ii) the matter does not relate to a claim arising as a result of a personal injury to the member;

  (iii) you are satisfied that the member does not wish to instruct some other *lawyer*; and

  (iv) no charge is made for your work unless those costs are recoverable from some other source;

(c) for a *company* limited by shares or guarantee of which:

  (i)   the *employer* or nominee of the *employer* is a shareholder or guarantor; or

  (ii) you are, or an officer of the *employer* is, appointed by the *employer* as an officer of the *company*,

  provided the *employer* is acting in pursuance of its statutory powers;

(d) for lenders in connection with new mortgages arising from the redemption of mortgages to the local authority, provided:

  (i)   neither you nor any other *employee* acts on behalf of the borrowers; and

  (ii) the borrowers are given the opportunity to be independently advised by a qualified conveyancer of their choice;

(e) for a *charity* or voluntary organisation whose objects relate wholly or partly to the *employer's* area;

(f) for a patient who is the subject of a Court of Protection Order where you are acting for a work colleague (under Rule 4.4 to 4.6 above) who is appointed as deputy for the patient; or

(g) for a child or young person subject to a Care Order in favour of the *employer* on an application to the Criminal Injuries Compensation Authority.

Law Centres, charities and other non-commercial advice services

4.16   If you are employed by a law centre or advice service operated by a charitable or similar non-commercial organisation you may give advice to and otherwise act for members of the public, provided:

(a) no funding agent has majority representation on the body responsible for the management of the service, and that body remains independent of central and local government;

(b) all fees you earn and costs you recover are paid to the organisation for furthering the provision of the organisation's services;

(c) the organisation is not described as a law centre unless it is a member of the Law Centres Federation; and

(d) the organisation has indemnity cover in relation to the *legal activities* carried out by you, reasonably equivalent to that required under the SRA Indemnity Insurance Rules.

4.17   Rule 4.16 above does not apply to an association formed for the benefit of its members.

The Crown, non-departmental public bodies and the Legal Aid Agency

4.18   If you are employed by the Crown, a non-departmental public body or the Legal Aid Agency (or any body established or maintained by the Legal Aid Agency), you may give legal advice to, and act for, *persons* other than your *employer* if in doing so you are carrying out the lawful functions of your *employer*.

Foreign law firms

4.19   Unless your employer is an *Exempt European Practice* you may provide legal services to your *employer's clients*, subject to the conditions set out in Rule 4.20 below, if you are a *solicitor* or an *REL* employed by:

(a) a practising *lawyer* of another jurisdiction who:

  (i)   is not struck off or suspended from the *register of foreign lawyers* or the *register of European lawyers*; and

  (ii) is not *practising* in that context as a *solicitor* or as an *REL*; or

(b) a business whose *managers* and *interest holders* are all practising through that business as *lawyers* of jurisdictions other than England and Wales, and do not include any person who:

  (i)   is struck off or suspended from the *register of foreign lawyers* or the *register of European lawyers*; or

  (ii) is *practising* through or in the context of that business as a *solicitor* or as an *REL*.

4.20   You must meet the following conditions if acting, under Rule 4.19 above, for anyone other than your *employer*.

(a) Even if you are qualified to do such work for your *employer*, you must not do, or supervise or assume responsibility for doing any of the following:

  (i)   drawing or preparing any instrument or papers comprising *reserved legal activities* under section 12(1)(c) or (d) of the *LSA*;

  (ii) exercising any right of audience, or right to conduct litigation (including making any application or lodging any document relating to litigation), before a *court* or immigration tribunal; or

      (iii) providing any immigration advice or immigration services, unless the *employer*, or a senior fellow *employee*, is registered with the Immigration Services Commissioner.

    (b) You must ensure that the work you do is covered by professional indemnity insurance reasonably equivalent to that required under the SRA Indemnity Insurance Rules.

    (c) You must:

      (i) inform your *client* that your *employer* is not regulated by the *SRA* and that the *SRA's* compulsory insurance scheme does not apply, and either give or confirm this information in writing, if you are a *solicitor*, and you are held out to a *client* as a *solicitor* (or as an English or Welsh *lawyer*) in connection with work you are doing for that *client*; and

      (ii) ensure that if you are identified on the notepaper as a *solicitor* (or as an English or Welsh *lawyer*) the notepaper also states that your *employer* is not regulated by the *SRA*.

4.21   Rule 4.20(c) above should also be read as referring to an *REL* being held out or identified as a *lawyer*, or under the *REL's* title from their home state.

In-house practice overseas

4.22   Rules 4.10 and 4.11 (Pro bono work) apply to your *in-house practice* where you are employed in a body outside England and Wales.

4.23   The other provisions of Rule 4 (In-house practice) do not apply to your *in-house practice* where you are employed in a body outside England and Wales, but you must comply with Rules 4.24 and 4.25 below.

4.24   Subject to 4.25 below, you may act as an *in-house lawyer*, but only for:

    (a) your *employer*;

    (b) a company or organisation controlled by your *employer* or in which your *employer* has a substantial measure of control;

    (c) a company in the same group as your *employer*;

    (d) a company which controls your *employer*; or

    (e) an *employee* (including a *director* or a company secretary) of a company or organisation under (a) to (d) above, provided that the matter relates to or arises out of the work of that company or organisation, does not relate to a claim arising as a result of a personal injury to the *employee*, and no charge is made for your work unless those costs are recoverable from another source.

4.25   If you are a *solicitor* registered in another state under the *Establishment Directive* with the professional body for a local legal profession you may *practise in-house* to the extent that a member of that legal profession is permitted to do so.

Regulatory bodies

4.26   If you are employed by a regulatory body you may in carrying out the function of the *employer* give legal advice to other *persons* and, where those functions are statutory, may act generally for such *persons*.

Guidance notes

(i)   This rule applies to you if you are a solicitor or REL (or in limited circumstances an RFL) working in in-house practice, which is generally when you are working otherwise than through a regulated legal practice such as an authorised body or an authorised non-SRA firm. However, these provisions also apply to you if you are a solicitor, REL or RFL when working in a licensed body or an authorised non-SRA firm but are doing work, for example, for the firm itself which is outside the scope of the firm's own authorisation.

(ii)   The general principle, subject to limited exceptions, is that your employer itself will need to be authorised if, in your capacity as an employee and as part of your employer's business, you wish to provide reserved legal services to the public (see LSA, section 15(4)). The provisions of 4.4 to 4.26, regarding acting in an in-house capacity for clients other than your employer, are subject to the provisions of the LSA which may nonetheless require your employer to obtain authorisation, for example members of an association may be "the public or a section of the public" for the purposes of the LSA. Such issues should be kept under review as your position may change e.g. your employer's business may develop in such a way that it requires authorisation.

(iii)   If you are a solicitor working in-house (whether in or outside England and Wales) you must comply with Rule 9 (Practising certificates). For further guidance on the need for a practising certificate see our website. Examples of situations where you will be practising as a solicitor, and will therefore need a practising certificate, include:

(a)   you are employed as a solicitor;

(b)   you are held out, on stationery or otherwise, as a solicitor for your employer;

(c)   you administer oaths;

(d)   you appear before a court or tribunal in reliance upon your qualification as a solicitor;

(e)   you instruct counsel;

(f)   you undertake work which is prohibited to unqualified persons under the provisions of Part 3 of the LSA, unless you are supervised by, and acting in the name of, a solicitor with a practising certificate or another qualified person;

(g)   your only qualification as a lawyer is that you are a solicitor, and:

(A) you are employed or held out as a lawyer;

(B) you undertake work in another jurisdiction which is reserved to lawyers;

(C) you are registered in a state other than the UK under the Establishment Directive; or

(D) you are a registered foreign legal consultant in another jurisdiction.

(iv) In England and Wales a number of statutory exceptions apply to qualify (ii). Certain in-house government solicitors are allowed to practise as solicitors without practising certificates. Some reserved work can be undertaken by non-solicitors working for local government, and therefore by non-practising solicitors working for local government. See also Rules 9, 10 and 11.

(v) A solicitor acting only as a justices' clerk in England and Wales is not practising as a solicitor and can instruct counsel without a practising certificate.

(vi) If you are an in-house solicitor the address of your employer's legal department is the place (or one of the places) where you practise and must therefore be notified to the SRA.

(vii) If you handle client money, the SRA Accounts Rules will apply to you unless you are exempted under Rule 5 of those rules.

(viii) If you are working in-house as the senior legal adviser of a company or a local authority you should have direct access to the board or to the council and its committees, and should try to ensure that your terms of employment provide for such access. "Direct access" does not mean that all instructions and advice must pass directly to and from the council, committee or board, but you must have direct access where necessary.

(ix) An in-house solicitor may act for work colleagues, subject to certain safeguards, provided the matter relates to and arises out of the person's work for the employer. This will cover matters that relate directly to the fellow employee's work but would not, for example, permit reserved legal services to be offered as a benefit under an employment package. Those working in-house will need to consider whether they are allowed to act on a case by case basis and, in particular, the extent to which there is a direct relationship between the work colleague's employment and the reserved legal activity.

(x) The ability of in-house solicitors to act for clients on a pro bono basis is limited by the LSA, which requires that, in general, the provision of reserved legal services to the public is carried out through an authorised body. There is no such limitation under the LSA in respect of unreserved services, such as providing legal advice. Rule 4.10 sets out the parameters within which in-house solicitors may provide reserved services on a pro bono basis, reflecting the position under the LSA. To determine whether you can undertake reserved legal activities within 4.10, one question will be whether the activities to be undertaken can be regarded as part of the business of the employer. Relevant factors are likely to be:

(a) relevancy of such work to the employer's business;

(b) whether the work is required of the employee by the employer;

(c) how often such work is carried out;

(d) where such work is carried out;

(e) when such work is carried out;

(f) whether such work is explicitly carried out on the employer's behalf;

(g) who provides the necessary professional indemnity insurance;

(h) the extent to which the employer relies on or publicises such work;

(i) whether the employer provides management, training or supervision in relation to such work;

(j) whether the employer specifically rewards the employee in any way in relation to such work;

(k) how many employees carry out the work, and the overall proportion of their time spent on such work;

(l) the extent to which such work complements or enhances the employer's business.

All the circumstances, and the context, will be critical to your decision about whether you may act, for example the work will not necessarily be part of the employer's business merely because it is carried out in office hours, or at the employer's premises.

There will be some situations which are likely to be easier to judge. If there is a clear relationship with the employer's business, acting will not be permissible. For example, you are likely to be prevented from acting:

(A) where the employer describes its business as including the provision of pro bono services;

(B) where the work may boost the employer's business by providing extra business opportunities or creating contacts.

(xi) If you are employed as a solicitor or REL by an insurer which runs a commercial legal telephone advice service, the restrictions in Rule 4.14 will not apply to prevent you acting for an insured in accordance with Rule 4.13.

(xii) If you are employed as a solicitor or REL by a law centre or advice service operated by a charitable or similar non-commercial organisation, you can advise and act for members of the public provided you comply with Rule 4.16 and 4.17. A solicitor or REL who works as a volunteer for such an advice service must comply with the SRA Indemnity Insurance Rules unless exempted by a waiver. If your employer obtains authorisation as a licensed body you will not need to rely on the exceptions in Rule 4.

(xiii)   As the in-house employee of a foreign law firm under Rule 4.19 and 4.20 you may not do reserved work for clients or (unless your employer is separately authorised) immigration work. You must also comply with special requirements as to insurance and "health warnings". Note also, that if you are employed by a foreign law firm and a principal, interest holder or director of the firm is a solicitor, Rule 4.19 and 4.20 will not apply unless the solicitor is dually qualified and is practising only as a lawyer of another jurisdiction in the context of that business.

(xiv)   By contrast, employment overseas by a foreign law firm will not usually fall within the definition of in-house practice in the Glossary if your employer is a lawyer or a law firm.

(xv)   If you are a solicitor, REL or RFL practising as a manager, employee, member or interest holder of an authorised non-SRA firm, neither Rule 4, nor the bulk of the SRA Code of Conduct, nor the SRA Accounts Rules, will be relevant to you when you do work of a type that is within the scope of the firm's authorisation. See Chapter 13 of the SRA Code of Conduct (Application and waivers provisions).

(xvi)   If you are a solicitor, REL or RFL practising as a manager, employee, member or interest holder of an authorised non-SRA firm, you must comply with Rule 4, with the SRA Code of Conduct, and with the SRA Accounts Rules, as if you were an in-house solicitor or REL when you do work of a type which is outside the scope of the firm's authorisation – see Rule 4.3 and the definition of "in-house practice" in the Glossary.

(xvii)   Note that if you are a solicitor, REL or RFL and you are a manager, member or interest holder of an authorised non-SRA firm, or employed in such a firm in connection with the provision of any legal services, it must be:

(a)   in your capacity as a solicitor, REL or RFL, or

(b)   in the capacity of an individual authorised by an approved regulator other than the SRA, if you are so authorised, or

(c)   in both such capacities;

except that if you are a solicitor who is a director of an authorised non-SRA firm or employed in such a firm in connection with the provision of any legal services, you must be practising in your capacity as a solicitor, even if also in some other capacity. See Rule 11.2 and 11.3, as well as section 1A(d) of the SA.

Rule 5: Authorised bodies

Practice from an office in England and Wales

5.1   An *authorised body* may *practise* from an office in England and Wales in the following ways only:

(a) as a stand-alone *firm*;

(b) as a *manager*, *member* or *interest holder* of another *authorised body*;

(c) as a *manager*, *member* or *interest holder* of an *authorised non-SRA firm*, in which case you must comply with any terms and requirements imposed on that firm's authorisation; or

(d) as an executor, trustee or nominee *company*, or a *company* providing company secretarial services, wholly owned and operated by another *authorised body*.

Practice from an office outside England and Wales

5.2   An *authorised body* may *practise* from an office outside England and Wales in the following ways only:

(a) as a stand-alone *firm*, provided that if any of the body's *managers* or *interest holders* are non-lawyers and the office is in an *Establishment Directive state* other than the *UK*, the rules for local *lawyers* would permit a local *lawyer* to practise through a business of that composition and structure;

(b) as a *manager*, *member* or *interest holder* of a business which has no office in England and Wales and meets all the following conditions:

   (i)   the business carries on the provision of legal advice or assistance, or representation in connection with the application of the law or resolution of legal disputes;

   (ii) a controlling majority of the *managers* and the *interest holders* are *lawyers* practising as such and/or *bodies corporate* in which *lawyers* practising as such constitute a controlling majority of the *managers* and *interest holders*;

   (iii) if any of the business's *managers* or *interest holders* are non-lawyers and any *manager* or *interest holder* is subject to the rules for local *lawyers*, the composition and structure of the business complies with those rules; and

   (iv) if any of the business's *managers* or *interest holders* are non-lawyers and the office is in an *Establishment Directive state* other than the *UK*, the rules for local *lawyers* would permit a local *lawyer* to practise through a business of that composition and structure;

(c) as an executor, trustee or nominee *company*, or a *company* providing company secretarial services, wholly owned and operated by another *authorised body*.

5.3   Nothing in rule 5.2 above prevents an *authorised body* from practising through an *overseas practice* for which it is the *responsible authorised body*.

Guidance notes

(i)   See Part 3 of these rules for the formation and eligibility criteria for recognised bodies and licensed bodies.

(ii)   Authorised bodies can have a complex structure, involving multi-layered ownership. But note that a partnership cannot be a partner in another partnership which is an authorised body because a partnership does not have separate legal identity (although, as an exception, an overseas partnership with separate legal identity could be a partner in a partnership which is an authorised body).

(iii)   The rules do not prevent an authorised body being a manager, member or interest holder of a recognised body or an authorised non-SRA firm which has an office outside England and Wales.

(iv)   An authorised body may practise through one or more overseas practices, which do not themselves require authorisation by the SRA. However, when considering whether authorisation is required for offices overseas, authorised bodies should consider the activities to be carried on from those offices, and note that rule 8.4 of the SRA Authorisation Rules provides that an authorised body may not carry on an activity unless through a body and individual who is authorised to carry on that activity.

Rule 6: Managers and employees authorised by another approved regulator

6.1   If you are a *manager* or *employee* of an *authorised body* and you are not a *solicitor* but you are authorised by an *approved regulator* other than the *SRA*, you must not:

(a)   be held out in any way which suggests that you are, or are entitled to *practise* as, a *solicitor*;

(b)   undertake the following *reserved work* in England and Wales, unless authorised by your *approved regulator* to do so:

  (i)   advocacy in open *court*;

  (ii)   the conduct of *court* litigation;

  (iii)   the administration of oaths and statutory declarations;

(c)   undertake advocacy in chambers in England and Wales, unless authorised by your *approved regulator* or acting under instructions given by a person qualified to supervise that *reserved work*;

(d)   undertake the following *reserved work* in England and Wales, unless authorised by your *approved regulator* or acting under the supervision of a person qualified to supervise that *reserved work*:

  (i)   the preparation of *court* documents;

  (ii)   the preparation of instruments and the lodging of documents relating to the transfer or charge of land;

(iii) the preparation of papers on which to found or oppose a grant of probate or a grant of letters of administration;

(iv) the preparation of trust deeds disposing of capital.

Guidance notes

(i) Rule 16 permits lawyers and firms authorised by another approved regulator to be interest holders and managers of an authorised body.

(ii) An individual authorised by another approved regulator cannot practise as a sole practitioner regulated by the SRA as the SRA can only authorise and regulate sole solicitors and RELs.

(iii) Where, in order to satisfy statutory requirements, there is a need for an individual doing reserved work to be supervised or directed by someone in the firm, this can only be undertaken by a person of equivalent or higher status.

(iv) A lawyer of England and Wales who is an individual authorised by another approved regulator is subject to the SRA's regulatory arrangements in relation to practice outside England and Wales if he or she is a manager of an authorised body.

Rule 7: Managers and employees who are not lawyers

7.1 If you are a *manager* or *employee* of an *authorised body* and you are not a *lawyer of England and Wales*, an *RFL* or a *lawyer* of an *Establishment Directive profession*, you must not:

(a) be held out in any way which suggests that you are, or are entitled to *practise* as, a *lawyer of England and Wales*;

(b) undertake the following *reserved work* in England and Wales:

(i) advocacy in open *court*;

(ii) the conduct of *court* litigation;

(iii) the administration of oaths and statutory declarations;

(c) undertake advocacy in chambers in England and Wales, except under instructions given by a person qualified to supervise that *reserved work*;

(d) undertake the following *reserved work* in England and Wales, except at the direction and under the supervision of a person qualified to supervise that *reserved work*:

(i) the preparation of *court* documents;

(ii) the preparation of instruments and the lodging of documents relating to the transfer or charge of land;

(iii) the preparation of papers on which to found or oppose a grant of probate or a grant of letters of administration;

(iv) the preparation of trust deeds disposing of capital.

Guidance note

(i)   A non-lawyer manager is subject to the SRA's regulatory arrangements in relation to legal practice outside England and Wales if he or she is a manager of an authorised body.

PART 2: RIGHTS OF PRACTICE

Rule 8: Reserved work and immigration work

Solicitors

8.1   As a *solicitor*, provided that you comply with Rule 9.1, you are authorised by the *SRA*:

  (a) to undertake the following *reserved work*:

  (i)   the exercise of any right of audience which *solicitors* had immediately before 7 December 1989;

  (ii) the exercise of any additional right of audience if you have a relevant higher courts advocacy qualification awarded by the *SRA* or another *approved regulator*;

  (iii) the conduct of, and the preparation of documents in, *court* and immigration tribunal proceedings;

  (iv) the preparation of instruments and the lodging of documents relating to the transfer or charge of land;

  (v)   the preparation of trust deeds disposing of capital;

  (vi) the preparation of papers on which to found or oppose a grant of probate or a grant of letters of administration;

  (vii) the administration of oaths and statutory declarations; and

  (b) to undertake *immigration work* not included under (a) above.

RELs

8.2   As an *REL*, you are authorised by the *SRA*:

  (a) to undertake the following *reserved work*:

  (i)   the exercise of any right of audience which *solicitors* had immediately before 7 December 1989;

  (ii) the exercise of any additional right of audience provided that you have a relevant higher courts advocacy qualification awarded by the *SRA* or another *approved regulator*;

  (iii) the conduct of, and the preparation of documents in, *court* and immigration tribunal proceedings;

    (iv) the preparation of instruments and the lodging of documents relating to the transfer or charge of land, provided you are a member of a profession listed under regulation 12 of the European Communities (Lawyer's Practice) Regulations 2000;

    (v) the preparation of trust deeds disposing of capital;

    (vi) the preparation of papers on which to found or oppose a grant of probate or a grant of letters of administration, provided you are a member of a profession listed under regulation 13 of the European Communities (Lawyer's Practice) Regulations 2000;

    (vii) the administration of oaths and statutory declarations; and

  (b) to undertake *immigration work* not included under (a) above.

8.3   When as an *REL* you exercise a right of audience before a *court* under 8.2(a)(i) or (ii), conduct *court* litigation under 8.2(a)(iii) or prepare *court* documents under 8.2(a)(iii) you must act in conjunction with a *solicitor* or barrister authorised to do that work.

RFLs

8.4   As an *RFL* working within Rule 3 you are authorised by the *SRA*:

  (a) to undertake the following *reserved work*:

    (i) advocacy before immigration tribunals; and

    (ii) the conduct of, and the preparation of documents in, immigration tribunal proceedings; and

  (b) to undertake immigration services which are not *reserved work* and are not included under (a) above, and to provide immigration advice.

Recognised bodies

8.5   Recognised bodies

  (a) A *recognised body* is authorised by the *SRA* to undertake the following *reserved work*:

    (i) advocacy before a *court* or immigration tribunal provided the *manager* or *employee* exercising the right of audience is authorised by the *SRA*, or otherwise entitled, to do so;

    (ii) the conduct of proceedings in a *court* or immigration tribunal;

    (iii) the preparation of documents in proceedings before a *court* or immigration tribunal;

    (iv) the preparation of instruments and the lodging of documents relating to the transfer or charge of land, provided the body has a *manager* who is:

- (A) an individual who is authorised to do that work, or

- (B) a *body corporate* which has a *manager* who is authorised to do that work;

(v) the preparation of trust deeds disposing of capital;

(vi) the preparation of papers on which to found or oppose a grant of probate or a grant of letters of administration, provided the body has a *manager* who is an individual authorised to do that work, or a *body corporate* with a *manager* who is authorised to do that work; and

(vii) the administration of oaths and statutory declarations.

(b) A *recognised body* is authorised to undertake immigration services which are not within (a) above, and to provide immigration advice.

Licensed bodies

8.6   A *licensed body* is authorised by the *SRA* to undertake the *reserved legal activities* and *immigration work* specified in the authorisation granted to the body under Rule 6 of the *SRA Authorisation Rules*.

Recognised sole practices

8.7   Recognised sole practices

(a) A *recognised sole practice* in which the *sole practitioner* is a *solicitor* is authorised by the *SRA*:

(i) to provide any *reserved work* which the *sole practitioner* is authorised to provide under Rule 8.1 above, and any other advocacy service through an *employee* of the *recognised sole practice* exercising a right of audience as authorised by the *SRA*, or otherwise entitled, to do; and

(ii) to undertake immigration services which are not within (i) above, and provide immigration advice.

(b) A *recognised sole practice* in which the *sole practitioner* is an *REL* is authorised by the *SRA*:

(i) to provide any *reserved work* which the *sole practitioner* is authorised to provide under Rule 8.2 above, and any other advocacy service through an *employee* of the *recognised sole practice* exercising a right of audience as authorised by the *SRA*, or otherwise entitled, to do; and

(ii) to undertake *immigration work* which is not within (i) above.

Guidance notes

(i)   Reserved work is work that is defined in Schedule 2 to the LSA as a "reserved legal activity". Certain categories of reserved work (rights of audience in chambers, reserved instrument activities and probate activities) can be done by an unqualified person under the supervision of a manager or fellow employee qualified to do that work – see Schedule 3 to the LSA.

(ii) Immigration work (immigration advice and immigration services) is restricted to certain persons under the Immigration and Asylum Act 1999. Immigration services relating to courts or immigration tribunals are reserved work – advocacy, the conduct of cases, and the preparation of papers. The court work is subject to the normal restriction on court work. Immigration Tribunal work can be done by RFLs who are practising as such. Other immigration work is not reserved work, but can only be done by an authorised person such as a solicitor, a barrister, a legal executive, a member of an Establishment Directive profession, or an RFL practising as such, or under the supervision of an authorised person, or under an exemption given by the Office of the Immigration Services Commissioner.

(iii) The Financial Services and Markets Act 2000 reserves the provision of "regulated activities" to persons authorised by the Financial Conduct Authority (FCA). Certain "regulated activities", ancillary to the provision of a professional service, are exempt from regulation by the FCA when carried out by firms authorised by the SRA – see the SRA Financial Services (Scope) Rules. For the definition of "regulated activity" see the activities specified in the Financial Services and Markets Act 2000 (Regulated Activities) Order 2001 (SI 2001/544).

(iv) The SRA does not authorise notarial activities. This does not prevent individuals, in an SRA authorised firm, providing notarial services where personally authorised to do so by the Master of the Faculties within paragraph 7 of Schedule 2 to the LSA.

(v) See also Rule 8.4 of the SRA Authorisation Rules which provides that an authorised body may not carry on an activity unless through a body and individual who is authorised to carry on that activity.

(vi) In the case of solicitors and RELs who undertake criminal advocacy, see also the SRA QASA Regulations.

Rule 9: Practising certificates

9.1 If you are *practising* as a *solicitor* (including *in-house*), whether in England and Wales or overseas, you must:

(a) have in force a practising certificate issued by the *SRA*; or

(b) be exempt under section 88 of the *SA* from holding a practising certificate.

9.2 You will be *practising* as a *solicitor* if you are involved in legal practice and:

(a) your involvement in the firm or the work depends on your being a *solicitor*;

(b) you are held out explicitly or implicitly as a *practising solicitor*;

(c) you are employed explicitly or implicitly as a *solicitor*; or

(d)   you are deemed by section 1A of the *SA* to be acting as a *solicitor*.

9.3   In 9.2 above "legal practice" includes not only the provision of legal advice or assistance, or representation in connection with the application of the law or resolution of legal disputes, but also the provision of other services such as are provided by *solicitors*.

9.4   If you are a *solicitor* who was formerly an *REL*, and you are *practising* from an office in the *UK* as a *lawyer* of an *Establishment Directive profession*, you must have in force a practising certificate issued by the *SRA*, even if you are not *practising* as a *solicitor*.

Guidance notes

(i)   Rule 9 includes, in rule form, the requirements of sections 1 and 1A of the SA. The issuing of practising certificates under that Act is the responsibility of the SRA. For further guidance on the need for a practising certificate see our website.

(ii)   If you practise as a solicitor, whether in a firm or in-house, without having a practising certificate, you will commit a criminal offence, as well as a breach of the rules, unless you are entitled to rely on the exemption in section 88 of the SA.

Rule 10: Sole practitioners

10.1   If you are a *solicitor* or *REL* you must not *practise* as a *sole practitioner* unless:

(a)   the *SRA* has authorised your *practice* as a *recognised sole practice*, or

(b)   [Deleted]

(c)   you are authorised to *practise* as a *sole practitioner* by an *approved regulator* other than the *SRA*.

10.2   If you are a *solicitor* or *REL* you will not be regarded as *practising* as a *sole practitioner* and you are exempt from the obligation for your *practice* to be a *recognised sole practice* if:

(a)   your *practice* is conducted entirely from an office or offices outside England and Wales;

(b)   your *practice* consists entirely of work as a temporary or permanent *employee* and any *firm* which employs you takes full responsibility for you as an *employee*; or

(c)   your *practice* consists entirely of:

     (i)   providing professional services without remuneration for friends, relatives, companies wholly owned by you or your family, or registered *charities*; and/or

     (ii)   administering oaths and statutory declarations; and/or

     (iii)   activities which could constitute *practice* but are done in the course of discharging the functions of any of the offices or appointments listed in paragraph (i)(E) of the definition of *private practice*.

Rule 11: Participation in legal practice

11.1   If you are a *solicitor*, *REL* or *RFL* and you are:

(a)   a *manager*, *member* or *interest holder* of:

    (i)   a *recognised body*; or

    (ii)   a *body corporate* which is a *European corporate practice* and is a *manager* of a *recognised body*; or

(b)   a *manager*, *member* or *owner* of:

    (i)   a *licensed body*; or

    (ii)   a *body corporate* which is a *European corporate practice* and is a *manager* of a *licensed body*;

it must be in your capacity as a *solicitor*, *REL* or *RFL* (whether or not you are held out as such);

(c)   employed in connection with the provision of legal services in England and Wales, by an *authorised body*;

it must be in your capacity as a *solicitor*, in accordance with section 1A of the *SA*, an *REL* or an *RFL* (whether or not you are held out as such);

(d)   *Practising* in accordance with (a), (b) or (c) above does not prevent you from *practising* also as an individual authorised by an *approved regulator* other than the *SRA* or providing services as a member of a non-lawyer profession.

11.2   Subject to 11.3 below, if you are a *solicitor*, *REL* or *RFL* and you are:

(a)   a *manager*, *member* or *interest holder* of:

    (i)   an *authorised non-SRA firm* which is not licensed under Part 5 of the *LSA*; or

    (ii)   a *body corporate* which is a *manager* of such an *authorised non-SRA firm*;

(b)   a *manager*, *member* or *owner* of an *authorised non-SRA firm* which is licensed under Part 5 of the *LSA*; or

(c)   an *employee* who is employed in connection with the provision of legal services in England and Wales, by an *authorised non-SRA firm*;

it must be in your capacity as a *solicitor*, *REL* or *RFL* or as an individual authorised by an *approved regulator* other than the *SRA* (whether or not you are held out as such) but this does not prevent you from *practising* in both capacities or providing services as a member of a non-lawyer profession in addition to *practising* as a *lawyer*.

11.3   If you are a *solicitor* who is employed by, or is a *director* of, an *authorised non-SRA firm*, section 1A of the *SA* will require you to *practise* through that firm in the capacity of *solicitor*, even if also *practising* in some other capacity.

11.4   No *solicitor* or *REL*, while a prisoner in any prison, may commence, prosecute or defend any action, suit or other contentious proceedings, or appear as an advocate in any such proceedings, unless he or she does so as a litigant in person and not as a *solicitor* or *REL*.

Guidance note

(i)   A solicitor, REL or RFL is required to be involved in a recognised body in that capacity even if they merely have a small interest in the firm. There is greater flexibility in licensed bodies where a solicitor, REL or RFL is permitted to have a small share in a licensed body without being treated as practising merely because of that involvement. For example, a solicitor could have a small interest in a licensed body through a pension fund even though not practising.

Rule 12: Persons who must be "qualified to supervise"

12.1   The following persons must be "*qualified to supervise*":

    (a)   a *sole practitioner*;

    (b)   one of the *lawyer managers* of an *authorised body* or of a *body corporate* which is a *legally qualified body* and which is a *manager* of the *authorised body*;

    (c)   one of the *solicitors* or *RELs* employed by a law centre in England and Wales, unless the law centre is licensed under Part 5 of the *LSA* in which case the provisions in Rule 12.1(b) will apply; or

    (d)   one *in-house solicitor* or *in-house REL* in any department in England and Wales where *solicitors* and/or *RELs*, as part of their employment:

        (i)   do publicly funded work; or

        (ii)   do or supervise advocacy or the conduct of proceedings for members of the public before a *court* or immigration tribunal.

12.2   To be "*qualified to supervise*" for the purpose of 12.1 a person must:

    (a)   have completed the training specified from time to time by the *SRA* for this purpose; and

    (b)   be a practising *lawyer*, and have been entitled to practise as a *lawyer* for at least 36 months within the last ten years; and

must be able to demonstrate this if asked by the *SRA*.

12.3   The following persons must ensure that their firm has at least one *manager* who is practising as a *lawyer* and has been entitled to practise as a *lawyer* for a minimum of 36 months within the last 10 years:

(a) a *solicitor manager* of a firm which is not an *authorised body* and which is practising from an office outside England and Wales, and *solicitors* control the firm, either directly as *partners, members* or *interest holders*, or indirectly by their ownership of *bodies corporate* which are *partners, members* or *interest holders*; and

(b) a *solicitor* or *REL manager* of a firm which is not an *authorised body* and which is practising from an office in Scotland or Northern Ireland, and *solicitors* and/or *RELs* control the firm, either directly as *partners, members* or *interest holders*, or indirectly by their ownership of *bodies corporate* which are *partners, members* or *interest holders*.

12.4   You must not set up as a *solicitor sole practitioner* outside England and Wales, or as an *REL sole practitioner* in Scotland or Northern Ireland, unless you have been entitled to *practise* as a *lawyer* for a minimum of 36 months within the last 10 years.

Guidance notes

(i)   The person "qualified to supervise" under Rule 12.2 does not have to be personally entitled by law to supervise all work undertaken by the firm. Responsibility for the overall supervision framework, including compliance with legal supervisory requirements, rests with the authorised body and its managers, or the recognised sole practitioner.

(ii)   In satisfying the requirement for 36 months entitlement to practise you can for example rely on a period as a lawyer of another jurisdiction. In calculating the 36 months, any period of entitlement to practise as a lawyer of another jurisdiction can be taken into account in addition to your time entitled to practise as a solicitor.

(iii)   Waivers may be granted in individual cases. See Rule 21.

(iv)   The training presently specified by the SRA is attendance at or participation in any course(s), or programme(s) of learning, on management skills involving attendance or participation for a minimum of 12 hours. The courses or programmes do not have to be CPD accredited in order to satisfy the requirement. It is not normally necessary to check with the SRA before undertaking a course or programme unless the course is unusual and outside the mainstream of management training. Advice may be sought from the Professional Ethics Guidance Team.

(v)   Controlling the firm in Rule 12.3 means constituting the largest (or equal largest) share of control of the firm either as individual managers or by their share in the control of bodies which are managers.

PART 3: FORMATION AND ELIGIBILITY CRITERIA FOR RECOGNISED BODIES, RECOGNISED SOLE PRACTICES AND LICENSED BODIES

Rule 13: Eligibility criteria and fundamental requirements for recognised bodies and recognised sole practices

Recognised bodies

13.1   To be eligible to be a *recognised body*, a body must be a *legal services body* namely a *partnership*, *company* or *LLP* of which:

(a)   at least one *manager* is:

  (i)   a *solicitor* with a current practising certificate, or

  (ii)   an *REL*, or

  (iii)   (in the case of a *partnership* or *LLP*) a *body corporate* which is a *legally qualified body* with at least one *manager* who is a *solicitor* with a current practising certificate or an *REL*; and

(b)   all of the *managers* and *interest holders* are *lawyers* and *legally qualified bodies*.

Services requirement for a recognised body or recognised sole practice

13.2   The business of a *recognised body* or *recognised sole practice* may consist only of the provision of:

(a)   professional services of the sort provided by individuals *practising* as *solicitors* and/or *lawyers* of other jurisdictions; and

(b)   professional services of the sort provided by notaries public, but only if a notary public is a *manager* or *employee* of a *recognised body*; and

(c)   the following services (whether or not they are also included in paragraph (a))

  (i)   alternative dispute resolution;

  (ii)   financial services;

  (iii)   estate agency;

  (iv)   management consultancy;

  (v)   company secretarial services;

  (vi)   other professional and specialist support services to business including human resources, recruitment, systems support, outsourcing, transcription and translating;

  (vii)   acting as a parliamentary agent;

  (viii) practising as a lawyer of another jurisdiction;

(ix) acting as a bailiff;

(x) accountancy services;

(xi) education and training activities; and

(xii) authorship, journalism and publishing.

Recognised sole practices

13.3   A *sole practitioner's practice* is eligible to be a *recognised sole practice* if the *sole practitioner*:

(a) is a *solicitor* or *REL*;

(b) will be *practising* as a *sole practitioner* from an office in England and Wales; and

(c) is not, and is not about to be made, subject to a condition on his or her practising certificate or registration.

Guidance notes

(i)   Although most organisations which involve non-lawyers as managers or interest holders must be licensed bodies, there is a limited exception under section 72(2) of the LSA which permits a small degree of non-lawyer involvement in recognised bodies. Where one or more bodies are involved in a firm as a manager or owner/interest holder, and in those bodies non-authorised persons have only a de minimis (less than 10%) control by way of voting rights, then the firm will remain a legal services body requiring recognition under the AJA. Where the control is 10% or more, the firm will be a licensable body.

(ii)   Rule 13.2 lists the services that can be carried out within a recognised body or a recognised sole practice: either solicitor services, notary services, services of a lawyer or as exceptions to these services under section 9(1A) of the Administration of Justice Act 1985. Professional services "of the sort that can be carried out by solicitors" include any legal activity under the LSA. Nothing in Rule 13.2 affects any requirements that may be imposed by legislation or non SRA-regulation in relation to the listed activities. See also the SRA Property Selling Rules 2011 in relation to estate agency services.

Rule 14: Eligibility criteria and fundamental requirements for licensed bodies

14.1   To be eligible to be a *licensed body*, a body must comply with the *lawyer manager* requirement set out in Rule 14.2 below and be a "licensable body", as defined under section 72 of the *LSA*, and as set out in Rule 14.3 to 14.6 below.

14.2   At all times at least one *manager* of a *licensed body* must be an individual who is:

(a) a *solicitor* with a current practising certificate;

(b) an *REL*;

(c) a *lawyer of England and Wales* and who is authorised by an *approved regulator* other than the *SRA*; or

(d) registered with the *BSB* under regulation 17 of the European Communities (Lawyer's Practice) Regulations 2000 (SI 2000/1119).

14.3   A body ("B") is a *licensable body* if a *non-authorised person*:

(a) is a *manager* of B, or

(b) is an *interest holder* of B.

14.4   A body ("B") is also a *licensable body* if:

(a) another body ("A") is a *manager* of B, or is an *interest holder* of B, and

(b) *non-authorised persons* are entitled to exercise, or control the exercise of, at least 10% of the *voting rights* in A.

14.5   A body may be a *licensable body* by virtue of both 14.3 and 14.4.

14.6   For the purposes of this rule, a *non-authorised person* has an indirect interest in a *licensable body* if the body is a *licensable body* by virtue of 14.4 and the *non-authorised person* is entitled to exercise, or control the exercise of, *voting rights* in A.

Rule 15: Formation, registered office and practising address

15.1   An *authorised body* which is a *partnership* may be formed under the law of any country and may be a legal *person*.

15.2   An *authorised body* which is an *LLP* must be incorporated and registered in England and Wales, Scotland or Northern Ireland under the Limited Liability Partnerships Act 2000.

15.3   An *authorised body* which is a *company* must be:

(a) incorporated and registered in England and Wales, Scotland or Northern Ireland under Parts 1 and 2 of the Companies Act 2006;

(b) incorporated in an *Establishment Directive state* and registered as an overseas company under Part 34 of the Companies Act 2006; or

(c) incorporated and registered in an *Establishment Directive state* as a *societas Europaea*.

15.4   An *authorised body* must have at least one *practising address* in England and Wales.

15.5   An *authorised body* must have its registered office at a *practising address* in England and Wales if the *authorised body* is registered in England and Wales:

(a) under Parts 1 and 2 of the Companies Act 2006;

(b) under the Limited Liability Partnerships Act 2000; or

(c) as a *societas Europaea.*

Guidance note:

(i) See also the reporting requirements relating to the practising address and registered addresses of your overseas practices set out in:

(a) Rule 4.4 of the SRA Authorisation Rules;

(b) Rule 18.2 of the SRA Practice Framework Rules; and

(c) Rule 3.2 of the SRA Overseas Rules.

(ii) See also the requirements relating to the practising address of a recognised sole practice in Rule 6 of the SRA Authorisation Rules.

Rule 16: Composition of a recognised body and a licensed body

16.1 Provided that the requirements for all *recognised bodies* and *licensed bodies* set out in Rule 13 or Rule 14, as appropriate, are met, a *recognised body* or a *licensed body* may have all or any of the following as a *partner* (if it is a *partnership*), a *member* (if it is an *LLP*), or a *director, member* or *shareowner* (if it is a *company*):

(a) a *lawyer of England and Wales* (including a *solicitor* with a current practising certificate);

(b) an *REL*;

(c) an *RFL*;

(d) an *EEL*;

(e) in the case of a *partnership* or an *LLP*, a *body corporate* which is a *legally qualified body*;

(f) in the case of a *company*, a *legally qualified body*, save that only an individual may be a *director* of a *recognised body* which is a *company*;

provided that, where necessary, they comply with the approval requirements in Part 4 of the *SRA Authorisation Rules.*

16.2 If the *authorised body* is a *licensed body*, then the list of permitted *partners, members* of an *LLP* or, in the case of a *company, directors*, registered *members* or *shareowners* at 16.1(a) to (f) shall include:

(a) a *licensed body* or another body licensed under Part 5 of the *LSA* by an *approved regulator* other than the *SRA*; and

(b) any other individual or *body corporate*;

subject to any necessary approval as a *manager* or *owner* under Part 4 (Approval of managers, owners and compliance officers) of the *SRA Authorisation Rules,* save that only an individual may be a *director* of a *licensed body* which is a *company*.

16.3   An *authorised body* which is an *LLP* must have at least two *members*.

Guidance notes

(i)   See 22.3 below regarding the position of firms which have non-lawyer managers prior to 6 October 2011.

(ii)   Although a legal services body can have a variety of types of manager, only a solicitor or an REL may be a sole practitioner.

(iii)   Where, in line with Rule 16, a firm has persons other than solicitors as managers (in particular where European lawyers are involved), any list of the managers will need to:

- (a)   identify any solicitor as a solicitor;
- (b)   in the case of any lawyer or notary of an Establishment Directive state other than the UK:
    - (A)   identify the jurisdiction(s) – local or national as appropriate – under whose professional title the lawyer or notary is practising;
    - (B)   give the professional title(s), expressed in an official language of the Establishment Directive state(s) concerned; and
    - (C)   if the lawyer is an REL, refer to that lawyer's registration with the SRA;
- (c)   indicate the professional qualification(s) of any other lawyer and the country or jurisdiction of qualification of any RFL not included in (b) above;
- (d)   identify any individual non-lawyer as a non-lawyer; and
- (e)   identify the nature of any body corporate, if this is not clear from its name.

In addition, whenever an REL (whether or not a manager) is named on letterhead used in England and Wales by any firm or in-house practice, the firm or the employer will need to follow the guidance in (iii)(b) above.

Rule 17: Authorised bodies which are companies

Record of non-member shareowners

17.1   Keeping a record

- (a)   A *recognised body* which is a *company* with shares must keep a record of any non-*member interest holders*, and retain the record for at least three years after their interest ceases;
- (b)   A *licensed body* which is a *company* with shares must keep a record of any non-*member owners*, and retain the record for at least three years after their ownership ceases.

17.2   A *member* who holds a share as nominee for a non-*member shareowner* in an *authorised body* must keep the *authorised body* informed of all facts necessary to keep an accurate and up-to-date record in accordance with Rule 17.1.

Rule 18: Information and documentation

18.1   An *authorised body* must supply any information and documentation relating to its composition and structure or to any of its *managers, employees, members* or *shareowners* or the *sole practitioner*, as and when requested to do so by the *SRA*.

18.2   Notwithstanding any requirement to obtain approval of a *manager, owner, COLP* or *COFA* under Part 4 of the *SRA Authorisation Rules*, an *authorised body* must notify the *SRA* within seven days of any change to its:

    (a) name;

    (b) registered office and/or any of its *practising addresses*;

    (c) *managers*;

    (d) *interest holders*, if it is a *recognised body*, and in the case of a *recognised body* which is a *company*, this includes *members* and *shareowners*;

    (e) *owners*, if it is a *licensed body*, and in the case of a *licensed body* which is a *company*, this includes *members* and *shareowners*;

    (f) *COLP*;

    (g) *COFA*; or

    (h) *overseas practices*, including any contact details and practising/registered addresses of its *overseas practices*.

18.3   An *authorised body* must notify the *SRA* within seven days if it is an unlimited *company* and it is re-registered as limited under the *Companies Acts*.

18.4   If a *relevant insolvency event* occurs in relation to an *authorised body* its *managers*, or in the case of an *authorised body* which is an overseas company, its *directors*, must notify the *SRA* within seven days.

Guidance notes

(i)   There are other SRA reporting and information requirements that apply to individuals or firms. See for example:

    (a) Rules 3, 8.7, 8.8, 8.9 and 8.10 and 18, 23, 24 and 25 of the SRA Authorisation Rules

    (b) Rule 32 of the SRA Accounts Rules

    (c) Regulations 1.2, 4.3, 4.5, 4.8, 4.12, 4.13 and 15 of the SRA Practising Regulations

    (d) Chapter 10 of the SRA Code of Conduct

(e)   Rule 17.3 of the SRA Indemnity Insurance Rules 2013 or any subsequent rules thereto.

(ii)   In addition to the requirement to inform the SRA when certain persons leave the firm, there are the requirements in Rule 8 of the SRA Authorisation Rules for firms to seek approval, where necessary, before certain persons join the firm. This is more onerous than simply informing the SRA of changes that have taken place.

PART 4: COMPLIANCE WITH PRACTICE REQUIREMENTS

Rule 19: Compliance with practice requirements

19.1   An *authorised body* and its *managers* and *employees* must at all times ensure that they act in accordance with the requirements of the *SRA's regulatory arrangements* as they apply to them.

19.2   A *solicitor*, *REL* or *RFL* who is a *member* or *shareowner* of an *authorised body* which is a *company* must not cause, instigate or connive at any breach of the requirements imposed under the *SRA's regulatory arrangements* by the *authorised body* or any of its *managers* or *employees*.

19.3   An *employee* of an *authorised body* must not cause, instigate or connive at any breach of any requirements imposed under the *SRA's regulatory arrangements*.

19.4   The *partners* in an *authorised body* which is a *partnership* are responsible not only as *managers* but also, jointly and severally, as the *authorised body*.

Rule 20:

[Deleted]

Rule 21: Waivers

21.1   Subject to provisions relating to any statutory obligations or the *SRA's regulatory arrangements* affecting its ability to waive any requirements, the *SRA* Board shall have power to waive in writing the provisions of these rules for a particular purpose or purposes expressed in such waiver, and to attach conditions to or revoke such waiver, at its own discretion.

Guidance note

(i)   An applicant for a waiver must satisfy the SRA that the circumstances are sufficiently exceptional to justify a departure from the requirements of the rule in question, bearing in mind its purpose. Applications should be made to the Professional Ethics Guidance Team.

Rule 22: Transitional provisions and grace period

22.1 [Deleted]

22.2 Unless the context otherwise requires, references in these rules to:

(a) these rules, or a provision of these rules; and

(b) the *SRA Code of Conduct*, rules, regulations or *regulatory arrangements*, or a provision of the same,

include a reference to the equivalent rules, regulations or provisions previously in force.

22.3 A body that has, at the time these rules come into force, been recognised by the *SRA* under section 9 *AJA* and that does not comply with Rule 13.1(b) above shall continue to be treated as a *legal services body* for the purposes of these rules and the *SRA's regulatory arrangements* until:

(a) such time as it ceases to comply with the management and control requirements set out in Rule 22.4 below; or

(b) the end of the transitional period under Part 2 of Schedule 5 to the *LSA*, or such earlier time as the body may elect,

at which time it shall be a *licensed body* for the purposes of these rules and the *SRA's regulatory arrangements*.

22.4 The management and control requirements referred to in Rule 22.3 above are:

(a) At least 75% of the body's *managers* must be:

(i) individuals who are, and are entitled to *practise* as, *lawyers of England and Wales*, *lawyers* of *Establishment Directive professions* or RFLs; or

(ii) *bodies corporate* which are legally qualified bodies;

although a legally qualified body cannot be a *director* of a body which is a *company*;

(b) Individuals who are, and are entitled to *practise* as, *lawyers of England and Wales*, *lawyers* of *Establishment Directive professions* or *RFLs* must make up at least 75% of the ultimate beneficial ownership of the body; and

(c) Individuals who are, and are entitled to *practise* as, *lawyers of England and Wales*, *lawyers* of *Establishment Directive professions* or *RFLs*, and/or legally qualified bodies, must:

(i) exercise or control the exercise of at least 75% of the *voting rights* in the body; and

(ii) if the body is a *company* with shares, hold (as registered *members* of the *company*) at least 75% of the shares.

(d) Subject to Rule 13.1(b) above, every *interest holder* of the *recognised body*, and every *person* who exercises or controls the exercise of any *voting rights* in the body, must be:

    (i)   an individual who is, and is entitled to *practise* as, a *lawyer of England and Wales*, a *lawyer* of an *Establishment Directive profession* or an *RFL*;

    (ii)   a legally qualified body; or

    (iii)   an individual who is approved under regulation 3 of the SRA Recognised Bodies Regulations 2009, regulation 5 of the SRA Recognised Bodies Regulations 2011 or Part 4 of the *SRA Authorisation Rules* and, subject to (e) below, is a *manager* of the body.

(e)   An individual who is not entitled under (d)(i) above may be an *interest holder* of a *recognised body* without being a *manager* of the body if:

    (i)   the *recognised body* is a *company* which is wholly or partly owned by a *partnership* or *LLP* which is a *legally qualified body*;

    (ii)   the individual is approved under regulation 3 of the SRA Recognised Bodies Regulations 2009, regulation 5 of the SRA Recognised Bodies Regulations 2011 or Part 4 of the *SRA Authorisation Rules* and is a *manager* of the *partnership* or *LLP*; and

    (iii)   the individual is precluded under the *partnership* agreement or *members'* agreement from exercising or authorising any vote in relation to the *company*.

For the purposes of Rule 22.4 and for the purposes of section 9A(6)(h) and (6C) of the *AJA* "legally qualified body" means a body which would meet the services requirement in Rule 13.2 and is:

(A)   a *recognised body*;

(B)   an *authorised non-SRA firm* of which individuals who are, and are entitled to practise as, *lawyers of England and Wales*, *lawyers* of *Establishment Directive professions* or *RFLs* make up at least 75% of the ultimate beneficial ownership; or

(C)   a European corporate practice which is a *lawyers'* practice and is a body incorporated in an *Establishment Directive state*, or a *partnership* with separate legal identity formed under the law of an *Establishment Directive state*:

    (I)   which has an office in an *Establishment Directive state* but does not have an office in England and Wales;

    (II)   whose ultimate beneficial owners include at least one individual who is not a *lawyer of England and Wales* but is, and is entitled to practise as, a *lawyer* of an *Establishment Directive profession*;

    (III)   whose *managers* include at least one such individual, or at least one body corporate whose *managers* include at least one such individual;

(IV) 75% of whose ultimate beneficial ownership is in the hands of individuals who are, and are entitled to practise as, *lawyers* of *Establishment Directive professions*, *lawyers of England and Wales*, and/or *RFLs*; and

(V) 75% of whose *managers* comprise such individuals, and/or bodies corporate 75% of whose *managers* comprise such individuals.

22.5 [Deleted]

22.6 [Deleted]

22.7 [Deleted]

PART 5: INTERPRETATION

Rule 23: Interpretation

23.1 The SRA Handbook Glossary 2012 shall apply and, unless the context otherwise requires:

(a) all italicised terms shall be defined; and

(b) all terms shall be interpreted,

in accordance with the *Glossary*.

[F]   Glossary

SRA Handbook Glossary 2012

PART 1: INTRODUCTION AND PREAMBLE

Introduction

This section of the Handbook contains the SRA Handbook Glossary.

The SRA Handbook Glossary comprises a set of defined terms which are used in the SRA Handbook. Terms being used in their defined sense appear as italicised text within the individual sets of provisions of the SRA Handbook. The same terms in the SRA Handbook may appear as italicised text in some cases but not in others. Where they are not italicised, for reasons relating to the specific context, they are not being used in their defined sense and take their natural meaning in that context.

The Glossary also contains interpretation and transitional provisions.

Preamble

The SRA Handbook Glossary dated 18 April 2012 made by the Solicitors Regulation Authority Board.

Made under Part I, Part II, section 79 and 80 of, and paragraph 6B of Schedule 1 to, the Solicitors Act 1974; and section 9 and 9A of, and paragraphs 14A, 14B and 32 to 34 of Schedule 2 to, the Administration of Justice Act 1985; and section 83 of, and Schedule 11 to and paragraph 6 of Schedule 14 to, the Legal Services Act 2007; and paragraphs 2 and 3 of Schedule 14 to the Courts and Legal Services Act 1990.

Subject to the approval of the Legal Services Board under paragraph 19 of Schedule 4 to the Legal Services Act 2007 and coming into force on the day it is approved.

PART 2: GENERAL

Rule 1: Application

1.1   Subject to Rule 1.2 below:

(a)   the definitions set out at Rule 2 below shall apply to the corresponding term where this appears in italics in the *SRA Handbook*; and

(b)   the interpretation provisions set out at Rule 3 below shall apply to the *SRA Handbook*.

1.2   This Rule shall not apply to the SRA Indemnity Insurance Rules 2011, the SRA Indemnity (Enactment) Rules 2011 and the SRA Indemnity Rules 2011 until 1 October 2012.

Rule 2: Definitions

academic stage of training means the undertaking by an individual of the following programmes of study which satisfy the requirements of the *Joint Statement*:

    (i) a *QLD*;

    (ii) a *CPE*; or

    (iii) an *Exempting Law Degree*;

at an *approved education provider*.

accounting period has the meaning given in Rule 33 of the *SRA Accounts Rules*.

accreditation means either *full accreditation* or *provisional accreditation* under the *SRA QASA Regulations*, and references to "accredited" should be construed accordingly.

actively participate in means, in relation to a *separate business*, having any active involvement in the *separate business*, and includes:

    (i) any direct control over the business, and any indirect control through another *person* such as a spouse; and

    (ii) any active participation in the business or the provision of its services to customers.

adequate training during a period of *recognised training* means training:

    (i) and experience in at least three distinct areas of English law and practice;

    (ii) to enable a *trainee* to develop the skills needed to activities set out in the *Practice Skills Standards* and comply with the *Principles*;

    (iii) which is appropriately supervised; and

    (iv) which meets the requirements of regulation 12 of the *SRA Training Regulations* – Qualification and Provider Regulations.

adjudicator

    (i) in the *SRA Cost of Investigations Regulations* means a person not involved in the investigation or preparation of a case who is authorised by the *SRA* to make an *SRA finding*; and

    (ii) in the *SRA Disciplinary Procedure Rules* means a person not involved in the investigation or preparation of a case who is authorised by the *SRA* to take *disciplinary decisions*.

agreed fee has the meaning given in Rule 17.5 of the *SRA Accounts Rules*.

agreement provider has the meaning given by article 63J(3) of the *Regulated Activities Order* read with paragraphs (6) and (7) of that article.

agreement seller has the meaning given by article 63J(3) of the *Regulated Activities Order*.

AJA means the Administration of Justice Act 1985.

appellate body means the body with the power, by virtue of an order under section 80(1) of the *LSA*, to hear and determine appeals against decisions made by the *SRA* acting as a *licensing authority*.

applicant means:

  (i) for the purposes of the *SRA Compensation Fund Rules* a *person* or *persons* applying for a grant out of the Compensation Fund under Rule 3 of the *SRA Compensation Fund Rules*; and

  (ii) for the purposes of the *SRA Authorisation Rules* a *licensable body* or a *legal services body* that, or a *sole practitioner* who, makes an application to the *SRA* for *authorisation*.

application for admission means application to *us* for a *certificate of satisfaction* under section 3(1) of the *SA* and for admission as a *solicitor* under section 3(2) of the *SA*.

appointed person in the *SRA Indemnity Insurance Rules*, means any person who is designated as a fee-earner in accordance with any arrangements made from time to time between the *firm* and the Legal Services Commission pursuant to the provisions of the Access to Justice Act 1999 or the Lord Chancellor (or any body established by the Lord Chancellor to provide or facilitate the provision of services) pursuant to the provisions of the Legal Aid, Sentencing and Punishment of Offenders Act 2012, regardless of whether the services performed for the *firm* by that person in accordance with Rule 4.1 of those Rules are performed pursuant to such arrangements or otherwise, and who is engaged by the *firm* under a contract for services in the course of the *private practice* of the *firm*.

appointed representative has the meaning given in *FSMA*.

Apprenticeship Standard for a Solicitor (England) means the standard approved by the Department for Business, Innovation and Skills in November 2014 and as varied from time to time.

approved education provider means a provider recognised by *us* as providing a *QLD*, *CPE* and/or an *Exempting Law Degree*.

approved regulator means any body listed as an approved regulator in paragraph 1 of Schedule 4 to the *LSA* or designated as an approved regulator by an order under paragraph 17 of that Schedule.

ARP means the Assigned Risks Pool, namely, the arrangements by which certain *firms* obtained professional indemnity insurance against civil liability up to 30 September

2013 pursuant to and on the terms set out in the SRA Indemnity Insurance Rules 2012 (and prior variations thereof).

ARP manager means the manager of the *ARP* being any *person* from time to time appointed by the *SRA* to carry out all or any particular functions of the manager of the *ARP* or the *SRA* and any such *person*.

arrangement in relation to financial services, fee sharing and *referrals* in Chapters 1, 6 and 9 of the *SRA Code of Conduct*, means any express or tacit agreement between you and another *person*, whether contractually binding or not.

assessment organisation in the *QLTSR* means the organisation awarded the initial three year contract to provide the *QLTS assessments*, together with any other organisations subsequently authorised to provide the *QLTS assessments* after the initial three year period has expired.

assets includes money, documents, wills, deeds, investments and other property.

associate has the meaning given in paragraph 5 to Schedule 13 of the *LSA*, namely:

(i) "associate", in relation to a person ("A") and:

    (A) a shareholding in a body ("S"); or

    (B) an entitlement to exercise or control the exercise of voting power in a body ("V");

means a person listed in sub-paragraph (ii).

(ii) The persons are:

    (A) the spouse or civil partner of A;

    (B) a child or stepchild of A (if under 18);

    (C) the *trustee* of any settlement under which A has a life interest in possession (in Scotland a life interest);

    (D) an undertaking of which A is a *director*;

    (E) an *employee* of A;

    (F) a *partner* of A (except, where S or V is a *partnership* in which A is a *partner*, another *partner* in S or V);

    (G) if A is an undertaking:

        (I) a *director* of A;

        (II) a subsidiary undertaking of A; or

        (III) a *director* or *employee* of such a subsidiary undertaking;

    (H) if A has with any other person an agreement or arrangement with respect to the acquisition, holding or disposal of shares or other interests in S or V (whether or not they are interests within the meaning of section 72(3) of the *LSA*), that other person; or

(I) if A has with any other person an agreement or arrangement under which they undertake to act together in exercising their voting power in relation to S or V, that person.

associated firm means:

(i) a *partnership* with whom you have one *partner* in common;

(ii) an *LLP* or a *company* without shares with whom you have one *member* in common; or

(iii) a *company* with shares with whom you have one *owner* in common.

authorisation granted to a body under Rule 6 of the *SRA Authorisation Rules* means:

(i) recognition under section 9 of the *AJA*, if it is granted to a *legal services body*;

(ii) recognition under section 9 of the *AJA*, if it is granted to a *sole practitioner*; and

(iii) a licence under Part 5 of the *LSA*, if it is granted to a *licensable body*;

and the term *"certificate of authorisation"* shall be construed accordingly.

authorised activities means:

(i) any *reserved legal activity* in respect of which the body is authorised;

(ii) any *non-reserved legal activity* except, in relation to an *MDP*, any such activity that is excluded from *regulated activity* on the terms of the licence;

(iii) any other activity in respect of which a *licensed body* is regulated pursuant to Part 5 of the *LSA*; and

(iv) any other activity a *recognised body* carries out in connection with its *practice*.

authorised body means:

(i) a body that has been authorised by the *SRA* to practise as a *licensed body* or a *recognised body*; or

(ii) a *sole practitioner's practice* that has been authorised by the *SRA* as a *recognised sole practice*.

authorised distance learning providers means those providers authorised by *us* to provide distance learning courses delivered by methods including correspondence, webinar, webcast, podcast, DVD, video and audio cassettes, television or radio broadcasts and computer based learning programmes.

authorised education provider means a provider recognised by *us* as providing the *LPC* and/or the *PSC*.

authorised insurer means:

(i) a *person* who has permission under Part 4A of *FSMA* to effect or carry out contracts of insurance of a relevant class;

(ii) a *person* who carries on an insurance market activity, within the meaning of section 316(3) of *FSMA*;

(iii) an *EEA* firm of the kind mentioned in paragraph 5(d) of Schedule 3 to *FSMA*, which has permission under paragraph 15 of that Schedule (as a result of qualifying for authorisation under paragraph 12 of that Schedule) to effect or carry out contracts of insurance of a relevant class; or

(iv) a *person* who does not fall within paragraph (i), (ii) or (iii) and who may lawfully effect or carry out contracts of insurance of a relevant class in a member state other than the *UK*,

where "relevant class" has the meaning set out in section 87(1B) of the *SA* provided that this definition must be read with section 22 of *FSMA*, any relevant order under that section, and Schedule 2 to *FSMA*.

authorised non-SRA firm means a firm which is authorised to carry on *legal activities* by an *approved regulator* other than the *SRA*.

authorised person

(i) subject to sub-paragraph (ii) below, means a *person* who is authorised by the *SRA* or another *approved regulator* to carry on a *legal activity* and for the purposes of the *SRA Authorisation Rules* and the *SRA Practice Framework Rules* includes a *solicitor*, a *sole practitioner*, an *REL*, an *EEL*, an *RFL*, an *authorised body*, an *authorised non-SRA firm* and a *European corporate practice* and the terms "*authorised individual*" and "non-authorised person" shall be construed accordingly; and

(ii) in the *SRA Financial Services (Scope) Rules*, has the meaning given in section 31 of *FSMA*.

authorised role holder means *COLP*, *COFA*, *owner* or *manager* under Rules 8.5 and 8.6 of the *SRA Authorisation Rules* or *COLP* or *COFA* under Regulation 4.8 of the *SRA Practising Regulations*, and "authorised role" should be construed accordingly.

authorised training provider means an organisation, body, firm, company, in-house practice or individual authorised by *us* under the *SRA Training Regulations* to take and train a *trainee solicitor*.

bank has the meaning given in section 87(1) of the *SA*.

barrister means a person called to the Bar by one of the Inns of Court and who has completed pupillage and is authorised by the General Council of the Bar to practise as a barrister.

beneficiary means a *person* with a beneficial entitlement to funds held by the *Society* on *statutory trust*.

best list means a list of potential beneficial entitlements to *statutory trust monies* which, in cases where it is not possible to create a *reconciled list*, is, in the view of the *SRA*, the most reliable that can be achieved with a reasonable and proportionate level of work taking into account the circumstances of the *intervention* and the nature of the evidence available.

body corporate means a company, an *LLP* or a partnership which is a legal person in its own right.

broker funds arrangement means an arrangement between a *firm* and a *life office* (or operator of a *regulated collective investment scheme*) under which the *life office* (or operator of the *regulated collective investment scheme*) agrees to establish a separate fund whose composition may be determined by instructions from the *firm* and in which it is possible for more than one *client* to invest.

BSB means the Bar Standards Board.

building society means a building society within the meaning of the Building Societies Act 1986.

buyer includes a prospective buyer.

CAEF means a criminal advocacy evaluation form completed by a judge to record the competence of a *solicitor* or an *REL* to conduct *criminal advocacy* against the Statement of Standards contained in the *QASA*.

candidate means a *person* who is assessed by the *SRA* for approval as an *owner*, *manager* or *compliance officer* under Part 4 of the *SRA Authorisation Rules*.

CCBE means the Council of the Bars and Law Societies of Europe.

CCBE Code means the *CCBE's* Code of Conduct for European lawyers.

CCBE state means any state whose legal profession is a full member, an associate member or an observer member of the *CCBE*.

certificate of satisfaction means a certificate or a certifying letter from *us* confirming that *you* have satisfied the *SRA Training Regulations* and are of the proper *character and suitability* to be admitted as a *solicitor*.

cessation means where the *insured firm's practice* ceases during the *period of insurance* or after the *period of insurance* in circumstances where the *insured firm* has not obtained insurance complying with the *MTC* and incepting on and with effect from the day immediately following the expiration of the *policy period*.

cessation period means the period commencing on the expiry of the *extended indemnity period* where, during the *extended indemnity period* the relevant *firm* has not ceased *practice* or obtained a *policy* of *qualifying insurance* incepting with effect on and from the day immediately following expiration of the *policy period*, and ending on the date which is the earlier to occur of:

(i)   the date, if any, on which the *firm* obtains a *policy* of *qualifying insurance* incepting with effect on and from the day immediately following expiration of the *policy period*;

(ii) the date which is 90 days after the commencement of the *extended indemnity period*; or

(iii) the date on which the *insured firm's practice* ceases.

character and suitability satisfies the requirement of section 3 of the *SA* in order that an individual shall be admitted as a *solicitor*.

charity has the meaning given in section 1 of the Charities Act 2011.

circumstances means an incident, occurrence, fact, matter, act or omission which may give rise to a *claim* in respect of civil liability.

claim means a demand for, or an assertion of a right to, civil compensation or civil damages or an intimation of an intention to seek such compensation or damages. For these purposes, an obligation on an *insured firm* and/or any *insured* to remedy a breach of the Solicitors' Accounts Rules 1998 (as amended from time to time), or any rules (including, without limitation, the *SRA Accounts Rules*) which replace the Solicitors' Accounts Rules 1998 in whole or in part, shall be treated as a claim, and the obligation to remedy such breach shall be treated as a civil liability for the purposes of clause 1 of the *MTC*, whether or not any *person* makes a demand for, or an assertion of a right to, civil compensation or civil damages or an intimation of an intention to seek such compensation or damages as a result of such breach, except where any such obligation may arise as a result of the insolvency of a bank (as defined in section 87 of the *SA*) or a *building society* which holds client money in a client account of the *insured firm* or the failure of such bank or *building society* generally to repay monies on demand.

claim for redress has the meaning given in section 158 of the *LSA*.

claimant means:

(i)   in the *SRA Statutory Trust Rules*, a *person* making a claim to *statutory trust monies*; and

(ii) in the *SRA Indemnity Insurance Rules*, a *person* or entity which has made or may make a *claim* including a *claim* for contribution or indemnity.

client means:

(i)   the *person* for whom you act and, where the context permits, includes prospective and former clients;

(ii) in Parts 1–6 of the *SRA Accounts Rules*, the person for whom *you* act; and

(iii) in the *SRA Financial Services (Scope) Rules*, in relation to any *regulated activities* carried on by a *firm* for a trust or the estate of a deceased person (including a controlled trust), the trustees or personal representatives in their capacity as such and not any *person* who is a beneficiary under the trust or interested in the estate.

client account has the meaning given in Rule 13.2 of the *SRA Accounts Rules*.

client account (overseas) means an account at a bank or similar institution, subject to supervision by a public authority, which is used only for the purpose of holding *client money (overseas)*, and the title, designation or account details allow the account to be identified as belonging to the client or clients of a *solicitor* or *REL* or that they are being held subject to a *trust*.

client conflict for the purposes of Chapter 3 of the *SRA Code of Conduct*, means any situation where you owe separate duties to act in the best interests of two or more *clients* in relation to the same or related matters, and those duties conflict, or there is a significant risk that those duties may conflict.

client money has the meaning given in Rule 12 of the *SRA Accounts Rules*.

client money (overseas) means money held or received for a *client* in respect of legal services that you are providing or as *trustee*, and all other money which is not *office money (overseas)*. This includes money held or received:

(i) as *trustee*;

(ii) as agent, bailee, stakeholder, or as the donee of a power of attorney, or as a liquidator, trustee in bankruptcy, *Court of Protection deputy* or trustee of an occupational pension scheme;

(iii) for payment of unpaid *professional disbursements*;

(iv) for payment of taxes, duties or fees on behalf of clients or third parties;

(v) as a payment on account of *costs* and *disbursements* generally;

(vi) jointly with another person outside of your practice;

(vii) to the sender's order.

COFA means a compliance officer for finance and administration in accordance with Rule 8.5 of the *SRA Authorisation Rules*, or Regulation 4.8 of the *SRA Practising Regulations*, and in relation to a *licensable body* is a reference to its *HOFA*.

collective investment scheme means (in accordance with section 235 of *FSMA* (Collective Investment Schemes)) any arrangements with respect to property of any description, including money, the purpose or effect of which is to enable *persons* taking part in the arrangements (whether by becoming owners of the property or any part of it or otherwise) to participate in or receive profits or income arising from the acquisition, holding, management or disposal of the property or sums paid out of such profits or income, which are not excluded by the Financial Services and Markets Act (Collective Investment Schemes) Order 2001 (SI 2001/1062).

COLP means compliance officer for legal practice in accordance with Rule 8.5 of the *SRA Authorisation Rules* or Regulation 4.8 of the *SRA Practising Regulations*, and in relation to a *licensable body* is a reference to its *HOLP*.

Companies Acts means the Companies Act 1985 and the Companies Act 2006.

company means a company incorporated in an *Establishment Directive state* and registered under the *Companies Acts* or a *societas Europaea*.

competing for the same objective for the purposes of Chapter 3 of the *SRA Code of Conduct* means any situation in which two or more *clients* are competing for an "objective" which, if attained by one *client*, will make that "objective" unattainable to the other *client* or *clients*, and "objective" means, for the purposes of Chapter 3, an asset, contract or business opportunity which two or more *clients* are seeking to acquire or recover through a liquidation (or some other form of insolvency process) or by means of an auction or tender process or a bid or offer which is not public.

complaint means an oral or written expression of dissatisfaction which alleges that the complainant has suffered (or may suffer) financial loss, distress, inconvenience or other detriment.

compliance officer is a reference to a body's *COLP* or its *COFA*.

compulsory professional indemnity insurance means the insurance you are required to have in place under the *SIIR*.

CONC means the *FCA's* Consumer Credit sourcebook.

conflict of interests means any situation where:

    (i)   you owe separate duties to act in the best interests of two or more *clients* in relation to the same or related matters, and those duties conflict, or there is a significant risk that those duties may conflict (a "client conflict"); or

    (ii) your duty to act in the best interests of any *client* in relation to a matter conflicts, or there is a significant risk that it may conflict, with your own interests in relation to that or a related matter (an "own interest conflict").

connected person means:

    (i)   any *associated firm*;

    (ii) anyone with whom you are related by blood, marriage or adoption, or with whom you are living together in a civil or domestic partnership;

    (iii) any *owner* or *employee* of your *firm* or of an *associated firm*, or anyone with whom that *owner* or *employee* is related by blood, marriage or adoption, or with whom they are living together in a civil or domestic partnership;

(iv) any *company* of which you are a *director* or *employee*, or any *LLP* of which you are a *member* or *employee*, or any *company* in which you, either alone or with any other connected person or persons, are entitled to exercise, or control the exercise of, one-third or more of the voting power at any general meeting;

(v) any *company* of which any of the *persons* mentioned in (i) and (ii) above is a *director* or *employee*, or any *LLP* of which any of them is a *member* or *employee*, or any *company* in which any of them, either alone or with any other connected person or persons, is entitled to exercise, or control the exercise of, one-third or more of the voting power at any general meeting; and

(vi) any other "associate" as defined in section 32 of the Estate Agents Act 1979.

connected practice means a body providing legal services, established outside England and Wales which is not an overseas practice or an excluded body but is otherwise connected to an authorised body in England and Wales, by virtue of:

(i) being a parent undertaking, within the meaning of section 1162 of the Companies Act 2006, of the authorised body;

(ii) being jointly managed or owned, or having a partner, member or owner in common, or controlled by or, with the authorised body;

(iii) participating in a joint enterprise or across its practice generally, sharing costs, revenue or profits related to the provision of legal services with the authorised body; or

(iv) common branding;

and in this definition:

(A) a "body" means a natural person or company, limited liability partnership or partnership or other body corporate or unincorporated association or business entity; and

(B) an "excluded body" means a body which is part of:

(I) a Verein or similar group structure involving more than one body providing legal services in respect of which the authorised body in England and Wales connected to it is not regarded as being the body which is the headquarters of that Verein or similar group structure or a significant part of it; or

(II) a joint practice, alliance or association or association with the authorised body in England and Wales connected to it which is controlled by a body providing legal services outside of England and Wales; or

(III) a group of affiliated bodies providing legal services which is not managed or controlled by an authorised body in England and Wales.

(C) A "joint enterprise" means any contractual arrangements between two or more independent bodies which provide legal services, for profit and/or other defined purpose or goal which apply generally between them, not just agreed on a matter by matter basis.

(D) "Common branding" means the use of a name, term, design, symbol, words or a combination of these that identifies two or more legal practices as distinct from other legal practices or an express statement that a legal practice is practising in association with one or more other named firms.

connected with means in relation to a *separate business* for the purpose of Chapter 12 of the *SRA Code of Conduct*:

(i) where an *owner* or *manager* of an *authorised body* is a *partner, owner, director, member* or member of the governing body of the *separate business*;

(ii) being a *subsidiary company* of the same *holding company* as the *separate business*; or

(iii) being a *subsidiary company* of the *separate business*.

continuous payment authority means consent given to a *client* for a *firm* to make one or more requests to a payment service provider for one or more payments from the *client's payment account*, but excluding:

(i) a direct debit to which the direct debit guarantee applies; and

(ii) separate consent given by a *client* to a *firm*, following the making of the *regulated credit agreement*, for the *firm* to make a single request to a payment service provider for one payment of a specified amount from the *client's* payment account on the same day as the consent is given or on a specified day.

contract of insurance means (in accordance with article 3(1) of the *Regulated Activities Order*) any contract of insurance which is a *long-term insurance contract* or a *general insurance contract*.

contractually based investment has the meaning given by article 3(1) of the *Regulated Activities Order* but does not include an *investment* which falls within the definition of a packaged product.

contributions means contributions previously made to the *fund* in accordance with Part III of the Solicitors' Indemnity Rules 2007 (or any earlier corresponding provisions), and any additional sums paid in accordance with Rule 16 of the *SRA Indemnity Rules*.

controller has the meaning given in section 422 of *FSMA*.

costs means *your fees* and *disbursements*.

Council has the meaning given in section 87 of the *SA*.

court means any court, tribunal or inquiry of England and Wales, or a British court martial, or any court of another jurisdiction.

Court of Protection deputy

    (i)   for the purposes of the *SRA Accounts Rules* includes a deputy who was appointed by the Court of Protection as a receiver under the Mental Health Act 1983 before the commencement date of the Mental Capacity Act 2005; and

    (ii) for the purposes of the *SRA Authorisation Rules* also includes equivalents in other *Establishment Directive states*.

CPD means continuing professional development, namely, the training requirement(s) set by *us* to ensure *solicitors* and *RELs* maintain competence.

CPD training record means a record of all *CPD* undertaken to comply with the *SRA Training Regulations* Part 3 – CPD Regulations.

CPD year means each year commencing 1 November to 31 October.

CPE means the Common Professional Examination, namely, a course, including assessments and examinations, approved by the JASB for the purposes of completing the *academic stage of training* for those who have not satisfactorily completed a *QLD*.

credit agreement has the meaning given by article 60B(3) of the *Regulated Activities Order*.

credit broking means an activity of the kind specified in article 36A of the *Regulated Activities Order*.

credit-related regulated activity means any of the following activities specified in Part 2 or 3A of the *Regulated Activities Order*:

    (i)   entering into a regulated credit agreement as lender (article 60B(1);

    (ii) exercising, or having the right to exercise, the lender's rights and duties under a regulated credit agreement (article 60B(2));

    (iii) credit broking (article 36A);

    (iv) debt adjusting (article 39D(1) and (2));

    (v) debt counselling (article 39E(1) and (2));

    (vi) debt collecting (article 39F(1) and (2));

    (vii) debt administration (article 39G(1) and (2));

    (viii)entering into a regulated consumer hire agreement as owner (article 60N(1));

    (ix) exercising, or having the right to exercise, the owner's rights and duties under a regulated consumer hire agreement (article 60N(2));

(x) providing credit information services (article 89A);

(xi) providing credit references (article 89B);

(xii) operating an electronic system in relation to lending (article 36H);

(xiii)agreeing to carry on a regulated activity (article 64) so far as relevant to any of the activities in (i) to (xii);

which is carried on by way of business and relates to a specified investment applicable to that activity or, in the case of (x) and (xi), relates to information about a person's financial standing.

credit token means a card, check, voucher, coupon, stamp, form, booklet or other document or thing given to a *client* by a person carrying on a *credit-related regulated activity* ("the provider"), who undertakes that:

(i) on production of it (whether or not some other action is also required) the provider will supply cash, goods or services (or any of them) on credit; or

(ii) where, on the production of it to a third party (whether or not any other action is also required), the third party supplies cash, goods and services (or any of them), the provider will pay the third party for them (whether or not deducting any discount or commission), in return for payment to the provider by the *client* and the provider shall, without prejudice to the definition of credit, be taken to provide credit drawn on whenever a third party supplies the *client* with cash, goods or services; and

the use of an object to operate a machine provided by the person giving the object or a third party shall be treated as the production of the object to that person or third party.

criminal advocacy means advocacy in all hearings arising out of a police-led or Serious Fraud Office-led investigation and prosecuted in the criminal courts by the Crown Prosecution Service or the Serious Fraud Office but does not include hearings brought under the Proceeds of Crime Act 2002.

date of notification the date of any notification or notice given is deemed to be:

(i) the date on which the communication is sent electronically to the recipient's e-mail or fax address;

(ii) the date on which the communication is delivered to or left at the recipient's last notified *practising address* if the recipient is *practising*, or to the recipient's last notified contact address if the recipient is not *practising*; or

(iii) seven days after the communication has been sent by post or document exchange to the recipient's last notified *practising address* if the recipient is *practising*, or to the recipient's last notified contact address if the recipient is not *practising*.

debt management plan means a non-statutory agreement between a *client* and one or more of the *client's* lenders the aim of which is to discharge or liquidate the *client's* debts, by making regular payments to a third party which administers the plan and distributes the money to the lenders.

decision period is the period specified in Rule 5 of the *SRA Authorisation Rules*.

defaulting practitioner means:

(i) a *solicitor* in respect of whose act or default, or in respect of whose *employee's* act or default, an application for a grant is made;

(ii) an *REL* in respect of whose act or default, or in respect of whose *employee's* act or default, an application for a grant is made;

(iii) a *recognised body* in respect of whose act or default, or in respect of whose *manager's* or *employee's* act or default, an application for a grant is made;

(iv) an *RFL* who is a *manager* of a *partnership*, *LLP* or *company* together with a *solicitor*, an *REL* or a *recognised body*, and in respect of whose act or default or in respect of whose *employee's* act or default, an application for a grant is made; or

(v) a *licensed body* in respect of whose act or default, or in respect of whose *owner's*, or *manager's* or *employee's* act or default, an application for a grant is made;

and the expressions "defaulting solicitor", "defaulting *REL*", "defaulting recognised body", "defaulting *RFL*" and "defaulting licensed body" shall be construed accordingly.

defence costs means legal costs and disbursements and investigative and related expenses reasonably and necessarily incurred with the consent of the *insurer* in:

(i) defending any proceedings relating to a *claim*; or

(ii) conducting any proceedings for indemnity, contribution or recovery relating to a *claim*; or

(iii) investigating, reducing, avoiding or compromising any actual or potential *claim*; or

(iv) acting for any *insured* in connection with any investigation, inquiry or disciplinary proceeding (save in respect of any disciplinary proceeding under the authority of the *Society* (including, without limitation, the *SRA* and the *Tribunal*));

and does not include any internal or overhead expenses of the *insured firm* or the *insurer* or the cost of any *insured's* time.

difference in conditions policy means a contract of professional indemnity insurance, made between one or more *participating insurers* and a *firm*, which provides cover including the *MTC* as modified in accordance with paragraph 2 of Appendix 3 to the *SRA Indemnity Insurance Rules*.

director means a director of a company; and in relation to a *societas Europaea* includes:

(i) in a two-tier system, a member of the management organ and a member of the supervisory organ; and

(ii) in a one-tier system, a member of the administrative organ.

disbursement means, in respect of those activities for which the practice is regulated by the *SRA*, any sum spent or to be spent on behalf of the *client* or trust (including any VAT element).

disciplinary decision means a decision, following an *SRA finding*, to exercise one or more of the powers provided by:

(i) section 44D(2) and (3) of the *SA*;

(ii) paragraph 14B(2) and (3) of Schedule 2 to the *AJA*; or

(iii) section 95 or section 99 of the *LSA*;

or otherwise to give a *regulated person* a written rebuke or to publish details of a written rebuke or a direction to pay a penalty in accordance with the *SRA Disciplinary Procedure Rules*.

discipline investigation means:

(i) subject to sub-paragraph (ii), an investigation by the *SRA* to determine whether a person should be subject to an *SRA finding*, a *disciplinary decision* or an application to the *Tribunal* under Rule 10 of the *SRA Disciplinary Procedure Rules*; and

(ii) for the purposes of the *SRA Cost of Investigations Regulations*, an investigation by the *SRA* to determine whether a *regulated person* should be subject to an *SRA finding* or an application to the *Tribunal*.

discrimination has the meaning set out in the Equality Act 2010, namely if, because of a protected characteristic as set out in that Act, *person* A treats *person* B less favourably than A treats or would treat others.

disqualified refers to a *person* who has been disqualified under section 99 of the *LSA* by the *SRA* or by any other *approved regulator*,

and references to "disqualify" and "disqualification" should be construed accordingly.

document in Chapter 10 of the *SRA Code of Conduct*, includes documents, whether written or electronic, relating to the *firm's client accounts* and *office accounts*.

EEA means European Economic Area.

EEL means exempt European *lawyer*, namely, a member of an *Establishment Directive profession*:

(i) registered with the *BSB*; or

(ii) based entirely at an office or offices outside England and Wales, who is not a *lawyer of England and Wales* (whether entitled to *practise* as such or not).

eligible former principal means a *principal* of a *previous practice* where:

(i) that *previous practice* ceased on or before 31 August 2000; and

(ii) a *relevant claim* is made in respect of any matter which would have given rise to an entitlement of the *principal* to indemnity out of the *fund* under the Solicitors' Indemnity Rules 1999 had the claim been notified to Solicitors Indemnity Fund Limited on 31 August 2000; and

(iii) the *principal* has not at any time been a "principal" of the *relevant successor practice* ("principal" having the meaning applicable to the *SIIR*); and

(iv) at the time that the *relevant claim* is made the *principal* is not a "principal" in "private practice" ("principal" and "private practice" having the meanings applicable to the *SIIR*).

employee means an individual who is:

(i) engaged under a contract of service by a *firm* or its wholly owned service company;

(ii) engaged under a contract for services, made between a *firm* or organisation and:

　(A) that individual;

　(B) an employment agency; or

　(C) a *company* which is not held out to the public as providing legal services and is wholly owned and directed by that individual; or

(iii) a *solicitor*, *REL* or *RFL* engaged under a contract of service or a contract for services by an *authorised non-SRA firm*;

(iv) a *solicitor*, *REL* or *RFL* engaged under a contract of service or a contract for services by a person, business or organisation,

under which the *firm*, *authorised non-SRA firm*, person, business, or organisation has exclusive control over the individual's time for all or part of the individual's working week; or in relation to which the *firm* or organisation has designated the individual as a fee earner in accordance with arrangements between the *firm* or organisation and the Lord Chancellor (or any body established by the Lord Chancellor to provide or facilitate the provision of services) pursuant to the provisions of the Legal Aid, Sentencing and Punishment of Offenders Act 2012, save that:

(A) for the purposes of the *SRA Financial Services (Scope) Rules*, means an individual who is employed in connection with the *firm's regulated activities* under a contract of service or under a contract for services such that he or she is held out as an employee or consultant of the *firm*; and

(B) for the purposes of the *SRA Indemnity Insurance Rules*, means any person other than a *principal*:

(I) employed or otherwise engaged in the *insured firm's practice* (including under a contract for services) including, without limitation, as a *solicitor*, lawyer, *trainee solicitor* or trainee lawyer, consultant, associate, locum tenens, agent, *appointed person*, office or clerical staff member or otherwise;

(II) seconded to work in the *insured firm's practice*; or

(III) seconded by the *insured firm* to work elsewhere;

but does not include any person who is engaged by the *insured firm* under a contract for services in respect of any work where that person is required, whether under the *SRA Indemnity Insurance Rules* or under the rules of any other professional body, to take out or to be insured under separate professional indemnity insurance in respect of that work.

employer means a:

(i) *firm* which engages an individual under a contract of service either on its own behalf or through its wholly-owned service company;

(ii) *firm* or organisation which has engaged an individual under a contract for services made between the firm or organisation and:

(A) that individual;

(B) an employment agency; or

(C) a company which is not held out to the public as providing legal services and is wholly owned and directed by that individual; or

(iii) an *authorised non-SRA firm* which engages a *solicitor*, *REL* or *RFL* under a contract of service or a contract for services;

(iv) a person, business or organisation which engages a *solicitor*, *REL* or *RFL* under a contract of service or a contract for services,

under which the *firm*, *authorised non-SRA firm*, person, business or organisation has exclusive control over the individual's time for all or part of the individual's working week; or in relation to which the *firm* or organisation has designated the individual as a fee earner in accordance with arrangements between the *firm* or organisation and the Lord Chancellor (or any body established by the Lord Chancellor to provide or facilitate the provision of services) pursuant to the provisions of the Legal Aid, Sentencing and Punishment of Offenders Act 2012.

entitled to practise for the purposes of the *QLTSR* means having the right to practise without restrictions or conditions as a *qualified lawyer* of the *recognised jurisdiction*.

equivalent means means learning which is assessed and for which qualification(s) or certificates have been granted and/or work based experiential learning which *we* determine is of at least an equivalent level and standard of that required by all or any part of the *solicitor* qualification and training framework as set out in the *SRA Training Regulations*. *We* will assess equivalence in accordance with guidance *we* may issue from time to time.

established

(i) For the purpose of the definition of "overseas practice", the status of an individual as being established outside England and Wales may be indicated by any of the following factors:

(A) a requirement for a work permit;

(B) the intention to reside outside England and Wales for a period of six months or longer;

(C) a requirement for authorisation with local regulatory body;

(D) an overseas practising address nominated in mySRA;

(E) an employment contract with a legal practice established outside England and Wales.

(ii) An individual who is temporarily seconded, assigned or transferred to work in an overseas practice, being supervised and managed for the duration of his or her secondment, transfer or assignment, by *managers* in the overseas practice, will be treated as *practising overseas*.

Establishment Directive means the Establishment of Lawyers Directive 98/5/EC.

Establishment Directive profession means any profession listed in Article 1.2(a) of the *Establishment Directive*, including a solicitor, barrister or advocate of the *UK*.

Establishment Directive state means a state to which the *Establishment Directive* applies.

European corporate practice means a *lawyers'* practice which is a body incorporated in an *Establishment Directive state*, or a partnership with separate legal identity formed under the law of an *Establishment Directive state* and which is regulated as a *lawyers'* practice:

(i) which has an office in an *Establishment Directive state* but does not have an office in England and Wales;

(ii) whose ultimate beneficial owners include at least one individual who is not a *lawyer of England and Wales* but is, and is entitled to practise as, a *lawyer* of an *Establishment Directive profession*;

(iii) whose *managers* include at least one such individual, or at least one *body corporate* whose *managers* include at least one such individual; and

(iv) of which *lawyers* are entitled to exercise, or control the exercise of, more than 90% of the *voting rights*.

European cross-border practice has the meaning set out in Rule 2.1 of the *SRA European Cross-border Practice Rules*.

excess means the first amount of a *claim* which is not covered by the insurance.

execution-only means a *transaction* which is effected by a *firm* for a *client* where the *firm* assumes on reasonable grounds that the *client* is not relying on the *firm* as to the merits or suitability of that *transaction*.

Exempt European Practice means:

(i)   a *lawyer's* practice formed in an *Establishment Directive state* which is regulated as such in that state and which is a structure in which *lawyers* are permitted to practise in that state; and

(ii) whose ultimate beneficial owners do not include any *practising lawyers of England and Wales*; and

(iii) whose main place of business is situated and carried on in an *Establishment Directive state* other than the United Kingdom; and

(iv) which does not carry on any *reserved legal activity*.

exempt person in the *SRA Financial Services (Scope) Rules* means a *person* who is exempt from the *general prohibition* as a result of an exemption order made under section 38(1) or as a result of section 39(1) or 285(2) or (3) of *FSMA* and who, in engaging in the activity in question, is acting in the course of business in respect of which that *person* is exempt.

Exempting Law Degree means a *QLD* incorporating an *LPC*, approved by *us*.

existing instructions means instructions to carry out *legal activities* received by a *firm* from a client, which the *firm* has accepted, on terms that have been agreed by the client, prior to the *firm* becoming subject to cover under the *cessation period*.

expired run-off claim means any claim made against the *fund* for indemnity under the *SRA Indemnity Rules* in respect of which no *preceding qualifying insurance* remains in force to cover such claim, by reason only of:

(i)   the run-off cover provided or required to be provided under the policy having been activated; and

(ii) the sixth anniversary of the date on which cover under such *qualifying insurance* would have ended but for the activation of such run-off cover having passed; or

(iii) (in the case of a firm in default or a run-off firm) the period of run-off cover provided or required to be provided under arrangements made to cover such claim through the *ARP* having expired.

expired run-off cover means either:

(i) (unless (ii) below applies) the terms of the ARP policy in force at the time immediately prior to the date on which run-off cover was triggered under the *preceding qualifying insurance*, excluding clause 5 (Run-off cover) of the *MTC*, as if it were a contract between Solicitors Indemnity Fund Limited and the firm or person making an *expired run-off claim*; or

(ii) where they are provided to Solicitors Indemnity Fund Limited prior to payment of the *claim*, the terms of the *preceding qualifying insurance*, provided that:

  (A) references in the *preceding qualifying insurance* to the qualifying insurer that issued such insurance shall be read as references to Solicitors Indemnity Fund Limited;

  (B) any obligation owed by any *insured* under the *preceding qualifying insurance* to the qualifying insurer which issued such insurance shall be deemed to be owed to Solicitors Indemnity Fund Limited in place of such qualifying insurer, unless and to the extent that Solicitors Indemnity Fund Limited in its absolute discretion otherwise agrees;

  (C) the obligations of the *fund* and/or any *insured* in respect of an *expired run-off claim* shall neither exceed nor be less than the requirements of the *MTC* which, in accordance with the applicable *SIIR*, such *preceding qualifying insurance* included or was required to include.

Solicitors Indemnity Fund Limited shall be under no obligation to take any steps to obtain the terms of any such *preceding qualifying insurance*, which for these purposes includes the terms on which it was written in respect of the *insured firm* or person in question, and not merely a standard policy wording.

extended indemnity period means the period commencing at the end of the *policy period* and ending on the date which is the earlier to occur of:

(i) the date, if any, on which the *firm* obtains a *policy* of *qualifying insurance* incepting on and with effect from the day immediately following the expiration of the *policy period*;

(ii) the date which is 30 days after the end of the *policy period*; or

(iii) the date on which the *insured firm's practice* ceases.

FCA means the Financial Conduct Authority.

fees means *your* own charges or profit costs (including any VAT element).

fee sharer means another *person* or business who or which shares *your* fees.

financial benefit includes any commission, discount or rebate, but does not include your *fees* or interest earned on any *client account*.

financial institution means any undertaking or unincorporated association which carries on a business of lending money (which may include mortgage lending) or otherwise providing or issuing credit including, without limitation, any bank or *building society*.

Financial Services Register means the record maintained by the *FCA* as required by section 347 of *FSMA* and including those *persons* who carry on, or are proposing to carry on, *insurance mediation activities*.

firm means:

   (i)   save as provided in paragraphs (ii) and (iii) below, an *authorised body* or a body or *person* which should be authorised by the *SRA* as a *recognised body* or whose practice should be authorised as a *recognised sole practice* (but which could not be authorised by another *approved regulator*); and for the purposes of the *SRA Code of Conduct* and the *SRA Accounts Rules* can also include in-house practice;

   (ii)   in the *SRA Indemnity Insurance Rules*:

      (A)   any *recognised body* (as constituted from time to time); or

      (B)   any *solicitor* or *REL* who is a *sole practitioner*, unless that *sole practitioner* is a *non-SRA firm*; or

      (C)   any *partnership* (as constituted from time to time) which is eligible to become a *recognised body* and which meets the requirements applicable to *recognised bodies* set out in the *SRA Practice Framework Rules* and the *SRA Authorisation Rules*, unless that *partnership* is a *non-SRA firm* or an *Exempt European Practice*; or

      (D)   any *licensed body* in respect of its *regulated activities*;

      whether before or during any relevant *indemnity period*;

   (iii)   in the *SRA European Cross-border Practice Rules*, means any business through which a *solicitor* or *REL* carries on *practice* other than *in-house practice*.

firm (overseas) means any business through which a *solicitor* or *REL* carries on practice other than in-house practice.

foreign lawyer means an individual who is not a *solicitor* or barrister of England and Wales, but who is a member, and entitled to practise as such, of a legal profession regulated within a jurisdiction outside England and Wales.

foundations of legal knowledge means those foundations of law the study of which is prescribed by *us* and the *BSB* for the purpose of completing the *academic stage of training* by undertaking a *QLD* or *CPE* and passing the assessments and examinations set during that course.

FSMA means the Financial Services and Markets Act 2000.

full accreditation means *accreditation* to conduct *criminal advocacy* under the *SRA QASA Regulations*, and references to "fully accredited" should be construed accordingly.

full route to qualification means that the applicant has not completed a shortened or fast-track route to qualification, which would be evidenced if non-domestic lawyers are not assessed on all the same outcomes/subjects/practices in the law of that jurisdiction as domestic candidates, prior to qualification.

full time in relation to a period of *recognised training*, means working 32 hours a week or more.

fund means the fund maintained in accordance with the *SRA Indemnity Rules*.

funeral plan contract has the meaning given in article 59 of the *Regulated Activities Order*.

general client account has the meaning given in Rule 13.5(b) of the *SRA Accounts Rules*.

general insurance contract means any *contract of insurance* within Part I of Schedule 1 to the *Regulated Activities Order*.

general prohibition has the meaning given in section 19(2) of *FSMA*.

high-cost short-term credit means a *regulated credit agreement*:

    (i)   which is a borrower-lender agreement or a P2P agreement;

    (ii) in relation to which the APR is equal to or exceeds 100%;

    (iii) either:

        (A) in relation to which a financial promotion indicates (by express words or otherwise) that the credit is to be provided for any period up to a maximum of 12 months or otherwise indicates (by express words or otherwise) that the credit is to be provided for a short term; or

        (B) under which the credit is due to be repaid or substantially repaid within a maximum of 12 months of the date on which the credit is advanced;

    (iv) which is not secured by a mortgage, charge or *pledge*; and

    (v) which is not:

        (A) a *credit agreement* in relation to which the lender is a community finance organisation; or

        (B) a home credit loan agreement, a bill of sale loan agreement or a borrower-lender agreement enabling a borrower to overdraw on a current account or arising where the holder of a current account overdraws on the account without a pre-arranged overdraft or exceeds a pre-arranged overdraft limit.

higher courts means the Crown Court, High Court, Court of Appeal and Supreme Court in England and Wales.

higher courts advocacy qualification means, subject to regulation 6 of the *SRA Higher Rights of Audience Regulations*, one of the qualifications referred to in regulation 3 of those regulations to exercise extended rights of audience in the *higher courts*.

HOFA means a Head of Finance and Administration within the meaning of paragraph 13(2) of Schedule 11 to the *LSA*.

holding company has the meaning given in the Companies Act 2006.

HOLP means a Head of Legal Practice within the meaning of paragraph 11(2) of Schedule 11 to the *LSA*.

home purchaser has the meaning given by article 63F(3) of the *Regulated Activities Order*.

immigration work means the provision of immigration advice and immigration services, as defined in section 82 of the Immigration and Asylum Act 1999.

indemnity period means:

(i) in the *SRA Indemnity Insurance Rules*, the period of one year starting on 1 September 2000, 2001 or 2002, the period of 13 calendar months starting on 1 September 2003, or the period of one year starting on 1 October in any subsequent calendar year; and

(ii) in the *SRA Indemnity Rules*, the period of one year commencing on 1 September in any calendar year from 1987 to 2002 inclusive, the period of 13 calendar months commencing on 1 September 2003, and the period of one year commencing on 1 October in any subsequent calendar year.

independent financial adviser means an adviser who provides unbiased and unrestricted advice based on a comprehensive and fair analysis of the relevant market and discloses this in writing to the *client*.

individual pension contract means a *pension policy* or *pension contract* under which contributions are paid to:

(i) a *personal pension scheme* approved under section 630 of the Income and Corporation Taxes Act 1988, whose sole purpose is the provision of annuities or lump sums under arrangements made by individuals in accordance with the scheme; or

(ii) a retirement benefits scheme approved under section 591(2)(g) of the Income and Corporation Taxes Act 1988, for the provision of relevant benefits by means of an annuity contract made with an insurance company of the *employee's* choice.

in-house practice means *practice* as a *solicitor*, *REL* or *RFL* (as appropriate) in accordance with Rules 1.1(c)(ii), 1.1(d)(ii), 1.1(e), 1.2(f), 2.1(c)(ii), 2.1(d)(ii), 2.1(e), 2.2(f), 3.1(b)(ii) or 3.1(c)(ii) of the *SRA Practice Framework Rules* and "in-house" shall be construed accordingly.

Insolvency Code of Ethics means the Code of Ethics produced by the *Joint Insolvency Committee* and adopted by the *SRA*.

insolvency event means in relation to a *participating insurer*:

   (i)   the appointment of a provisional liquidator, administrator, receiver or an administrative receiver; or

  (ii) the approval of a voluntary arrangement under Part I of the Insolvency Act 1986 or the making of any other form of arrangement, composition or compounding with its creditors generally; or

 (iii) the passing of a resolution for voluntary winding up where the winding up is or becomes a creditors' voluntary winding up under Part IV of the Insolvency Act 1986; or

  (iv) the making of a winding up order by the court; or

  (v) the making of an order by the court reducing the value of one or more of the *participating insurer's* contracts under section 377 of *FSMA*; or

  (vi) the occurrence of any event analogous to any of the foregoing insolvency events in any jurisdiction outside England and Wales.

insolvency practice means accepting an appointment or acting as an appointment holder as an insolvency practitioner within the terms of the Insolvency Act 1986 and other related legislation.

insurance mediation activity means any of the following activities specified in the *Regulated Activities Order* which is carried on in relation to a *contract of insurance* or rights to or interests in a *life policy*:

   (i)   dealing in *investments* as agent;

  (ii) arranging (bringing about) deals in *investments*;

 (iii) making arrangements with a view to *transactions* in *investments*;

  (iv) assisting in the administration and performance of a *contract of insurance*;

  (v) advising on *investments*;

  (vi) agreeing to carry on a *regulated activity* in (i) to (v) above.

insurance mediation officer means the individual within the management structure of the *firm* who is responsible for an *insurance mediation activity*.

insurance undertaking means an undertaking, whether or not an *insurer*, which carries on insurance business.

insured in the *SRA Indemnity Insurance Rules* means each person and entity named or described as a person to whom the insurance extends and includes, without limitation, those referred to in clause 1.3 in the *MTC* and, in relation to *prior practices* and *successor practices* respectively, those referred to in clauses 1.5 and 1.7 of the *MTC*.

insured firm means the *firm* (as defined for the purposes of the *SRA Indemnity Insurance Rules*) which contracted with the *insurer* to provide the insurance.

insured firm's practice means:

(i)   the legal *practice* carried on by the *insured firm* as at the commencement of the *period of insurance*; and

(ii) the continuous legal *practice* preceding and succeeding the *practice* referred to in paragraph (i) (irrespective of changes in ownership of the *practice* or in the composition of any *partnership* which owns or owned the *practice*).

insurer means:

(i)   for the purposes of the SRA Financial Services (Conduct of Business) Rules 2001 a firm with permission to effect or carry out *contracts of insurance* (other than a bank); and

(ii) for the purposes of the *SRA Indemnity Insurance Rules* the underwriter(s) of the insurance.

interest includes a sum in lieu of interest.

interest holder means a *person* who has an interest or an indirect interest, or holds a *material interest*, in a body (and "indirect interest" and "interest" have the same meaning as in the *LSA*), and references to "holds an interest" shall be construed accordingly.

international lawyers means lawyers who are not basing their application on a professional qualification as a *qualified lawyer* gained within the *UK* or within the EEA or Switzerland.

intervened practitioner means the *solicitor, recognised body, licensed body, REL* or *RFL* whose *practice* or *practices* are the subject of an *intervention*.

intervention means the exercise of the powers specified in section 35 of and Schedule 1 to the *SA*, or section 9 of and paragraphs 32 to 35 of Schedule 2 to the *AJA*, or section 89 of and paragraph 5 of Schedule 14 to the Courts and Legal Services Act 1990, or section 102 of and Schedule 14 to the *LSA*.

introducer means any person, business or organisation who or that introduces or refers *clients* to your business, or recommends your business to *clients* or otherwise puts you and *clients* in touch with each other.

investment means any of the *investments* specified in Part III of the *Regulated Activities Order*.

investment trust means a closed-ended *company* which is listed in the *UK* or another member state and:

(i) is approved by HM Revenue and Customs under section 842 of the Income and Corporation Taxes Act 1988 (or, in the case of a newly formed *company*, has declared its intention to conduct its affairs so as to obtain approval); or

(ii) is resident in another member state and would qualify for approval if resident and listed in the *UK*.

investment trust savings scheme means a dedicated service for investment in the securities of one or more *investment trusts* within a particular marketing group (and references to an "investment trust savings scheme" include references to securities to be acquired through that scheme).

ISA means an Individual Savings Account, namely, an account which is a scheme of investment satisfying the conditions prescribed in the Individual Savings Account Regulations 1998 (S.I. 1998/1870).

Joint Insolvency Committee means the Committee formed by the Insolvency Service, the recognised professional bodies under the Insolvency Act 1986 and other related legislation, and appointed lay representatives.

Joint Statement means the Joint Statement on Qualifying Law Degrees, prepared jointly by *us* and the *BSB*, setting out the conditions a law degree course must meet in order to be recognised by *us* as a *QLD*.

knowledge of any matter, includes any matter of which you may reasonably be expected to have knowledge.

LASPO means the Legal Aid, Sentencing and Punishment of Offenders Act 2012.

lawyer means a member of one of the following professions, entitled to practise as such:

(i) the profession of solicitor, barrister or advocate of the *UK*;

(ii) a profession whose members are authorised to carry on *legal activities* by an *approved regulator* other than the *SRA*;

(iii) an *Establishment Directive profession* other than a *UK* profession;

(iv) a legal profession which has been approved by the *SRA* for the purpose of *recognised bodies* in England and Wales; and

(v) any other regulated legal profession specified by the *SRA* for the purpose of this definition.

lawyer-controlled body means:

(i) an *authorised body* in which *lawyers of England and Wales* constitute the national group of *lawyers* with the largest (or equal largest) share of control of the body either as individual *managers* or by their share in the control of bodies which are *managers*;

(ii) for the purposes of Part 7 (Overseas practice) of the *SRA Accounts Rules* the definition at sub-paragraph (i) above applies save that the second reference to "lawyers" is to be given its natural meaning and the references to *managers* are to be read as *managers (overseas)*.

lawyer of England and Wales means:

(i) a *solicitor*; or

(ii) an individual who is authorised to carry on *legal activities* in England and Wales by an *approved regulator* other than the *SRA*, but excludes a member of an *Establishment Directive profession* registered with the *BSB* under the *Establishment Directive*.

lead insurer means the insurer named as such in the contract of insurance, or, if no lead insurer is named as such, the first-named insurer on the relevant certificate of insurance.

legal activity has the meaning given in section 12 of the *LSA*, and includes any *reserved legal activity* and any other activity which consists of the provision of legal advice or assistance, or representation in connection with the application of the law or resolution of legal disputes.

Legal Ombudsman means the scheme administered by the Office for Legal Complaints under Part 6 of the *LSA*.

legal or equitable mortgage includes a legal or equitable charge and, in Scotland, a heritable security.

legally qualified body means any of the following:

(i) a *recognised body*;

(ii) a *licensed body* of which *lawyers* are entitled to exercise, or control the exercise of, 90% or more of the *voting rights* of that *licensed body*;

(iii) an *authorised non-SRA firm* of which *lawyers* are entitled to exercise, or control the exercise of, 90% or more of the *voting rights* of that *authorised non-SRA firm*; or

(iv) a *European corporate practice*,

and for the purposes of section 9A(6)(h) and (6C) of the *AJA* means a body which would meet the requirement in Rule 13.2 of the *SRA Practice Framework Rules*.

legal services body means a body which meets the criteria in Rule 13.1 of the *SRA Practice Framework Rules*.

Level 7 Higher Apprenticeship in Legal Practice (Wales) means the standard approved by the Welsh Government in March 2015 and as varied from time to time.

licensable body means a body which meets the criteria in Rule 14 (Eligibility criteria and fundamental requirements for licensed bodies) of the *SRA Practice Framework Rules*.

licensed body means a body licensed by the *SRA* under Part 5 of the *LSA*.

licensing authority means an *approved regulator* which is designated as a licensing authority under Part 1 of Schedule 10 to the *LSA*, and whose licensing rules have been approved for the purposes of the *LSA*.

life office means a *person* with permission to effect or carry out *long-term insurance contracts*.

life policy means a *long-term insurance contract* other than a *pure protection contract* or a *reinsurance contract*, but including a *pension policy*.

LLP means a limited liability partnership incorporated under the Limited Liability Partnerships Act 2000.

local authority means any of those bodies which are listed in section 270 of the Local Government Act 1972 or in section 21(1) of the Local Government and Housing Act 1989.

long-term care insurance contract has the meaning given in Part II of Schedule 1 to the *Regulated Activities Order*.

long-term insurance contract has the meaning given in Part II of Schedule 1 to the *Regulated Activities Order*.

LPC means a Legal Practice Course, namely, a course, the satisfactory completion of which is recognised by *us* as satisfying, in part, the vocational stage of training.

LSA means the Legal Services Act 2007.

manager means:

    (i)   a *member* of an *LLP*;

    (ii) a *director* of a *company*;

    (iii) a *partner* in a *partnership*; or

(iv) in relation to any other body, a member of its governing body.

manager (overseas) means:

(i) a member of an *LLP*;

(ii) a director of a company;

(iii) a *partner* in a *partnership*; or

(iv) in relation to any other body, a member of its governing body.

market making means where a *firm* holds itself out as willing, as principal, to buy, sell or subscribe for *investments* of the kind to which the *transaction* relates at prices determined by the *firm* generally and continuously rather than in respect of each particular *transaction*.

master policy means a policy referred to in Rule 5 of the *SRA Indemnity Rules*.

master policy insurer means an insurer under a *master policy*.

material interest has the meaning given to it in Schedule 13 to the *LSA*; and a person holds a "material interest" in a body ("B"), if that person:

(i) holds at least 10% of the shares in B;

(ii) is able to exercise significant influence over the management of B by virtue of the person's shareholding in B;

(iii) holds at least 10% of the shares in a parent undertaking ("P") of B;

(iv) is able to exercise significant influence over the management of P by virtue of the person's shareholding in P;

(v) is entitled to exercise, or control the exercise of, voting power in B which, if it consists of *voting rights*, constitutes at least 10% of the *voting rights* in B;

(vi) is able to exercise significant influence over the management of B by virtue of the person's entitlement to exercise, or control the exercise of, *voting rights* in B;

(vii) is entitled to exercise, or control the exercise of, voting power in P which, if it consists of *voting rights*, constitutes at least 10% of the *voting rights* in P; or

(viii) is able to exercise significant influence over the management of P by virtue of the person's entitlement to exercise, or control the exercise of, *voting rights* in P;

and for the purpose of this definition, "person" means:

(i) the *person*,

(ii) any of the *person's* associates, or

(iii) the *person* and any of the *person's* associates taken together;

and "parent undertaking" and "voting power" are to be construed in accordance with paragraphs 3 and 5 of Schedule 13 to the *LSA*.

MDP means a *licensed body* which is a multi-disciplinary practice providing a range of different services, only some of which are regulated by the *SRA*.

member

(i) means:

(A) in relation to a *company*, a *person* who has agreed to be a member of the *company* and whose name is entered in the *company's* register of members; and

(B) in relation to an *LLP*, a member of that *LLP*; save that

(ii) for the purposes of the *SRA Indemnity Rules*, means a member of a practice, being:

(A) any principal (including any *principal*) therein;

(B) any *director* or officer thereof, in the case of a *recognised body* or a *licensed body* which is a *company*;

(C) any member thereof in the case of a *recognised body* or a *licensed body* which is an *LLP*;

(D) any *recognised body* or a *licensed body* which is a *partner* or held out to be a *partner* therein and any officer of such *recognised body* or a *licensed body* which is a *company*, or any member of such *recognised body* or a *licensed body* which is an *LLP*;

(E) any person employed in connection therewith (including any *trainee solicitor*);

(F) any *solicitor* or *REL* who is a consultant to or associate in the practice;

(G) any *foreign lawyer* who is not an *REL* and who is a consultant or associate in the practice; and

(H) any *solicitor* or *foreign lawyer* who is working in the practice as an agent or locum tenens, whether he or she is so working under a contract of service or contract for services;

and includes the estate and/or personal representative(s) of any such persons.

members of the public for the purposes of Chapter 8 of the *SRA Code of Conduct*, does not include:

(i) a current or former *client*;

(ii) another *firm* or its *manager*;

(iii) an existing or potential professional or business connection; or

(iv) a commercial organisation or public body.

mixed payment has the meaning given in Rule 18.1 of the *SRA Accounts Rules*.

MTC means the minimum terms and conditions with which a *policy* of *qualifying insurance* is required by the *SRA Indemnity Insurance Rules* to comply, a copy of which is annexed as Appendix 1 to those Rules.

non-lawyer means:

    (i)   an individual who is not a *lawyer* practising as such; or

    (ii) a *body corporate* or *partnership* which is not:

        (A) an *authorised body*;

        (B) an *authorised non-SRA firm*; or

        (C) a business, carrying on the practice of *lawyers* from an office or offices outside England and Wales, in which a controlling majority of the *owners* and *managers* are *lawyers*;

save in Part 7 (Overseas) of the *SRA Accounts Rules* where the term "lawyer" is to be given its natural meaning.

non-mainstream regulated activity means a *regulated activity* of a *firm* regulated by the *FCA* in relation to which the conditions in the Professional Firms' Sourcebook (5.2.1R) are satisfied.

non-registered European lawyer means:

    (i)   in the *SRA Indemnity Rules*, a member of a legal profession which is covered by the *Establishment Directive*, but who is not:

        (A) a *solicitor*, *REL* or *RFL*,

        (B) a barrister of England and Wales, Northern Ireland or the Irish Republic, or

        (C) a Scottish advocate; and

    (ii) in the *SRA Financial Services (Scope) Rules*, a member of a profession covered by the *Establishment Directive* who is based entirely at an office or offices outside England and Wales and who is not a solicitor, *REL* or *RFL*.

non-reserved legal activity means a legal activity that falls within section 12(3)(b) of the *LSA*.

non-solicitor employer means any *employer* other than a *recognised body*, *recognised sole practice*, *licensed body* or *authorised non-SRA firm*.

non-SRA firm means a *sole practitioner*, *partnership*, *LLP* or *company* which is not authorised to practise by the *SRA*, and which is either:

    (i)   authorised or capable of being authorised to practise by another *approved regulator*; or

(ii) not capable of being authorised to practise by any *approved regulator*.

occupational pension scheme means any scheme or arrangement which is comprised in one or more documents or agreements and which has, or is capable of having, effect in relation to one or more descriptions or categories of employment so as to provide benefits, in the form of pensions or otherwise, payable on termination of service, or on death or retirement, to or in respect of earners with qualifying service in an employment of any such description or category.

office account means an account of the *firm* for holding *office money* and/or *out-of-scope money*, or other means of holding *office money* or *out-of-scope money* (for example, the office cash box or an account holding money regulated by a regulator other than the *SRA*).

office money has the meaning given in Rule 12 of the *SRA Accounts Rules*.

office money (overseas) means money which belongs to you or your *overseas practice*. This includes money held or received in respect of:

(i) the running of your *overseas practice*, for example sales tax on your practice's *fees*;

(ii) *fees* due to you or your *overseas practice* against a bill or written notification of *costs* incurred which has been delivered to the *client* or paying party; and

(iii) *disbursements* already paid by you or your *overseas practice*;

(iv) *disbursements* incurred but not yet paid by you or your *overseas practice*, but excluding unpaid *professional disbursements*.

opt-out means a *transaction* resulting from a decision by an individual to opt-out of or decline to join a final salary or money-purchase *occupational pension scheme* of which he or she is a current member, or which he or she is, or at the end of a waiting period will become, eligible to join, in favour of an *individual pension contract* or contracts.

out-of-scope money means money held or received by an *MDP* in relation to activities that are not *regulated activities*.

overseas means outside England and Wales.

overseas practice

(i) means:

(A) a branch office of an *authorised body*;

(B) a *subsidiary company* of an *authorised body*;

(C) a subsidiary undertaking, within the meaning of section 1162 of the Companies Act 2006, of an *authorised body*;

(D) an entity whose business, management or ownership are otherwise in fact or law controlled by an *authorised body*;

(E) an individual acting as a representative (whether as an employee or agent) of an *authorised body*; or

(F) a sole principal whose business, management or ownership are otherwise in fact or law controlled by an *authorised body*,

established outside England and Wales and providing legal services; and

(ii) in the *SRA Indemnity Rules* means a *practice* carried on wholly from an *overseas* office or offices, including a *practice* deemed to be a *separate practice* by virtue of paragraph (ii) of the definition of *separate practice*.

own interest conflict for the purpose of Chapter 3 of the *SRA Code of Conduct*, means any situation where your duty to act in the best interests of any *client* in relation to a matter conflicts, or there is a significant risk that it may conflict, with your own interests in relation to that or a related matter.

owner means, in relation to a body, a *person* with any interest in the body, save that:

(i) in the *SRA Authorisation Rules*, the *SRA Practice Framework Rules* and the *SRA Practising Regulations* owner means any *person* who holds a *material interest* in an *authorised body*, and in the case of a *partnership*, any *partner* regardless of whether they hold a *material interest* in the *partnership*; and

(ii) for the purposes of the *SRA Principles* and the *SRA Code of Conduct* means a *person* who holds a *material interest* in the body; and

(iii) for the purposes of the *SRA Suitability Test* includes owners who have no active role in the running of the business as well as owners who do,

and "own" and "owned by" shall be construed accordingly.

panel solicitors means any solicitors appointed by the Solicitors Indemnity Fund in accordance with Rule 14.15 of the *SRA Indemnity Rules*.

participating insurer means an *authorised insurer* which has entered into a *participating insurer's agreement* with the *Society* which remains in force for the purposes of underwriting new business at the date on which the relevant contract of *qualifying insurance* is made.

participating insurer's agreement means an agreement in such terms as the *Society* may prescribe setting out the terms and conditions on which a *participating insurer* may provide professional indemnity insurance to *solicitors* and others in *private practice* in England and Wales.

partner means a *person* who is or is held out as a partner in a *partnership*.

partnership means a body that is not a *body corporate* in which *persons* are, or are held out as, *partners*, save that in the *MTC* means an unincorporated *insured firm* in which *persons* are or are held out as *partners* and does not include an *insured firm* incorporated as an *LLP*.

part-time in relation to a *period of recognised training* means working fewer than 32 hours a week.

pawn means any article subject to a *pledge*.

pawnee means a person who takes any article in pawn and includes any person to whom the rights and duties of the original *pawnee* have passed by assignment or operation of law.

payment includes any form of consideration whether any benefit is received by you or by a third party (but does not include the provision of hospitality that is reasonable in the circumstances) and "pay" and "paid" shall be construed accordingly.

pension contract means a right to benefits obtained by the making of contributions to an *occupational pension scheme* or to a *personal pension scheme*, where the contributions are paid to a *regulated collective investment scheme*.

pension policy means a right to benefits obtained by the making of contributions to an *occupational pension scheme* or to a *personal pension scheme*, where the contributions are paid to a *life office*.

pension transfer means a *transaction* resulting from a decision by an individual to transfer deferred benefits from a final salary *occupational pension scheme*, or from a money-purchase *occupational pension scheme*, in favour of an *individual pension contract* or contracts.

PEP means a personal equity plan within the Personal Equity Plan Regulations 1989.

period of insurance means the period for which the insurance operates.

person includes a body of persons (corporate or unincorporated).

person under investigation means a *person* subject to a *discipline investigation*.

person who has an interest in a licensed body means a *person* who has an interest or an indirect interest in a *licensed body* as defined by sections 72(3) and (5) of the *LSA*.

person who lacks capacity under Part 1 of the Mental Capacity Act 2005 includes a "patient" as defined by section 94 of the Mental Health Act 1983 and a person made the subject of emergency powers under that Act, and equivalents in other *Establishment Directive states*.

personal pension scheme means any scheme or arrangement which is not an *occupational pension scheme* or a *stakeholder pension scheme* and which is comprised in one or more instruments or agreements, having or capable of having effect so as to provide benefits to or in respect of people on retirement, or on having reached a particular age, or on termination of service in an employment.

plan provider has the meaning given by article 63B(3) of the *Regulated Activities Order* read with paragraphs (7) and (8) of that article.

pledge means a *pawnee's* rights over an article taken in *pawn*.

policy means a contract of professional indemnity insurance made between one or more *persons*, each of which is a *participating insurer*, and a *firm*.

policy default

(i) means in the *SRA Indemnity Insurance Rules* a failure on the part of a *firm* or any *principal* of that *firm*:

   (A) to pay for more than two months after the due date for payment all or any part of the premium or any other sum due in respect of a *policy*; or

   (B) to reimburse within two months a *participating insurer* in respect of any amount falling within a *firm's policy* excess which has been paid on an *insured's* behalf to a *claimant* by a *participating insurer*;

(ii) for the purposes of this definition, the due date for payment means, in respect of any *policy* or any payment to be made under any *policy*:

   (A) the date on which such payment fell due under the terms of the *policy* or any related agreement or arrangement; or

   (B) if a *firm* was first required under the *SIIR* to effect such a *policy* prior to the date on which it did so, the date if earlier on which such payment would have fallen due had such *policy* been effected by the *firm* when it was first required to do so under the *SIIR*.

policy period means the *period of insurance* in respect of which risks may attach under a *policy*, but excluding the *extended indemnity period* and the *cessation period*.

practice means the activities, in that capacity, of:

(i) a *solicitor*;

(ii) an *REL*, from an office or offices within the *UK*;

(iii) a member of an *Establishment Directive profession* registered with the *BSB* under the *Establishment Directive*, carried out from an office or offices in England and Wales;

(iv) an *RFL*, from an office or offices within England and Wales, as:

   (A) an *employee* of a *recognised sole practice*; or

(B) a *manager, employee, member* or *interest holder* of an *authorised body* or a *manager, employee* or owner of an *authorised non-SRA firm*;

(v) an *authorised body*;

(vi) a *manager* of an *authorised body*;

(vii) a person employed in England and Wales by an *authorised body*;

(viii)a *lawyer of England and Wales*; or

(ix) an *authorised non-SRA firm*;

and "practise" and "practising" should be construed accordingly; save for in:

(i) the *SRA Indemnity Insurance Rules* where "practice" means the whole or such part of the *private practice* of a *firm* as is carried on from one or more offices in England and Wales;

(ii) the *SRA Indemnity Rules* where it means a practice to the extent that:

(A) in relation to a *licensed body*, it carries on *regulated activities*; and

(B) in all other cases, it carries on *private practice* providing professional services as a sole *solicitor* or *REL* or as a *partnership* of a type referred to in Rule 6.1(d) to 6.1(f) and consisting of or including one or more *solicitors* and/or *RELs*, and shall include the business or practice carried on by a *recognised body* in the providing of professional services such as are provided by individuals practising in *private practice* as *solicitors* and/or *RELs* or by such individuals in *partnership* with *RFLs*, whether such practice is carried on by the *recognised body* alone or in *partnership* with one or more *solicitors, RELs* and/or other *recognised bodies*; and

(iii) in the *SRA Overseas Rules* where it shall be given its natural meaning.

practice from an office includes *practice* carried on:

(i) from an office at which you are based; or

(ii) from an office of a *firm* in which you are the *sole practitioner*, or a *manager*, or in which you have an ownership interest, even if you are not based there,

save that for the purposes of Part 7 (Overseas) of the *SRA Accounts Rules* the term "practice" is to be given its natural meaning, and references to "firm" and "manager" are to be read as references to "*firm (overseas)*" and to "*manager (overseas)*";

and "practising from an office" and "practises from an office" should be construed accordingly.

practice of a lawyer of a CCBE state means the activities of a *lawyer* of a *CCBE state* in that capacity.

Practice Skills Standards means the standards published by *us* which set out the practice skills *trainees* will develop during the *period of recognised training* and use when qualified.

practising address means, in relation to an *authorised body*, an address from which the body provides services consisting of or including the carrying on of activities which it is authorised to carry on.

practising overseas means the conduct of a practice:

- (i)   of an overseas practice;
- (ii) of a manager, member or owner of an overseas practice in that capacity;
- (iii) of a solicitor *established* outside England and Wales for the purpose of providing legal services in an overseas jurisdiction; and
- (iv) of an REL *established* in Scotland or Northern Ireland for the purpose of providing legal services in those jurisdictions.

preceding qualifying insurance means, in the case of any *firm* or person who makes an *expired run-off claim*, the policy of *qualifying insurance* which previously provided run-off cover in respect of that *firm* or person, or which was required to provide such cover, or (in the case of a firm in default or a run-off firm) arrangements to provide such run-off cover through the *ARP*.

pre-contract deposit means the aggregate of all payments which constitute pre-contract deposits from a *buyer* in relation to the proposed sale of a *property*.

prescribed means prescribed by the *SRA* from time to time.

previous practice means any *practice* which shall have ceased to exist as such for whatever reason, including by reason of:

- (i)   any death, retirement or addition of *principals*; or
- (ii) any split or cession of the whole or part of its practice to another without any change of *principals*.

previous regulations in the *SRA Higher Rights of Audience Regulations* means either the Higher Courts Qualification Regulations 1992, the Higher Courts Qualification Regulations 1998, or the Higher Courts Qualification Regulations 2000, or the Solicitors Higher Rights of Audience Regulations 2010.

principal

- (i)   subject to paragraphs (ii) to (iv) means:
    - (A)   a *sole practitioner*;
    - (B)   a *partner* in a *partnership*;

(C) in the case of a *recognised body* which is an *LLP* or *company*, the *recognised body* itself;

(D) in the case of a *licensed body* which is an *LLP* or *company*, the *licensed body* itself;

(E) the principal *solicitor* or *REL* (or any one of them) employed by a *non-solicitor employer* (for example, in a law centre or in commerce and industry); or

(F) in relation to any other body, a member of its governing body;

(ii) in the *SRA Authorisation Rules*, *SRA Practice Framework Rules* and *SRA Practising Regulations*, means a *sole practitioner* or a *partner* in a *partnership*;

(iii) in the *SRA Indemnity Insurance Rules* means:

  (A) where the *firm* is or was:

   (I) a *sole practitioner* – that practitioner;

   (II) a *partnership* – each *partner*;

   (III) a *company* with a share capital – each *director* of that *company* and any *person* who:

    (01) is held out as a *director*; or

    (02) beneficially owns the whole or any part of a share in the *company*; or

    (03) is the ultimate beneficial owner of the whole or any part of a share in the *company*;

   (IV) a *company* without a share capital – each *director* of that *company* and any *person* who:

    (01) is held out as a *director*; or

    (02) is a *member* of the *company*; or

    (03) is the ultimate owner of the whole or any part of a *body corporate* or other legal person which is a *member* of the *company*;

   (V) an *LLP* – each *member* of that *LLP*, and any *person* who is the ultimate owner of the whole or any part of a *body corporate* or other legal person which is a *member* of the *LLP*;

  (B) where a *body corporate* or other legal person is a *partner* in the *firm*, any *person* who is within paragraph (A)(III) of this definition (including sub-paragraphs (01) and (03) thereof), paragraph (A)(IV) of this definition (including sub-paragraphs (01) and (03) thereof), or paragraph (A)(V) of this definition;

(iv) in the *SRA Indemnity Rules*, means:

(A) a *solicitor* who is a *partner* or a sole *solicitor* within the meaning of section 87 of the *SA*, or an *REL* who is a *partner*, or who is a sole practitioner, or an *RFL* or *non-registered European lawyer* who is a *partner*, and includes any *solicitor*, *REL*, *RFL* or *non-registered European lawyer* held out as a principal; and

(B) additionally in relation to a *practice* carried on by a *recognised body* or a *licensed body* alone, or a *practice* in which a *recognised body* or a *licensed body* is or is held out to be a *partner*:

    (I) a *solicitor*, *REL*, *RFL* or *non-registered European lawyer* (and in the case of a *licensed body* any other person) who:

        (01) beneficially owns the whole or any part of a share in such *recognised body* or *licensed body* (in each case, where it is a *company* with a share capital); or

        (02) is a member of such *recognised body* or *licensed body* (in each case, where it is a *company* without a share capital or an *LLP* or a *partnership* with legal personality); or

    (II) a *solicitor*, *REL*, *RFL* or *non-registered European lawyer* (and in the case of a *licensed body* any other person) who is:

        (01) the ultimate beneficial owner of the whole or any part of a share in such *recognised body* or *licensed body* (in each case, where the *recognised* body or *licensed body* is a *company* with a share capital); or

        (02) the ultimate owner of a member or any part of a member of such *recognised body* or *licensed body* (in each case, where the *recognised body* or *licensed body* is a *company* without a share capital or an *LLP* or a *partnership* with legal personality).

prior practice means each *practice* to which the *insured firm's practice* is ultimately a *successor practice* by way of one or more mergers, acquisitions, absorptions or other transitions, but does not include any such *practice* which has elected to be insured under run-off cover in accordance with clause 5.6(a) of the *MTC*.

private legal practice means the provision of services in *private practice* as a *solicitor* or *REL* including, without limitation:

    (i) providing such services in England, Wales or anywhere in the world, whether alone or with other lawyers in a *partnership* permitted to practise in England and Wales by Rule 12 of the Solicitors' Code of Conduct 2007 or by the *SRA Practice Framework Rules*, a *recognised body* or a *licensed body* (in respect of its *regulated activities*); and

    (ii) the provision of such services as a secondee of the *insured firm*; and

(iii) any *insured* acting as a personal representative, *trustee*, attorney, notary, insolvency practitioner or in any other role in conjunction with a *practice*; and

(iv) the provision of such services by any *employee*; and

(v) the provision of such services pro bono publico;

but does not include:

(vi) practising as an *employee* of an employer other than a *solicitor*, an *REL*, a *partnership* permitted to practise in England and Wales by Rule 12 of the Solicitors' Code of Conduct 2007 or by the *SRA Practice Framework Rules*, a *recognised body* or a *licensed body* (in respect of its *regulated activities*); or

(vii) discharging the functions of any of the following offices or appointments:

(A) judicial office;

(B) Under Sheriffs;

(C) members and clerks of such tribunals, committees, panels and boards as the *Council* may from time to time designate but including those subject to the Tribunals and Inquiries Act 1992, the Competition Commission, Legal Services Commission Review Panels, Legal Aid Agency Review Panels and Parole Boards;

(D) Justices' Clerks; or

(E) Superintendent Registrars and Deputy Superintendent Registrars of Births, Marriages and Deaths and Registrars of Local Crematoria.

private loan means a loan other than one provided by an institution which provides loans on standard terms in the normal course of its activities.

private practice

(i) for the purposes of the *SRA Indemnity Insurance Rules*:

(A) in relation to a *firm* which is a *licensed body* means its *regulated activities*; and

(B) subject to paragraph (A) of this definition, in relation to all *firms* includes without limitation all the professional services provided by the *firm* including acting as a personal representative, trustee, attorney, notary, insolvency practitioner or in any other role in conjunction with a *practice*, and includes services provided pro bono publico,

but does not include:

(C) *practice* carried on by a *solicitor* or *REL* in the course of employment with an employer other than a *firm*; or

(D) *practice* carried on through a *non-SRA firm* or by an *REL* through an *Exempt European Practice*; or

(E) discharging the functions of any of the following offices or appointments:

  (I) judicial office;

  (II) Under Sheriffs;

  (III) members and clerks of such tribunals, committees, panels and boards as the *Council* may from time to time designate but including those subject to the Tribunals and Inquiries Act 1992, the Competition Commission, Legal Services Commission Review Panels, Legal Aid Agency Review Panels and Parole Boards;

  (IV) Justices' Clerks;

  (V) Superintendent Registrars and Deputy Superintendent Registrars of Births, Marriages and Deaths and Registrars of Local Crematoria; or

  (VI) such other offices as the *Council* may from time to time designate;

(F) *practice* consisting only of providing professional services without remuneration for friends, relatives, or to companies wholly owned by the *solicitor* or *REL's* family, or registered charities; or

(G) in respect of a sole *solicitor* or a sole *REL*, *practice* consisting only of:

  (I) providing professional services without remuneration for friends, relatives, or to companies wholly owned by the *solicitor* or *REL's* family, or registered charities; and/or

  (II) administering oaths and statutory declarations; and/or

  (III) activities which could constitute *practice* but are done in the course of discharging the functions of any of the offices or appointments listed in paragraphs (E)(I) to (VI) above.

(ii) for the purposes of the *SRA Indemnity Rules* "private practice" shall be deemed to include:

  (A) the acceptance and performance of obligations as trustees; and

  (B) notarial practice where a solicitor notary operates such notarial practice in conjunction with a solicitor's practice, whether or not the notarial fees accrue to the benefit of the solicitor's practice;

but does not include:

  (C) practice to the extent that any fees or other income accruing do not accrue to the benefit of the *practice* carrying on such practice (except as provided by paragraph (B) in this definition);

  (D) practice by a *solicitor* or *REL* in the course of his or her employment with an employer other than a *solicitor*, *REL*, *recognised body*, *licensed body* or *partnership* such as is referred to in Rule 6.1(d) to 6.1(f); in which connection and for the avoidance of doubt:

(I) any such *solicitor* or *REL* does not carry on private practice when he or she acts in the course of his or her employment for persons other than his or her employer;

(II) any such *solicitor* or *REL* does not carry on private practice merely because he or she uses in the course of his or her employment a style of stationery or description which appears to hold him or her out as a *principal* or *solicitor* or *foreign lawyer* in private practice; or

(III) any practice carried on by such a *solicitor* outside the course of his or her employment will constitute private practice;

(E) discharging the functions of the following offices:

(I) judicial office;

(II) Under Sheriffs;

(III) members and clerks of such tribunals, committees, panels and boards as the *Council* may from time to time designate but including those subject to the Tribunals and Inquiries Act 1992, the Competition Commission, Legal Services Commission Review Panels and Parole Boards;

(IV) Justices' Clerks;

(V) Superintendent Registrars and Deputy Superintendent Registrars of Births, Marriages and Deaths and Registrars of Local Crematoria;

(VI) such other offices as the *Council* may from time to time designate.

professional activity means a professional activity which is regulated by the *SRA*.

professional contact means professional contact which is regulated by the *SRA*.

professional disbursement means, in respect of those activities for which the practice is regulated by the *SRA*, the fees of counsel or other *lawyer*, or of a professional or other agent or expert instructed by *you*, including the fees of interpreters, translators, process servers, surveyors and estate agents but not travel agents' charges.

professional principles are as set out in section 1(3) of the *LSA*:

(i) that authorised persons should act with independence and integrity;

(ii) that authorised persons should maintain proper standards of work;

(iii) that authorised persons should act in the best interests of their *clients*;

(iv) that persons who exercise before any *court* a right of audience, or conduct litigation in relation to proceedings in any *court*, by virtue of being author-ised persons should comply with their duty to the *court* to act with independ-ence in the interests of justice; and

(v) that the affairs of *clients* should be kept confidential,

and in this definition "authorised persons" has the meaning set out in section 18 of the *LSA*.

professional services means, for the purposes of the *SRA Financial Services (Scope) Rules*, services provided by a *firm* in the course of its *practice* and which do not constitute carrying on a *regulated activity*.

prohibited referral fee means

(i) a *payment* prohibited by section 56 of *LASPO*; or

(ii) a *payment* made to or by you which appears to the *SRA* to be a referral fee for the purposes of section 57(7) of *LASPO*, unless you show that the *payment* was made as consideration for the provision of services or for another reason and not as a referral fee.

property includes an interest in property.

property selling means things done by any person in the course of a business (including a business in which they are *employed*) pursuant to instructions received from another person (in this definition referred to as the "*client*") who wishes to dispose of or acquire an interest in land:

(i) for the purpose of, or with a view to, effecting the introduction to the *client* of a third person who wishes to acquire or, as the case may be, dispose of such an interest; and

(ii) after such an introduction has been effected in the course of that business, for the purpose of securing the disposal or, as the case may be, the acquisition of that interest.

provisional accreditation means accreditation to conduct *criminal advocacy* under the *SRA QASA Regulations* but which requires further steps to be taken to obtain *full accreditation*, and references to "provisionally accredited" should be construed accordingly.

PSC means the Professional Skills Course, namely, a course normally completed during the training contract, building upon the *LPC*, providing training in Financial and Business Skills, Advocacy and Communication Skills, and Client Care and Professional Standards. Satisfactory completion of the PSC is recognised by *us* as satisfying, in part, the vocational stage of training.

publicity includes all promotional material and activity, including the name or descrip-tion of your *firm*, stationery, advertisements, brochures, websites, directory entries, media appearances, promotional press releases, and direct approaches to potential *clients* and other *persons*, whether conducted in person, in writing, or in electronic form, but does not include press releases prepared on behalf of a *client*.

pure protection contract means:

  (i) a *long-term insurance contract*:

    (A) under which the benefits are payable only in respect of death or of incapacity due to injury, sickness or infirmity;

    (B) which has no surrender value or the consideration consists of a single premium and the surrender value does not exceed that premium; and

    (C) which makes no provision for its conversion or extension in a manner which would result in its ceasing to comply with (A) or (B); or

  (ii) a *reinsurance contract* covering all or part of a risk to which a *person* is exposed under a *long-term insurance contract*.

QASA means the Quality Assurance Scheme for Advocates (Crime) developed by the Joint Advocacy Group and described in full in the QASA Handbook published from time to time and available at: **http://www.sra.org.uk**.

QLD means a qualifying law degree, namely, a degree or qualification awarded by a body approved by the JASB for the purposes of completing the *academic stage of training*, following a course of study which includes:

  (i) the study of the *foundations of legal knowledge*; and

  (ii) the passing of appropriate assessments set in those foundations.

QLTR means the Qualified Lawyers Transfer Regulations 1990 and 2009.

QLTSR means the *SRA* Qualified Lawyers Transfer Scheme Regulations 2010 and 2011.

QLTS assessments means the suite of assessments approved by *us* and provided by the *assessment organisation*.

QLTT means the Qualified Lawyers Transfer Test, namely, the test which some lawyers are required to pass under the *QLTR*.

qualified lawyer means either:

  (i) a lawyer whose qualification *we* have determined:

    (A) gives the lawyer rights of audience;

    (B) makes the lawyer an officer of the court in the *recognised jurisdiction*; and

    (C) has been awarded as a result of a generalist (non-specialist) legal education and training; or

(ii) any other lawyer to whom *we* determine Directive 2005/36/EC on the recognition of professional qualifications applies.

qualified to supervise means a person complying with the requirements of Rule 12.2 of the *SRA Practice Framework Rules*.

qualifying insurance means a *policy* that provides professional indemnity insurance cover in accordance with the *MTC* but only to the extent required by the *MTC*.

re-accreditation means the process by which a *solicitor* or an *REL* demonstrates their competence and renews their *accreditation* under the *SRA QASA Regulations* at their existing level for a further five years.

recognised body means a body recognised by the *SRA* under section 9 of the *AJA*.

recognised jurisdiction means a jurisdiction where *we* have determined that:

(i) to become a *qualified lawyer* applicants have completed specific education and training at a level that is at least equivalent to that of an English/Welsh H-Level (e.g. Bachelor's) degree;

(ii) members of the *qualified lawyer's* profession are bound by an ethical code that requires them to act without conflicts of interest and to respect their client's interests and confidentiality; and

(iii) members of the *qualified lawyer's* profession are subject to disciplinary sanctions for breach of their ethical code, including the removal of the right to practise, and

all European jurisdictions to which Directive 2005/36/EC on the recognition of professional qualifications apply are "recognised jurisdictions" for the purposes of the *QLTSR*.

recognised sole practice means the *practice* of a sole *solicitor* or *REL* which is recognised by the *SRA* under section 9 of the *AJA*.

recognised sole practitioner means a *solicitor* or *REL* authorised by the *SRA* under section 1B of the *SA* to practise as a *sole practitioner*.

recognised training means training required under *SRA Training Regulations* Regulation 5.1, and "period of recognised training" and "recognise training" should be construed accordingly.

reconciled accounts means that all elements of the accounting records of an *intervened practitioner's practice* are consistent with each other.

reconciled list means a list of beneficial entitlements to *statutory trust monies* created from a set of *reconciled accounts*.

record of training means a record created and maintained by a *trainee*, which contains details of the work he or she has performed, how the *trainee* has acquired, applied and developed his or her skills by reference to the *Practice Skills Standards* and the *Principles*, and the *trainee's* reflections on his or her performance and development plans, and is verified by the individual(s) supervising the *trainee*.

referral includes any situation in which another person, business or organisation introduces or refers a *client* to your business, recommends your business to a *client* or otherwise puts you and a *client* in touch with each other.

register of European lawyers means the register of European lawyers maintained by the *SRA* under regulation 15 of the European Communities (Lawyer's Practice) Regulations 2000 (SI 2000/1119).

register of foreign lawyers means the register of foreign lawyers maintained by the *SRA* under the Courts and Legal Services Act 1990.

regular payment has the meaning given in Rule 19 of the *SRA Accounts Rules*.

Regulated Activities Order means the Financial Services and Markets Act 2000 (Regulated Activities) Order 2001.

regulated activity means:

    (i)   subject to sub-paragraph (ii) below:

        (A)   any *reserved legal activity*;

        (B)   any *non-reserved legal activity* except, in relation to an *MDP*, any such activity that is excluded on the terms of the licence;

        (C)   any other activity in respect of which a *licensed body* is regulated pursuant to Part 5 of the *LSA*; and

    (ii) in the *SRA Financial Services (Scope) Rules*, an activity which is specified in the *Regulated Activities Order*.

regulated collective investment scheme means:

    (i)   an investment *company* with variable capital;

    (ii) an authorised unit trust scheme as defined in section 237(3) of *FSMA*; or

    (iii) a scheme recognised under sections 264, 270 or 272 of *FSMA*.

regulated consumer hire agreement has the meaning given by article 60N(3) of the *Regulated Activities Order*.

regulated credit agreement has the meaning given by article 60B(3) of the *Regulated Activities Order*.

regulated home purchase plan has the meaning given by article 63F(3) of the *Regulated Activities Order*.

regulated home reversion plan has the meaning given by article 63B(3) of the *Regulated Activities Order*.

regulated individual means:

    (i)   a solicitor;

    (ii) an REL; and

    (iii) a manager, member or owner of an *overseas practice*.

regulated mortgage contract has the meaning given by article 61(3) of the *Regulated Activities Order*.

regulated person

    (i)   in the *SRA Indemnity Rules* has the meaning given in section 21 of the *LSA*;

    (ii) means, in the *SRA Disciplinary Procedure Rules*:

        (A) a *solicitor*;

        (B) an *REL*;

        (C) an *RFL*;

        (D) a *sole practitioner* in a *recognised sole practice*;

        (E) a *recognised body*;

        (F) a *manager* of a *recognised body*;

        (G) a *licensed body*;

        (H) a *manager* of a *licensed body*;

        (I) an *employee* of, or in, an *authorised body*, a *solicitor*, or an *REL*; or

        (J) to the extent permitted by law, any person who has previously held a position or role described in (A) to (I) above;

    (iii) for the purposes of the *SRA Cost of Investigations Regulations* means the persons at paragraph (ii) (A) to (I) above and also includes a *person who has an interest in a licensed body* and, to the extent permitted by law, any person who has previously held an interest in a *licensed body*.

regulated sale and rent back agreement has the meaning given by article 63J(3) of the *Regulated Activities Order*.

regulatory arrangements has the meaning given to it by section 21 of the *LSA*, and includes all rules and regulations of the *SRA* in relation to the authorisation, *practice*, conduct, discipline and qualification of persons carrying on *legal activities* and the accounts rules and indemnification and compensation arrangements in relation to their *practice*.

regulatory objectives has the meaning given to it by section 1 of the *LSA* and includes the objectives of protecting and promoting the public interest, supporting the constitutional principle of the rule of law, improving access to justice, protecting and promoting the interests of consumers, promoting competition in the provision of *legal activities* by *authorised persons*, encouraging an independent, strong, diverse and effective legal profession, increasing public understanding of the citizen's legal rights and duties, and promoting and maintaining adherence to the *professional principles*.

reinsurance contract means a *contract of insurance* covering all or part of a risk to which a *person* is exposed under a *contract of insurance*.

REL means registered European lawyer, namely, an individual registered with the *SRA* under regulation 17 of the European Communities (Lawyer's Practice) Regulations 2000 (SI 2000/ no.1119).

REL-controlled body means an *authorised body* in which *RELs*, or *RELs* together with *lawyers of England and Wales* and/or European lawyers registered with the *BSB*, constitute the national group of lawyers with the largest (or equal largest) share of control of the body, either as individual *managers (overseas)* or by their share in the control of bodies which are *managers (overseas)*, and for this purpose *RELs* and European lawyers registered with the *BSB* belong to the national group of England and Wales.

related authorised body means an *authorised body* which has a *manager, owner* or *sole practitioner* in common with another *authorised body*.

related body in relation to *in-house practice* means a body standing in relation to your *employer* as specified in Rule 4.7(a) to (d) or 4.15(c) of the *SRA Practice Framework Rules*.

relevant claim means a claim made on or after 1 September 2000 against a *relevant successor practice*.

relevant indemnity period in relation to *contributions* or indemnity means that *indemnity period* in respect of which such *contributions* are payable or such indemnity is to be provided in accordance with the *SRA Indemnity Rules*.

relevant insolvency event occurs in relation to a body if:

(i) a resolution for a voluntary winding up of the body is passed without a declaration of solvency under section 89 of the Insolvency Act 1986;

(ii) the body enters administration within the meaning of paragraph 1(2)(b) of Schedule B1 to that Act;

(iii) an administrative receiver within the meaning of section 251 of that Act is appointed;

(iv) a meeting of creditors is held in relation to the body under section 95 of that Act (creditors' meeting which has the effect of converting a *members' voluntary* winding up into a creditors' voluntary winding up);

(v) an order for the winding up of the body is made;

(vi) all of the *managers* in a body which is unincorporated have been adjudicated bankrupt; or

(vii) the body is an overseas company or a *societas Europaea* registered outside England, Wales, Scotland and Northern Ireland and the body is subject to an event in its country of incorporation analogous to an event as set out in paragraphs (i) to (vi) above.

relevant licensed body means a *licensed body* other than:

(i) an unlimited company, or an *overseas* company whose members' liability for the company's debts is not limited by its constitution or by the law of its country of incorporation; or

(ii) a nominee company only, holding *assets* for clients of another *practice*; and

(A) it can act only as agent for the other *practice*; and

(B) all the individuals who are *principals* of the *licensed body* are also *principals* of the other *practice*; and

(C) any fee or other income arising out of the *licensed body* accrues to the benefit of the other *practice*; or

(iii) a *partnership* in which none of the *partners* is a limited company, an *LLP* or a legal person whose *members* have limited liability.

relevant recognised body means a *recognised body* other than:

(i) an unlimited company, or an *overseas* company whose members' liability for the company's debts is not limited by its constitution or by the law of its country of incorporation; or

(ii) a nominee company only, holding *assets* for clients of another *practice*; and

(A) it can act only as agent for the other *practice*; and

(B) all the individuals who are *principals* of the *recognised body* are also *principals* of the other *practice*; and

(C) any fee or other income arising out of the *recognised body* accrues to the benefit of the other *practice*; or

(iii) a *partnership* in which none of the *partners* is a limited company, an *LLP* or a legal person whose *members* have limited liability; or

(iv) a *sole practitioner* that is a *recognised body*.

relevant successor practice means in respect of a *previous practice*, a *successor practice* or a "successor practice" (as defined in Appendix 1 to the *SIIR*) (as may be applicable) against which a *relevant claim* is made.

relevant work-based experience means experience which an *authorised training provider* may recognise as satisfying up to six months of the period of *recognised training*, and which:

(i) has been gained in the preceding three years;

(ii) was in English and Welsh law and practice and in one or more areas of law;

(iii) enabled the acquisition of one or more of the *Practice Skills Standards* and/or the *Principles*; and

(iv) was adequately supervised and appraised.

representative in the *SRA Compensation Fund Rules*, means the personal representative of a deceased *defaulting practitioner*; the *trustee* of a bankrupt *defaulting practitioner*; the administrator of an insolvent *defaulting practitioner*, or other duly appointed representative of a *defaulting practitioner*.

reserved legal activity has the meaning given in section 12 of the *LSA*, and includes the exercise of a right of audience, the conduct of litigation, reserved instrument activities, probate activities, notarial activities and the administration of oaths, as defined in Schedule 2 to the *LSA*.

reserved work means activities which *persons* are authorised by the *SRA* to carry out, or prohibited from carrying out, under the *SRA Practice Framework Rules*.

responsible authorised body in respect of an *overseas practice* means the *authorised body* referred to in whichever of paragraph (i)(A) to (F) of the definition of "overseas practice" is applicable to that practice.

retail investment product has the meaning given in the Financial Conduct Authority Handbook.

reversion seller has the meaning given by article 63B(3) of the *Regulated Activities Order*.

revocation in relation to a practising certificate or registration under the *SRA Practising Regulations* includes withdrawal of a practising certificate or registration for the purposes of the *SA* and cancellation of registration for the purposes of Schedule 14 to the Courts and Legal Services Act 1990.

RFL means registered foreign lawyer, namely, an individual registered with the *SRA* under section 89 of the Courts and Legal Services Act 1990.

running account credit means a facility under a *credit agreement* under which the borrower or another person is enabled to receive from time to time from the lender, or a third party, cash, goods or services to an amount or value such that, taking into account payments made by or to the credit of the borrower, the credit limit (if any) is not at any time exceeded.

SA means the Solicitors Act 1974.

secondment means the temporary transfer of a *trainee* to an organisation other than his or her *authorised training provider*, the *authorised training provider* remaining responsible for ensuring that the requirements of the *SRA Training Regulations* are met.

section 43 investigation means an investigation by the *SRA* as to whether there are grounds for the *SRA*:

    (i)   to make an order under section 43(2) of the *SA*; or

    (ii) to make an application to the *Tribunal* for it to make such an order.

security has the meaning given by article 3(1) of the *Regulated Activities Order* but does not include an *investment* which falls within the definition of a packaged product.

separate business means a business, wherever situated, which you *own*, are *owned by*, *actively participate in* or are *connected with* and which is not any of the following:

    (i)   an *authorised body*, an *authorised non-SRA firm*, or an *overseas practice*; or

    (ii) an *in-house practice* or practice overseas which is permitted by the *SRA Practice Framework Rules*.

separate designated client account has the meaning given in Rule 13.5(a) of the *SRA Accounts Rules*.

separate practice means:

    (i)   a *practice* in which the number and identity of the *principals* is not the same as the number and identity of the *principals* in any other *practice*. When the same *principals* in number and identity carry on *practice* under more than one name or style, there is only one *practice*;

    (ii) in the case of a *practice* of which more than 25% of the *principals* are *foreign lawyers*, any *overseas* offices shall be deemed to form a separate practice from the offices in England and Wales;

    (iii) in the case of an *overseas* office of a *practice*, the fact that a *principal* or a limited number of *principals* represent all the *principals* in the *practice* on a local basis shall not of itself cause that *overseas* office to be a separate practice provided that any fee or other income arising out of that office accrues to the benefit of the *practice*; and

    (iv) in the case of a *recognised body* or *licensed body* the fact that all of the shares in the *recognised body* or *licensed body* (as the case may be) are beneficially owned by only some of the *principals* in another *practice*, shall not, of itself, cause such a *recognised body* or *licensed body* (as the case may be) to be a separate practice provided that any fee or other income arising out of the *recognised body* or *licensed body* accrues to the benefit of that other *practice*.

shareowner means:

(i) a *member* of a company with a share capital, who owns a share in the body; or

(ii) a *person* who is not a *member* of a company with a share capital, but owns a share in the body, which is held by a *member* as nominee.

SIF means the Solicitors Indemnity Fund.

SIIR means the Solicitors' Indemnity Insurance Rules 2000 to 2010, the SRA Indemnity Insurance Rules 2011 to 2012 or the *SRA Indemnity Insurance Rules* or any rules subsequent thereto.

societas Europaea means a European public limited liability company within the meaning of Article 1 of Council Regulation 2157/2001/EC.

Society means the Law Society, in accordance with section 87 of the *SA*.

sole practitioner means a *solicitor* or an *REL practising* as a sole principal in a *practice* (other than an incorporated *practice*) and does not include a *solicitor* or an *REL practising in-house*, save for the purposes of:

(i) the *SRA Accounts Rules* and *SRA Indemnity Insurance Rules* where references to "practising" are to be given their natural meaning; and

(ii) the *SRA Authorisation Rules* where it includes (as the context may require) a *solicitor* or *REL* intending to *practise* as a sole principal in a *practice* (other than incorporated *practice*).

solicitor means a person who has been admitted as a solicitor of the Senior Courts of England and Wales and whose name is on the roll kept by the *Society* under section 6 of the *SA*, save that in the *SRA Indemnity Insurance Rules* includes a person who *practises* as a solicitor whether or not he or she has in force a practising certificate, and also includes *practice* under home title of a former *REL* who has become a solicitor.

SRA means the Solicitors Regulation Authority, and reference to the SRA as an *approved regulator* or *licensing authority* means the SRA carrying out regulatory functions assigned to the *Society* as an *approved regulator* or *licensing authority*.

SRA Accounts Rules means the SRA Accounts Rules 2011.

SRA Admission Regulations means the SRA Admission Regulations 2011.

SRA Authorisation Rules means the SRA Authorisation Rules 2011.

SRA Code of Conduct means the SRA Code of Conduct 2011.

SRA Compensation Fund Rules means the SRA Compensation Fund Rules 2011.

SRA Cost of Investigations Regulations means the SRA Cost of Investigations Regulations 2011.

SRA Disciplinary Procedure Rules means the SRA Disciplinary Procedure Rules 2011.

SRA European Cross-border Practice Rules means the SRA European Cross-border Practice Rules 2011.

SRA Financial Services (Scope) Rules means the SRA Financial Services (Scope) Rules 2001.

SRA finding means:

(i) for the purposes of the *SRA Disciplinary Procedure Rules*, a decision that the *SRA* is satisfied:

(A) that a *regulated person* (which for the avoidance of doubt, shall include a *solicitor*) has failed to comply with a requirement imposed by or made under the *SA*, the *AJA* or the *LSA*;

(B) in relation to a *solicitor*, that there has been professional misconduct; or

(C) that a *HOLP, HOFA, manager, employee, person who has an interest in a licensed body*, or any other person has (intentionally or through neglect) caused or substantially contributed to a significant breach of the terms of the *licensed body's* licence, or has failed to comply with duties imposed by section 90, 91, 92 or 176 of the *LSA* as appropriate,

and for the avoidance of doubt does not include:

(D) investigatory decisions such as to require the production of information or *documents*;

(E) directions as to the provision or obtaining of further information or explanation;

(F) decisions to stay or adjourn;

(G) authorisation of the making of an application to the *Tribunal*;

(H) authorisation of an *intervention* pursuant to the *SA*, the *AJA*, the Courts and Legal Services Act 1990 or Schedule 14 to the *LSA*;

(I) a letter of advice from the *SRA*;

and

(ii) for the purposes of the *SRA Cost of Investigations Regulations*, a decision that the *SRA* is satisfied:

(A) that a *regulated person* has failed to comply with a requirement imposed by or made under the *SA*, the *AJA* or the *LSA*;

(B)   in relation to a *solicitor*, that there has been professional misconduct.

SRA Handbook means the handbook published from time to time by the *SRA* and containing its *regulatory arrangements*.

SRA Handbook Glossary means the SRA Handbook Glossary 2012, and references to the "Glossary" shall be interpreted accordingly.

SRA Higher Rights of Audience Regulations means the SRA Higher Rights of Audience Regulations 2011.

SRA Indemnity Insurance Rules means the SRA Indemnity Insurance Rules 2013.

SRA Indemnity Rules means the SRA Indemnity Rules 2012.

SRA Insolvency Practice Rules means the SRA Insolvency Practice Rules 2012.

SRA Overseas Rules means the SRA Overseas Rules 2013.

SRA Practice Framework Rules means the SRA Practice Framework Rules 2011.

SRA Practising Regulations means the SRA Practising Regulations 2011.

SRA Principles means the SRA Principles in the *SRA Handbook* and "Principles" shall be interpreted accordingly.

SRA QASA Regulations means the SRA Quality Assurance Scheme for Advocates (Crime) Regulations 2013.

SRA Quality Assurance Scheme for Advocates (Crime) Notification Regulations means the SRA Quality Assurance Scheme for Advocates (Crime) Notification Regulations 2012.

SRA Statutory Trust Rules means the SRA Intervention Powers (Statutory Trust) Rules 2011.

SRA Suitability Test means the SRA Suitability Test 2011.

SRA Training Regulations means the SRA Training Regulations 2014.

stakeholder pension scheme means a scheme established in accordance with Part I of the Welfare and Pensions Reform Act 1999 and the Stakeholder Pension Scheme Regulations 2000.

statement of standards means the "statement of standards for solicitor higher court advocates" issued by *us*.

statutory trust means the trust created by Schedule 1 of the *SA*, or Schedule 14 of the *LSA*, over monies vesting in the *Society* following an *intervention*.

statutory trust account means an account in which *statutory trust monies* are held by the *Society*.

statutory trust monies means the monies vested in the *Society* under the *statutory trust*.

statutory undertakers means:

(i) any persons authorised by any enactment to carry on any railway, light railway, tramway, road transport, water transport, canal, inland navigation, dock, harbour, pier or lighthouse undertaking or any undertaking for the supply of hydraulic power; and

(ii) any licence holder within the meaning of the Electricity Act 1989, any public gas supplier, any water or sewerage undertaker, the Environment Agency, any public telecommunications operator, the Post Office, the Civil Aviation Authority and any relevant airport operator within the meaning of Part V of the Airports Act 1986.

subsidiary company has the meaning given in the Companies Act 2006.

substantially common interest for the purposes of Chapter 3 of the *SRA Code of Conduct*, means a situation where there is a clear common purpose in relation to any matter or a particular aspect of it between the *clients* and a strong consensus on how it is to be achieved and the *client conflict* is peripheral to this common purpose.

successor practice

(i) means a *practice* identified in this definition as 'B', where:

  (A) 'A' is the *practice* to which B succeeds; and

  (B) 'A's owner' is the owner of A immediately prior to transition; and

  (C) 'B's owner' is the owner of B immediately following transition; and

  (D) 'transition' means merger, acquisition, absorption or other transition which results in A no longer being carried on as a discrete legal *practice*.

(ii) B is a successor practice to A where:

  (A) B is or was held out, expressly or by implication, by B's owner as being the successor of A or as incorporating A, whether such holding out is contained in notepaper, business cards, form of electronic communications, publications, promotional material or otherwise, or is contained in any statement or declaration by B's owner to any regulatory or taxation authority; and/or

(B)   (where A's owner was a *sole practitioner* and the transition occurred on or before 31 August 2000) – the *sole practitioner* is a *principal* of B's owner; and/or

(C)   (where A's owner was a *sole practitioner* and the transition occurred on or after 1 September 2000) – the *sole practitioner* is a *principal* or *employee* of B's owner; and/or

(D)   (where A's owner was a *recognised body* or a *licensed body* (in respect of its *regulated activities*)) – that body is a *principal* of B's owner; and/or

(E)   (where A's owner was a *partnership*) – the majority of the *principals* of A's owner have become *principals* of B's owner; and/or

(F)   (where A's owner was a *partnership* and the majority of *principals* of A's owner did not become *principals* of the owner of another legal *practice* as a result of the transition) – one or more of the *principals* of A's owner have become *principals* of B's owner and:

(I)   B is carried on under the same name as A or a name which substantially incorporates the name of A (or a substantial part of the name of A); and/or

(II)   B is carried on from the same premises as A; and/or

(III)   the owner of B acquired the goodwill and/or *assets* of A; and/or

(IV)   the owner of B assumed the liabilities of A; and/or

(V)   the majority of staff employed by A's owner became *employees* of B's owner.

(iii)   Notwithstanding the foregoing, B is not a successor practice to A under paragraph (ii) (B), (C), (D), (E) or (F) if another *practice* is or was held out by the owner of that other *practice* as the successor of A or as incorporating A, provided that there is insurance complying with the *MTC* in relation to that other *practice*.

sum insured means the *insurer's* limit of liability under a *policy* in respect of any one *claim* (exclusive of *defence costs*).

supplementary run-off cover means run-off cover provided by the Solicitors Indemnity Fund following the expiry of run-off cover provided to a *firm* in accordance with the *SRA Indemnity Insurance Rules* or otherwise under a *policy* (but subject to compliance with the *MTC*).

temporary practice overseas means the situation where:

(i)   a *solicitor* is practising but not established overseas; or

(ii)   an *REL* is practising from an office in Scotland or Northern Ireland,

but the solicitor or REL is not *practising overseas*.

trainee solicitor means any person receiving *recognised training* with the express purpose of qualification as a *solicitor*, at an *authorised training provider* and "trainee" should be construed accordingly.

training principal means a *solicitor* or *barrister* nominated by an *authorised training provider* and who meets the requirements of regulation 13 of the SRA Training Regulations 2014 – Qualification and Provider Regulations to oversee *recognised training* within that organisation.

transaction means the purchase, sale, subscription or underwriting of a particular *investment*.

Tribunal means the Solicitors Disciplinary Tribunal which is an independent statutory tribunal constituted under section 46 of the *SA* but references to the Tribunal do not include the Tribunal when it is performing any function as an *appellate body*.

trustee includes a personal representative, and "trust" includes the duties of a personal representative.

turnover in the *SRA Compensation Fund Rules* means the amounts derived from the provision of goods and services in the most recent financial year, after deduction of:

(A) trade discounts,

(B) value added tax, and

(C) any other taxes based on the amounts so derived.

UK means United Kingdom.

UK qualified lawyer in the *QLTSR*, means solicitors and barristers qualified in Northern Ireland, solicitors and advocates qualified in Scotland and *barristers* qualified in England and Wales.

unadmitted person means a person who:

(i) has requested us to assess a *character and suitability* issue under regulation 6 of the SRA Training Regulations 2014 – Qualification and Provider Regulations;

(ii) has commenced a period of *recognised training* under regulation 5 of the SRA Training Regulations 2014 – Qualification and Provider Regulations;

(iii) is seeking to establish eligibility to apply for admission under regulation 2 of the *QLTSR*; or

(iv) is seeking admission pursuant to Directive 2005/36/EC;

but who has not been admitted as a *solicitor*, and "unadmitted persons" should be construed accordingly.

undertaking means a statement, given orally or in writing, whether or not it includes the word "undertake" or "undertaking", made by or on behalf of you or your *firm*, in the course of *practice*, or by you outside the course of *practice* but as a *solicitor* or *REL*, to someone who reasonably places reliance on it, that you or your *firm* will do something or cause something to be done, or refrain from doing something.

us means the *SRA*, and "our" and "ourselves" should be construed accordingly.

vocational stage means:

   (i)   the *LPC*;

  (ii) a required period of *recognised training*; and

 (iii) the *PSC*.

voting rights in a body includes the right to vote in a partners', members', directors' or shareholders' meeting, or otherwise in relation to the body, and "control the exercise of voting rights" shall be interpreted as including de facto as well as legal control over such rights.

we means the *SRA*, and "our" and "ourselves" should be construed accordingly.

without delay means, in normal circumstances, either on the day of receipt or on the next working day.

you means:

   (i)   for the purposes of the *SRA Training Regulations* any person intending to be a *solicitor*, other than those seeking admission under the *QLTSR*;

  (ii) for the purposes of the SRA Training Regulations 2011 Part 3 a *solicitor* or an *REL*;

 (iii) for the purposes of the *SRA Admission Regulations* any person intending to be a *solicitor*;

 (iv) for the purpose of the *QLTSR* a person seeking admission as a *solicitor* via transfer in accordance with those regulations;

  (v) for the purpose of the *SRA Suitability Test* any individual intending to be a *solicitor*, and any person seeking authorisation as an *authorised role holder* under the *SRA Authorisation Rules*;

 (vi) for the purposes of the *SRA Accounts Rules* (save for Part 7 (Overseas practice)):

      (A) a *solicitor*; or

      (B) an *REL*;

     in either case who is:

         (I) a *sole practitioner*;

     (II) a *partner* in a *partnership* which is a *recognised body, licensed body* or *authorised non-SRA firm*, or in a *partnership* which should be a *recognised body* but has not been recognised by the *SRA*;

     (III) an assistant, associate, professional support lawyer, consultant, locum or person otherwise employed in the practice of a *recognised body, licensed body, recognised sole practice* or *authorised non-SRA firm*; or of a *partnership* which should be a *recognised body* but has not been recognised by the *SRA*, or of a *sole practitioner* whose *practice* should be a *recognised sole practice* but has not been authorised by the *SRA*; and "employed" in this context shall be interpreted in accordance with the definition of "employee" for the purposes of the *SRA Code of Conduct*;

     (IV) employed as an in-house lawyer by a *non-solicitor employer* (for example, in a law centre or in commerce and industry);

     (V) a *director* of a *company* which is a *recognised body, licensed body* or *authorised non-SRA firm*, or of a *company* which is a *manager* of a *recognised body, licensed body* or *authorised non-SRA firm*;

     (VI) a member of an *LLP* which is a *recognised body, licensed body* or *authorised non-SRA firm*, or of an *LLP* which is a *manager* of a *recognised body, licensed body* or *authorised non-SRA firm*; or

     (VII) a *partner* in a *partnership* with separate legal personality which is a *manager* of a *recognised body, licensed body* or *authorised non-SRA firm*;

(C) an *RFL* practising:

     (I) as a *partner* in a *partnership* which is a *recognised body, licensed body* or *authorised non-SRA firm*, or in a *partnership* which should be a *recognised body* but has not been recognised by the *SRA*;

     (II) as the *director* of a *company* which is a *recognised body, licensed body* or *authorised non-SRA firm*, or as the *director* of a *company* which is a *manager* of a *recognised body, licensed body* or *authorised non-SRA firm*;

     (III) as a member of an *LLP* which is a *recognised body, licensed body* or *authorised non-SRA firm*, or as a member of an *LLP* which is a *manager* of a *recognised body, licensed body* or *authorised non-SRA firm*;

     (IV) as a *partner* in a *partnership* with separate legal personality which is a *manager* of a *recognised body, licensed body* or *authorised non-SRA firm*;

     (V) as an employee of a *recognised body, licensed body* or *recognised sole practice*; or

(VI) as an employee of a *partnership* which should be a *recognised body* but has not been authorised by the *SRA*, or of a *sole practitioner* whose *practice* should be a *recognised sole practice* but has not been authorised by the *SRA*;

(D) a *recognised body*;

(E) a *licensed body*;

(F) a *manager* or employee of a *recognised body* or *licensed body*, or of a *partnership* which should be a *recognised body* but has not been authorised by the *SRA*; or

(G) an employee in a *recognised sole practice*, or in a *sole practitioner* whose *practice* should be a *recognised sole practice* but has not been authorised by the *SRA*;

(vii) for the purposes of the *SRA Higher Rights of Audience Regulations* means a *solicitor* or an *REL*;

(viii)for the purposes of the *SRA Insolvency Practice Rules* means a *solicitor* or an *REL*;

(ix) for the purposes of the *SRA Quality Assurance Scheme for Advocates (Crime) Notification Regulations* means a *solicitor* or an *REL*; and

(x) for the purposes of the *SRA QASA Regulations* means a *solicitor* or an *REL*;

and references to "your" and "yourself" should be construed accordingly.

Rule 3: General Interpretation

3.1 Unless the context otherwise requires:

(a) the singular includes the plural and vice versa;

(b) words importing the masculine gender include the feminine and vice versa and references to the masculine or feminine include the neuter;

(c) the word "body" includes a *sole practitioner*, and a special body within the meaning of section 106 of the *LSA*;

(d) any explanatory notes, guidance notes and/or commentary are for the purposes of guidance only;

(e) any headings are for ease of reference only;

(f) any appendices to the provisions within the *SRA Handbook* will form part of the *SRA Handbook*;

(g) "in writing" includes any form of written electronic communication normally used for business purposes, such as emails;

(h) references to certificates, letters or other forms of written communication include references to those in both electronic and hard copy format; and

(i)   a reference to any statute, statutory provision, code or regulation includes any subordinate legislation (as defined by section 21(1) of the Interpretation Act 1978) made under it.